Type of First-rate
Early 19th C.

H.M.S. Inflexible ~ 1876

Fighting Sail

By the Same Author

CAPTAINS AND KINGS (Allen & Unwin)
AN INTRODUCTION TO BRITISH MARINE PAINTING (Batsford)
THE CROWN JEWELS (Penguin)
CAPTAIN MARRYAT: A Rediscovery (Constable)
THE DISCOVERY OF TAHITI (Folio Society)
BATTLE HONOURS OF THE ROYAL NAVY (George Philip)
A PORTRAIT OF LORD NELSON (Chatto)
EMMA HAMILTON AND SIR WILLIAM (Chatto)
THE GLORIOUS FIRST OF JUNE (Batsford)
GREAT SEA BATTLES (Weidenfeld & Nicolson)
A PORTRAIT GALLERY OF ENGLISH LITERATURE (Chatto)
THE SEA AND THE SWORD: The Baltic 1630–1945 (Cape)
NELSON'S BATTLES (Batsford)
CUNNINGHAM OF HYNDHOPE: Admiral of the Fleet (John Murray)
MARSHAL MANNERHEIM AND THE FINNS (Weidenfeld & Nicolson)
THE NAVY (Penguin)
THE LIFE AND LETTERS OF VICE-ADMIRAL LORD COLLINGWOOD (O.U.P.)
A JOURNEY TO THE NORTHERN CAPITALS (Allen & Unwin)
ADMIRAL OF THE FLEET: The Life of Sir Charles Lambe (Sidgwick & Jackson)
NELSON'S LAST DIARY and THE PRAYER BEFORE TRAFALGAR (Seeley, Service)
WITH WOLFE AT QUEBEC (Collins)
GREAT BATTLE FLEETS (Hamlyn)
THE LIFE-BOAT SERVICE: A History of the R.N.L.I. 1824–1974 (Cassell)
NELSON (Weidenfeld & Nicolson)
A CONCISE HISTORY OF THE BRITISH NAVY (Thames & Hudson)
COMMAND AT SEA (Cassell)
GREAT NAVAL ACTIONS (David & Charles)

FOR YOUNGER PEOPLE

NELSON AND THE AGE OF FIGHTING SAIL (Cassell)
CAPTAIN COOK AND THE SOUTH PACIFIC (Cassell)
THE BATTLE OF JUTLAND (Lutterworth Press)

British Plenty
Engraving by C. Knight

This depicts one of the few pleasures of life in the Royal Navy during the Revolutionary Wars. His ship is paid off, money is in his pocket and he is desperate for wine, women and song. But after a few nights of carousal, and very little remaining but oblivion, it is more than likely that the British tar was glad to return to the sea!

OLIVER WARNER

Fighting Sail

THREE HUNDRED YEARS OF WARFARE AT SEA

FOREWORD BY ADMIRAL OF THE FLEET THE EARL MOUNTBATTEN OF BURMA

CASSELL
LONDON

CASSELL LTD.
35 Red Lion Square, London WC1R 4SG
and at Sydney, Auckland, Toronto, Johannesburg,
an affiliate of
Macmillan Publishing Co., Inc.,
New York.

First published 1979

Designed by Simon Bell

ISBN 0 304 30003 9

Printed in Great Britain by
Richard Clay (The Chaucer Press) Ltd
Bungay, Suffolk

Lieutenant

Cook

Captain

To the memory of Oliver Warner
and to the Officers and Men of the Royal Navy
past and present

Midshipman

Sailor

Admiral

FOREWORD

by

ADMIRAL OF THE FLEET
THE EARL MOUNTBATTEN OF BURMA,

K.G., P.C., G.C.B., O.M., G.C.S.I., G.C.I.E., G.C.V.O., D.S.O., F.R.S.

As Oliver Warner has said, any survey of warfare under sail could scarcely lack variety and *Fighting Sail* certainly provides plenty of that. But the writing of the history itself has also proved varied. Originally planned as part of a series under the editorship of Correlli Barnett which was not pursued, Oliver Warner obtained his consent to follow up the idea and write the history in his own inimitable style. In August 1976 when he was in the middle of writing the book he suddenly died and Victoria Howard-Vyse was persuaded by his widow to finish the story.

Victoria Howard-Vyse first met Oliver Warner when he was writing the life of her great-great-great-uncle, the renowned Lord Collingwood who was Nelson's second-in-command at the Battle of Trafalgar, and thereafter she worked for him for eleven years until his death. She was therefore undoubtedly a first-class choice to continue Oliver's great work.

My father joined the Royal Navy in 1868, forty-one years after the Battle of Navarino which marked the end of the history of 'Fighting Sail'. At that time there were practically no armoured ships in the Navy and no breech-loading guns. Ships that had steam-power as well as sail were becoming more numerous, but fourteen knots was still considered a great speed when steaming on the measured mile. Four or five inches of iron on part of the waterline was all the protection that armour gave to the few ships that had it. The gunrooms, where the Midshipmen lived, were only just abaft the men's quarters on the lower deck and outside their mess were the chests which contained all their clothes and belongings and over which their hammocks were slung at night.

My father joined his first ship, the frigate *Ariadne*, in January 1869. She had been specially fitted out as a sort of Royal Yacht to take the Prince and Princess of Wales on a cruise in the Mediterranean. My father wrote in his diary that he disliked the life on board and all its surroundings; hard work night and day in all weathers, horrid and insufficient food, rough handling in the gunroom at all times and the terror of taking his share in drill aloft at sea without having had any preliminary exercises in a training ship. Despite all this, after the *Ariadne* paid off my father spent his month's leave making a full-rigged model of the ship.

I joined the Royal Navy in 1913 and retired from active service fifty-two years later in 1965. During this time I witnessed a great many changes and now today we are in the atomic age with the guided missile launcher replacing the gun turret and the nuclear reactor the boiler furnace. These changes are just as fundamental as that from sail-driven wooden walls to steam-driven iron-clads.

But one of the most fascinating aspects of maritime warfare is the almost timeless aspect of the basic parameters. Although enormous technological advances have taken place, the underlying concept of how ships are used in the furtherance of a maritime strategy remains very much the same as it was many hundreds of years ago when man first began to use the sea as an arena of military and political policy.

This story of three hundred years of warfare at sea is therefore not only fascinating but a valuable contribution to the history of our great maritime nation.

Mountbatten of Burma

A.F.

CONTENTS

'Play with your fancies; and in them behold
Upon the hempen tackle ship-boys climbing;
Hear the shrill whistle which doth order give
To sounds confus'd; behold the threaden sails,
Borne with th' invisible and creeping wind,
Draw the huge bottoms through the furrow'd sea,
Breasting the lofty surge.'

Henry V

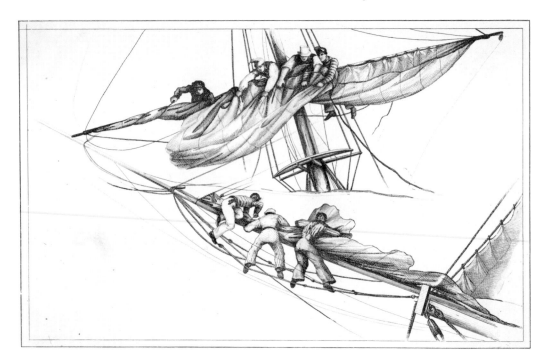

ACKNOWLEDGEMENTS

It would be impossible to make acknowledgement to all those who have given help in the production of this book without first recognizing the great honour and privilege of having Admiral of the Fleet The Earl Mountbatten of Burma write the Foreword for it.

Other acknowledgements are due to:

Colonel David Ascoli
Simon Bell, Esq.
Rear-Admiral W. P. Brock
William Brown, Esq.
Ralph Gillies Cole, Esq.
Group-Captain C. J. Collingwood, OBE, DFC
Miss Judith Collingwood
Lieutenant-General Sir George Collingwood, KBE, CB, DSO
Miss Mary Griffith
Major-General P. R. C. Hobart, CB, DSO, OBE, MC
Mrs. P. Holmes (National Maritime Museum)
Mrs. Victoria Howard-Vyse
William Howard-Vyse, Esq.
Commander A. S. King, RN (HMS *Collingwood*)
Captain G. A. de G. Kitchin, CBE, RN
Miss C. L. Macdonald
Mrs. J. Moore (National Maritime Museum)
His Grace the Duke of Northumberland, KG
Vice-Admiral R. D. Oliver, CB, CBE, DSC, RN
Lieutenant-Commander G. S. Pearson, RN
First Officer Anne Prees, WRNS (HMS *Collingwood*)
Miss J. Prendergast (National Portrait Gallery)
Earl Spencer
Captain John Steel, RN (late HMS *Collingwood*)

PREFACE

As first planned, this outline history of warfare in the age of sail was to have been one of a series under the editorship of Mr Correlli Barnett which would have considered land and sea fighting from classical times onwards. The project was not pursued, but with Mr Barnett's consent I have made use of some of the suggestions he put forward. I have, however, so varied his brief that he would be unlikely to recognize in the present work more than an echo of what he had in mind.

Any survey of warfare under sail, from its tentative beginnings to the affair at Navarino in 1827 where ships from the British, French and Russian navies combined to defeat a Turkish–Egyptian force, could scarcely lack variety. The span is of over three centuries. Many episodes are famous. The end was as gradual as the start, but soon after Navarino steam propulsion and the extension of the use of explosive shell affected everything. Whereas a ship of the time of the Spanish Armada would not have looked grossly out of place at Trafalgar, so gradually had methods changed during the intervening years, the pace soon quickened drastically. Within a century of the early ironclads, the nuclear-powered submarine had been designed.

Relative lack of grace in earlier times implied do diminution in the degree of tension on the part of those involved, either tactically, ship to ship, or in planning. However, sail had one special advantage: the vessels were pleasing to the eye, a fact of which artists made full use. That is why, although a writer may well falter in pursuing this particular subject, the graphic material at his disposal will certainly enrich his pages. Sir Philip Sidney put into eight words what we savour in so much of the older marine painting—'Oft cruel fighting well pictured forth do please'. But when we enjoy what is offered it is well to remember the suffering which was so often its basis.

O.W.
Haslemere, Surrey

ONE

THE DAY
OF THE CARRACK

Galley warfare — Revolutionary shipbuilding — The great sea voyages
Sea power — The carrack — Prestige ships — Armament
Aids to navigation — The Treaty of Tordesillas — The Navy of Henry VIII
Spanish commitments — San Juan de Uloa — The battle of Terceira
Preparations for the Spanish Armada

IN MANY VARIETIES OF HUMAN ACTIVITY change has been gradual rather than swift. For instance, no clear-cut stage marks a transition from sea warfare in which the oar-propelled galley was the principal vessel, to that in which the ship under sail, equipped with guns which could hit at some distance, was paramount.

Indeed, in certain areas, notably the Mediterranean, and the Baltic, with peculiar conditions of hydrography and coastline, the galley, mounting guns on a modest scale, and with sail for supplementary power, retained advantages after it had become obsolete elsewhere. It was pre-eminently useful in amphibious campaigning. It could operate in shallow waters where a sailing ship of size could not venture safely. It could get off, when beached, almost as easily as it could take the ground. It was adapted for ramming, the collision and smashing of oars being followed by hand-to-hand fighting such as was normal at sea, and remained a feature, though on a diminished scale, until the close of the sailing era.

Two of the last important battles in which galleys played a principal part took place, appropriately enough, not far from the scene of the great encounter of classical times between the Greeks and Persians at Salamis. A fight off Prevesa between Andrea Doria the Genoese, and Khayr al-Din of Algiers, gave Islam ascendancy in the eastern Mediterranean from 1538 until 1571, when there occurred the famous clash near Lepanto between the Turkish fleet and that of the Christian League. In both cases, artillery had importance. The power of the Moslem guns caused Andrea Doria to retreat at Prevesa, though his decision was complicated by orders not to engage unless he was sure of victory. At Lepanto, if most of the fighting was as grimly hand-to-hand as anything recorded, the guns of the Venetian galleasses, a blend of galley and sailing ship, were formidable in the Christian attack, doing much execution in the opening phases.

Future events had been foreshadowed in the previous century. For instance, at Zonchio, in the Morea south of Lepanto, in one of the numerous affrays between Venetians and Turks, who were striving for dominance in the area, a straight fight took place in August 1499 between ships under sail. This was when galleys and sailing ships formed mixed fleets, as they did for many decades. The magazine of the single Turkish ship caught fire, and her two Venetian opponents, which were close by, suffered so much from the blaze that all three vessels were destroyed. Grimani, the Venetian Captain-General, flew his flag in a galley, lost advantage thereby, and failed to prevent the Turks capturing the land base at Lepanto as a result of the battle.

A process of revolutionary shipbuilding began in the fifteenth century. During the earlier years most large ships had one tower-like mast and a single sail. They were the 'round ships', the beamy cargo-carriers of the seas, which had been familiar for generations. Fifty years later, large ships had three masts, sometimes more, and at least five or six sails. This was the radical improvement which enabled the transatlantic voyages of Columbus to succeed, and Vasco da Gama to establish the route to the Far East via the Cape of Good Hope. Somewhere near Calicut, on the Malabar coast of India, a skirmish took place in 1498 between the Portuguese and local vessels, the result of which showed that the adventurers from Europe, through superior ships and weapons, would be able to exploit the resources of the regions to which their skill and pertinacity had brought them. The conclusion was confirmed by victory over the Arabs off Diu in 1508.

The way of the Spanish in the New World was at first easier. There was no occasion for battle between Columbus's ships and the native craft they met with. Although the newcomers would not have it all their own way at sea in their areas of discovery, when opposition came it was from the continent from which they themselves had set out.

The illustrious early generation of oceanic pioneers, including Ferdinand Magellan, who led the first voyage of circumnavigation on behalf of Spain, though he himself did not survive to complete it, would scarcely have understood the phrase 'sea power', so familiar to modern ears, as having any other meaning than as an aspect of power in general. Ships, they would have said, were for trading, fishing, venturing. Fleets were for transporting troops for campaigning ashore, these troops being used in attack or defence as the case might be, if an enemy should be encountered when they were afloat. Until oceanic as opposed to coastal commerce became a regular activity on the part of leading countries, as it did soon after the discoveries of the later fifteenth century, sea power was not highly relevant in itself in matters of high policy. Once it became necessary to institute convoy and covering squadrons for the protection of merchantmen, matters altered radically.

Local supremacy was always important, and so was prestige. Huge ships were sometimes designed or built for ambitious rulers even before their best practical use had been worked out. As for local supremacy, a work known as the *Libel of English Policy* dating from the reign of Henry V, victor of Agincourt, believed to have been written by Adam de Moleyns, Bishop of Chichester, contained lines which were often quoted:

> Cherish merchandise; keep the admiralty
> That we be masters of the narrow sea.

Yet in England, as elsewhere, it was only after interests had extended far beyond what were indeed 'narrow seas', that specialist attention was increasingly given in ruling circles to maritime affairs. When the time came for theorizing, the root of the matter might have been expressed in the view that whereas no one can 'command' the sea, since this would imply occupation or at the very least effective supervision, 'sea power' is a form of strength which enables its possessor to send forces and to trade where he wishes, the same advantage being denied, when necessary, to others. Most of the situations through which warfare under sail came about accord with this proposition, with the proviso that as the sea is a means to an end rather than an end in itself, the deep-seated, reasonable notion of sea warfare being an adjunct of warfare in general held good.

II

If the galley and its larger, better-armed and more heavily-rigged development, the galleass, continued to find favour in the Mediterranean, there is evidence that well before the end of the fifteenth century the Venetians, and their rivals, the Genoese, were building ships which could be adapted to carry bigger guns than could have been used by oared vessels.

A print produced between 1470 and 1480 is valuable evidence. It shows a three-masted Venetian vessel. Her tower-like main mast is square-rigged, and is provided not only with a large top or circular platform but a triangular sail above it. The smaller foremast is also square-rigged. It has a top of more modest dimensions, and the mizen, aft, has the triangular lateen sail favoured in southern waters. The lateen sail was adopted for the mizen in other countries, including those of northern Europe, until, in the course of time, square rig on all three masts became common.

A favoured type of three-master, in both southern and northern waters, was known as the carrack. It was Mediterranean in origin and a specialization of Genoese builders. These ships, when fully developed, had tops on all three masts, and carried guns when necessary. A pronounced feature was an elaborate forecastle rising high above the waist of the ship and projecting well beyond the main structure of the hull. It was of a height perceptibly greater than that of the other considerable 'castle' aft.

The carrack, although not to be compared with its successor the galleon as an efficient vessel under sail, was impressive: for instance, a ship ordered by Henry V to be built at Bayonne, near the northern frontier of Spain, though not completed, would have been 186 feet from stem to stern. An English-built ship, the *Grâce Dieu* of 1418 which, though launched, was never actively employed, was burnt in 1439, and her remains lie in the mud of the Hamble River. She is believed to have been of 1,400 tons, enormous for her age. Both would have been used as troop-carriers.

Other countries were not behind in prestige building. The *Peter*, 150 feet long overall, deriving from La Rochelle, created a sensation when she reached Danzig in 1462. She is described as a 'carvel' or caravel, a rather uncertain term for a build of southern origin, lateen-sailed, and of smooth-sided construction, with planks edge to edge. This made for greater strength than the clincher or clinker building, with planks overlapping, which had been usual in the north.

Prestige ships included the *Great Michael*, built in Scotland at Newhaven, Midlothian, in 1511 on the orders of James V, and later sold to France. She was 240 feet long overall and was said to have 'wasted all the woods of Fife' to supply constructional needs. As an answer to such a grandiose design, the big *Henry Grâce à Dieu* was launched in England three years later, one of the achievements of Henry VIII, who inherited his father's interest in ships. Soon afterwards, in 1523, came the *Santa Anna*,

built for the Knights of Malta; the Swedish *Elefant* of 1532, signalizing the power of Gustavus Vasa, first of a warrior dynasty; and the Portuguese *São João* of 1534, which was referred to as a galleon, not a carrack.

Representations of the carrack are often of the highest interest. There is one of striking beauty in a stained-glass window on the south side of King's College Chapel, Cambridge. It was designed by a Fleming, Dirick Vellert, and put in place between 1526 and 1531. The detail purports to show St Paul departing from Miletus in New Testament times, but the ship is contemporary with the designer and the glazier, Galyon Hone. By the time they produced it, the height of the forecastle had been modified in relation to the rest of the ship.

Of much the same date is a painting at Greenwich, believed to be by Cornelis Anthoniszoon, of 'Portuguese Carracks off a Rocky Coast'. This shows the great main-sail, the squared stern tapering upwards, and the proud decoration of such vessels. They were leading examples in an age of seafaring reconnaissance, discovery and exploitation.

To arm ships in the most effective way brought many problems. Land guns, which had a long history and attained great size and weight, were not subject to limitations imposed by conditions at sea. From time to time heavy pieces had been mounted on upper decks, firing over the bulwarks, but in general, ships' armament was confined to light weapons. These were breech-loaded, and could stand along the bulwarks. They

Magellan discovering the Straits of Magellan,
c. *1480–1520*
Engraving after W. O. Brierly

Portuguese by birth, Ferdinand Magellan, before he took to the sea, was a page at the court of John II, and then enlisted for a voyage to India in 1505. After many more voyages, and an accident which lamed him for life, he fell into disfavour and transferred his allegiance to Spain. With the permission of Charles V, he set off on the first circumnavigation of the world in September 1519. On 21 October 1520, he discovered the straits later to bear his name, and is here depicted directing a seaman to plumb the depths to see if the water was deep enough to sail through. Reaching the Philippines, he led the natives in an attack on a neighbouring island and was killed. The *Vittoria*, only one of the squadron of five left, reached Seville in July 1522 with thirty-one of the 270 souls who had set out.

were man-killers, intended to reinforce the bows of archers and the wide range of hand weapons on board; they were of value both at a moderate distance or, if after close fighting, a boarding party succeeded in gaining a lodgement in the waist of a ship. A devastating fire could then be poured on the intruders from castles and tops. The smaller guns had odd names, murderer, saker, minion, falcon and falconet among them.

Heavier pieces were of two main types: the first was the ship-battering, short-range cannon and demi-cannon, firing shot of about 50 and 32 pounds respectively, ammunition being of iron or stone. The other was the culverin and demi-culverin, a long gun firing lighter shot further than the cannon. Culverins were in favour with nations with weatherly ships which could keep heavily-armed opponents at a distance. In due course, technical considerations caused heavier guns to be muzzle-loaded, since the detachable breech of the lighter gun had many drawbacks. It was only in the later nineteenth century, after the days of sail warfare were over, that breech-loading was reapplied to guns of large calibre as a result of improvements in method and manufacture.

The number of guns borne by individual ships was sometimes considerable. For instance, the *São João* is said to have carried no fewer than 366 when she took part in an attack on Tunis in 1535. This is not improbable, as hand-guns and swivel-mounted pieces were included in the total.

A profound change took place in numbers, size, and where guns were placed on board, when portholes were cut in the sides of ships through which to fire. Credit for the idea is sometimes given to a Frenchman, one Decharges of Brest, the year being 1501. What is beyond doubt is that the idea soon caught on and became usual. Representations of the *São João* show that she employed this method of broadside fire, and it was the cutting of portholes in hulls which led to a change in northern Europe from clinker to the stronger carvel building, particularly for vessels designed as men-of-war.

As the effect of shot was dependent on charges of gunpowder, the quantity and quality of this volatile blend of saltpetre, sulphur and charcoal was of the greatest importance. There was never enough of it if action was sustained, and the quality at first varied from the mediocre to the poor. Until a process of manufacturing saltpetre was discovered by a German in 1560, this ingredient came by tortuous channels mainly from Eastern sources, but a supplementary supply was derived from Morocco in the later half of the sixteenth century.

The development of aids to navigation was slow, and the problem of finding longitude accurately had to wait until the advent of a time-keeping instrument able to withstand the strains of sea travel and extremes of temperature. The solution was not found before the eighteenth century. A seaman such as Columbus had more to help him than his predecessors, but it was not much by later standards.

By the fifteenth century, cartographers had produced coastal charts called *portolani*, drawn on vellum and brilliantly embellished, Columbus's own brother being skilled in the art. Maps of the world as then known were inaccurate and inventive, and it was not until the 1570s that the 'atlas' of Gerard Mercator, a Fleming, was published on a projection still in use.

The Portuguese were the first to transform navigation by learning to observe the position of the sun by day and the Pole Star by night with the astrolabe—taking 'sights'. The instrument itself was of ancient origin and was adapted for sea service

5

shortly before 1480 by Johann Müller, a German mathematician, and Martin Behaim of Nuremberg, a geographer who had been at sea in a Portuguese ship. A simplified version was fitted with an alidade or sighting bar, and with a scale by which the altitude of a heavenly body could be measured. Seamen also used a cross-staff for a similar purpose, but it had the drawback that the observer had to look directly at the sun. The back-staff, freed from such a disadvantage, was not invented until 1594 by an Englishman, John Davis.

The mariner's compass, first noted in Europe in 1187 at Amalfi, was housed in a casing known as a binnacle, but magnetic variations were not understood. In shallower waters seamen made use of a sounding lead. Watches were measured at sea by means of half-hour sand-glasses, which were turned eight times in each watch, the turn being marked by a cry on deck or striking a bell. Breakages were frequent, and Magellan, for example, is known to have carried many spares.

As the direction and strength of the wind might alter during a watch, affecting the course and speed of the ship, a traverse board was used, fitted with pegs to record such variations as could be estimated by whoever was in charge on deck. Even with such aids, 'latitude sailing' gave manifold causes for error. They could be of such magnitude that Magellan's pilot underestimated the breadth of the Pacific by three thousand miles. The term 'dead reckoning', used to estimate a ship's whereabouts and based on courses steered and distances run rather than on 'sights', which were dependent on a clear atmosphere, accounted for some disastrous inaccuracies.

It was inevitable that the epoch-making fifteenth-century Iberian voyages should have led to divergences of interest between Spain and Portugal. Agreement was reached at last, and recorded in the Treaty of Tordesillas of 1494. As the result of an appeal, Pope Alexander VI, as Supreme Pontiff, divided the world into two. Portugal became paramount in Africa and in the Far East. Spain was established westerly, although the line of demarcation, not always precise, allowed Brazil to Portugal.

This division froze out all other Powers, at a time when discoveries were continual and technical developments proceeding fast. First to feel the effect was France, one of whose kings, François I, was later to remark ironically: 'I should very much like to see the clause in Adam's will which excludes me from a share of the world.' The Treaty was not many years old before raiders from French ports, who were considered to be pirates by the Spaniards, were making a nuisance of themselves in the Caribbean. Their success led to the arming of ships plying to and from the West Indies and the Spanish Main, the north-western littoral of South America. As early as 1526 they usually sailed in company, with protective squadrons in the focal areas of Cape St Vincent, the Canaries and the Azores.

Regular convoys were instituted in 1543, and were strengthened in the following years by an admiral of ability, Pero Menendez de Aviles. He planned the seizure of the Isles of Scilly, where he would have based ships to deal with raiders. The project was dropped after Menendez's death in 1574, which was as well for the interlopers. By that time they had accumulated valuable experience in waters officially Spanish, and acquired considerable pickings from wealth consigned to Europe.

It happened that during the earlier part of the sixteenth century, France and England had sovereign rulers in François I (1515–47) and Henry VIII (1509–47) whose reigns were almost concurrent. Both were concerned with maintaining a balance of power in Europe, and both paid much attention to their fleets as a source of strength. Of the two,

Henry VIII was the more farseeing. By the end of his life he had established an enduring structure of naval administration.

France was noted for fine ships, and continued so to be throughout the era of sail, but as her Continental interests were preponderant she never gave the same attention to sea affairs as was essential to England if the island was to flourish, or even keep its independence. Although Henry VIII was more than once at war with France, and had to suffer the humiliation of occasional landings by raiding parties, he determined to make his navy powerful and give it the best armament he could procure, sending abroad for skilled men.

If mixed fleets of galleys, galleasses and sailing ships were the rule in Henry's time, and tactics those of the galley, he had learnt from his predecessors the great potentialities of the heavily-armed sailing ship. He ordained a continuous series of buildings, adaptations and rebuildings throughout his reign, and created, from modest beginnings, a good fleet. He had inherited a dry dock at Portsmouth which could accommodate large ships. It had been completed by his father in 1496 at a total charge of £193. 0s. 6¾d. The first Tudor achieved one of the bargains for which he was famous. The second founded dockyards at Woolwich, Deptford and Chatham.

Henry had better luck with some of his smaller ships, which survived into the reign of his daughter, Elizabeth, and did good service with her fleet, than with two of his big carracks. His pride, the *Henry Grâce à Dieu*, known by various other names including the *Great Harry*, was a four-master, the mast aft of the mizen being known as a bonaventure. She had top-masts and top-gallant masts on the foremost three and a top-mast only on the bonaventure. As originally equipped she carried 184 guns, mostly light pieces, but she was entirely rebuilt between 1536 and 1539. She emerged with 21 heavy bronze guns, muzzle-loading, 130 iron guns, breech-loading, and 100 small guns. The heavier pieces were housed on two complete decks, with lighter weapons in the castles and elsewhere. Thus ordered, she was recognizably the ancestor of the three-decked man-of-war of later times, which served as flagships and were the most powerful vessels afloat. Alas, she was burnt in 1553, having seen no service of importance.

An earlier ship of Henry's had been the smaller *Mary Rose*, launched in the year of his accession. Like her more imposing sister she too was entirely rebuilt at about the same time, and supplied with every naval weapon then in use, including bronze cannon cast by one John Owen, whose name appeared on his handicraft, wrought-iron breech-loaders of some size, culverins, hand-guns, pikes and even long-bows. Examples of her armoury have been recovered from her hull, which lies in the sea-bed not far from Southsea Castle, for she also met a sad end.

This was in the summer of 1545 when the French, having organized an invading force, were about to attack Portsmouth, where the king took charge ashore. The orders to the Lord Admiral, John Dudley, afterwards Duke of Northumberland, were for a line abreast formation in two divisions to repel the attack. The van guard was to disorganize the enemy, and ships from the second, or 'main' body, were to complete the rout. There was also a 'wing', or flanking squadron, of galleys. Fighting had not gone beyond skirmishing when the *Mary Rose* met with disaster. Incompetently handled, and her heavy guns not secured, with her lower gun-ports open she heeled, filled and sank. The invasion failed, after the English had the better of an encounter off Shoreham, where French galleys fared badly against broadsides.

III

The brief reigns of Edward VI and Mary in England brought no maritime complications. Indeed, when Mary married Philip of Spain soon after her accession, the bridegroom could hire or make use of English ships. But when, in 1558, Elizabeth succeeded her half-sister, declining the hand of her bereaved brother-in-law, change was certain. Philip now had various causes for anxiety. Elizabeth was a Protestant; Philip the dedicated champion of Catholicism. The Queen gave her support, at first morally but later materially, to Philip's rebel subjects in the Netherlands, who were not to be put down even by the brutalities of his Governor, the Duke of Alva. Finally, her seamen grew bold in their encroachments overseas. The Spaniards often had the measure of French raiders, but they now had to guard against seamen who added illicit trading to other activities in areas forbidden them by a Papal edict for which they cared nothing.

Philip's commitments by sea were numerous. Although the Turks had suffered great loss at Lepanto they remained a threat, for galleys were expendable and could be built quickly. Spanish lines of communication were as vital in the Mediterranean as in northern seas, demanding vigilance and strength. The Atlantic and coastal traffic had to be protected, and there was even threat in the Pacific (known as the South Seas), particularly after Drake's depredations during the world voyage of 1577–80 which made him famous.

Drake had learnt much of his business under his kinsman, John Hawkins. He had escaped, like his leader, from an encounter with the Spaniards at San Juan de Uloa in Mexico in 1568. Hawkins had been treacherously attacked and got away only after a stiff fight in which he learnt the value of guns used at a distance.

At the time he was engaged in the unsavoury slave trade, shipping Negroes across the Atlantic to work for the Spaniards because most of the natives of the occupied regions preferred death to so doing. Local Spanish governors winked at the intrusion; indeed, as Hawkins's biggest ship, the *Jesus*, was well armed and the men of his squadron had some experience of fighting, he soon had the settlement at San Juan de Uloa at his mercy. Matters would have remained so had it not been for the appearance of a Spanish fleet commanded by Don Martin Henriques. Even so, the English were in a strong position and could have prevented the Spaniards from entering the harbour to water and provision had not Hawkins come to a written agreement with Henriques. This allowed the Spanish fleet to enter but safeguarded the English from attack.

Unfortunately, Henriques was a man for whom an agreement with a heretic, however solemn, had no validity if it could not be enforced—anyway, so he argued, the English had no business in those parts. He made covert plans to attack Hawkins, and would have overwhelmed him but for the alertness shown by the English. Even so, they lost the *Jesus*. She had been bought from the Hanseatic League, a trading confederacy of North German towns, by Henry VIII fifty years before, and, after being condemned as unfit for the Navy, Queen Elizabeth lent her to Hawkins as a slaver. This high-sided ship, in her poor condition, was 'wonderfully pierced with shot', and she had also to face an attack by fire-ships which led to a brief panic. Even so, before she sank she accounted for three Spaniards: the *Almirante*, which blew up, the *Capitana* and a merchantman which settled on the bottom. Total defeat had been staved off by skilful gunnery, the *Jesus* using three of the ship-smashing cannon type and seventeen of the culverin. Hawkins got his surviving men away, bitter at heart, vowing to avenge such

8

treachery. The Queen was to give him the chance to do so when she made him Treasurer of the Navy, an office in which he succeeded his father-in-law, Benjamin Gonson. From 1578 onwards, Hawkins rebuilt the English fleet in a manner which would have pleased that vigorous innovator, Henry VIII.

IV

On the death of the King of Portugal in 1580, Philip II decided to annex the country, to which he considered himself to have a right through his mother. The claimant to the throne, Dom Antonio, had no powerful following, and a Spanish fleet commanded by the Marquis of Santa Cruz, in conjunction with an army under Alva, soon had Lisbon at its mercy. Subjugation of the entire country followed in due course.

The conquest gave Philip much addition to his strength at sea, but it was on that element that he met with opposition. The Azores held out against him, helped by France, and it was not before July 1582 that there occurred off Terceira, in the island group, the earliest encounter of the highest significance in which galleys played no part. A fresco recording the action, which Philip caused to be painted for the Escorial by the Genoese artist Nicolas Granello, shows a mass of fighting ships. All are under sail.

Battle of Lepanto 1571

Lepanto, important as the last battle fought between galleys, also heralded the end of Turkish domination of the Mediterranean. The Christians, for once united, whose fleet embodied several ships lent by the Pope, under the command of Don John of Austria, finally won a hard-fought fight. The wounded included Cervantes, who lost his left hand. A result of Lepanto was that although most fleets retained galleys for years to come, emphasis was laid more and more upon the sailing ship.

9

Vasco da Gama c. *1460–1524*
Westermayer

One of the greatest of the early navigators. By his voyage of 1497–8, during which he rounded the Cape of Good Hope, crossed the Indian Ocean, naming St Helena on the way, and arriving at Calicut in May 1498, he began the Portuguese era of prosperity, and started trade between East and West. He was made Viceroy of India in 1524, with his headquarters at Goa, but died on Christmas Eve of that year.

The Spanish admiral was Santa Cruz. As this same nobleman had commanded the reserve of galleys at Lepanto eleven years earlier, playing a vital part in the Christian success, he became the strongest link between the old and the new naval warfare.

Having had intelligence of a forthcoming attempt on Philip's part to subdue the Azores, the French sent a considerable fleet to parry the threat, seventy ships in all, three English vessels being among them. In command was Philip Strozzi, a member of a Florentine family, several of whom served the French in military capacities. Santa Cruz arrived a week later, and after manoeuvres during which Strozzi gained the windward position, battle took place on 24 July.

10

JACQUES CARTIER 1491 – 1557

Jacques Cartier (1491–1557)
A montage picture from contemporary prints

The Breton, Jacques Cartier, led the first organized French expedition across the Atlantic in 1534, discovering the St Lawrence River. Two years later, he ventured further up the river, naming the Île d'Orléans after the French royal family, and got to Stadacona (Quebec) and Hochelaga (Montreal). Disappointed at not discovering rich minerals, he retired to St Malo, leaving the real discovery of Canada to Samuel de Champlain some sixty years later.

The Spaniards were greatly outnumbered. They had only twenty-five ships in all, although two of them were of the galleon type, built in Portugal. These were the *San Martin*, in which Santa Cruz flew his flag, and the *San Mateo*. The *San Martin* was armed with seventeen cannon and culverins on the lower deck, above which were a further seventeen large and small guns. Each piece had a professional gunner under whom were six soldiers.

As usual, the French ships sailed well, although in general they were smaller and less well armed than their opponents. Strozzi himself exchanged out of his 700-ton flagship into a nimbler vessel and, since he had the advantage in numbers, ordered four ships to concentrate on each of the largest Spaniards. The assault on the *San Mateo* was particularly fierce, and she was driven out of formation.

Fighting was at close range, at which Santa Cruz could use his cannon. He poured two broadsides into different French ships, one of which was soon in a sinking state; but after four hours' battery, the *San Mateo* was in straits, and Strozzi had actually boarded her when Santa Cruz who, by a brilliant feat, had managed to gain the wind, appeared through the smoke and attacked the French flagship. Most of the other Frenchmen held off, and the Spanish admiral was successful in capturing both his opponent and his ship. The remaining French fled. Two had been sunk, and others, 'broken with artillerie' according to a contemporary Spanish account, were abandoned. Santa Cruz just managed to tow the French flagship inshore, but his own force was by that time so much damaged that an immediate return to Spain was necessary. Conquest of the Azores was achieved a year later with a fleet numbering sixty, this time including twelve galleys and two galleasses.

Strozzi had been beaten because, at a critical stage in the action, his opponent gained the windward position and used his guns to shattering purpose. Added to this was the French defection. There were those who spoke of treachery, as was so often to be the case in sea fighting.

When the islands were at last occupied the Spanish captains were heard to exclaim: 'Now that we have all Portugal, England is ours!' The boast was rash, for the account of the fight brought back by the English captains confirmed Hawkins in the ideas he had been carrying out for some time in building and arming new royal ships, and in re-equipping older ones. This was the result both of his own experience in Mexico and of mature reflection. English ships must sail as well as the French, and should fight at ranges of their own choosing.

Elated by his successes—had he not proved himself both in galley and sail warfare?—Santa Cruz suggested a grand-scale seaborne assault on England. The King approved in principle, appointed the marquis 'Captain-General of the Ocean Sea' and laid down nine new galleons in his Biscay yards. The Portuguese fleet was refurbished, and even the date for the 'Enterprise of England' was fixed. It was to be 1587, and it was to be undertaken as a grand strategical and tactical operation making use of the forces under the Duke of Parma in the Netherlands. Although the menace was real enough, security was bad. By the earlier months of the critical year, the English Parliament had been given a precise idea of what might be in store.

TWO

THE SPANISH ARMADA

The galleon — Drake at Cadiz — The death of Santa Cruz
The Armada and Medina Sidonia — Actions in the Channel
Fire-ships at Calais — Battle off Gravelines
The Armada dispersed — Later alarms — The loss of the Revenge
Second raid on Cadiz

ELIZABETH OF ENGLAND was never better served by her leading men, and her nation in general, than during the crisis of the Spanish Armada. The Lord Treasurer, Burghley, was a statesman who had been concerned with the state of the Navy from the outset of the reign. Although reputedly a man of peace, naval and military advisers found him sympathetic to their suggestions, though there was never enough money for all they wanted.

Among key personalities, the Lord Admiral, Charles, Lord Howard of Effingham, although inexperienced at sea, had three assets: rank; willingness to delegate; and a sanguine nature. Accustomed to making the best of things, whatever the circumstances, he worked through encouragement. His second-in-command, Drake, was the best-known seaman living, his mere name a threat to Spain. At Court, Sir Walter Ralegh was not only a shrewd student of naval affairs, but his knowledge of the shipwright's art rivalled that of Hawkins. Howard's flagship, the *Ark Royal*, had been built privately as the *Ark Ralegh*, and presented to the Queen. Howard thought her 'the odd ship in the world for all conditions; and truly I think there can be no great ship make me change and go out of her. We can see no sail, great nor small, but how so ever they be off, we fetch them and speak with them.' This was a fine tribute to Ralegh's prescience.

By this time, the galleon had displaced the carrack as the principal ship of war. It was a type which was to be found, variously and continuously modified, in every considerable fleet, and it was to have a long life. Size differed as much as armament, and the decoration, as in the carrack, was usually superb. As a generalization, it could be said that the galleon, as well as having her forecastle set well back from the stem of the ship, was fitted with a low, projecting beak-head which may have owed something to the ram of the galley.

Other features were a squared stern, with galleries on both quarters. The interior was arranged with partial decks at various levels, for it was a principle that gun-ports should not be cut through the wales or heavy strakes running fore and aft. To do so would have weakened the longitudinal strength of the hull.

There were tops on the two forward masts, and usually on the mizen and on the bonaventure, when one was carried. The galleon was slimmer than the carrack. Typical dimensions were: length from stem to stern, 135 feet: length of keel, 100 feet: beam, 35 feet—giving rough proportions of 4:3:1.

Hawkins differentiated between 'race' and 'lofty-built' galleons and saw the advantages of each. The 'race-built' were comparatively low in the water. The 'lofty-built' were intended, in his own phrase, 'for majesty and terror of the enemy'. The *Ark Royal* was a typical example of an imposing ship—800 tons—which could also sail well. As for artillery, Sir William Wynter, Master of the Ordnance of the Navy, was persuaded to supply a preponderance of long and medium-range pieces, though the short-range cannon was not overlooked. Hawkins reduced the complements of ships of war since under normal conditions they would not need to find large boarding parties, and increased the seaman's pay from 6s. 8d. to 10s. a month.

By contrast, indeed, by tradition, Spain was conservative. In his earlier proposals for the Armada, Santa Cruz actually suggested that forty galleys should form part of the fleet, and this despite his own experience at Terceira. But he was over sixty years of age, and with an assurance of Spanish invincibility in all manner of sea warfare which was not wholeheartedly shared by his principal subordinates. These included Juan Martinez de Recalde, who had been his second at the Azores; the flamboyant Miguel de Oquendo; and Pedro de Valdes, who had been in action with the English off Ferrol, and was convinced of the paramount importance of artillery.

There was also conservatism in Spanish shipbuilding. The Casa de Contratacion of Seville had a monopoly in ships for the 'Indian Guard' whose duty was to safeguard the

14

treasure from the New World. It was behind the times in matters of design. Even the Portuguese galleons, which the king valued rightly as an addition to his strength, were not as handy as the newer-built English ships, which could sail within six points of the wind.

II

Two events which were to affect the 'Enterprise of England' occurred in the earlier months of 1587. Santa Cruz failed to intercept one of Drake's devastating raids on Spanish possessions in the New World. He returned to Lisbon with his squadron distressed by weather, while the English got back safely.

In April, Drake got his wish to strike what he called a 'home stroke' on Cadiz and elsewhere, his intention being to disrupt enemy preparations. The Queen changed her mind about the plan at the last minute, but her recall came too late. Drake was by that time on his way, accompanied by Sir William Borough, a notable man but one of a cautious school, with whom the commander soon fell out. This was chiefly because Drake had small faith in Councils of War, preferring to trust his experience, his keen instinct in the conduct of operations and his proved powers of leadership.

His force was well suited to its mission. He had four Queen's ships, the *Bonaventure*, 550 tons, and a flagship which had served him on his latest expedition; the *Golden Lion*, 500 tons; the *Dreadnought*, 400 tons; and the *Rainbow*, 500 tons, a medium-sized galleon of the latest build. There were also fourteen private and mer-chant ships and seven pinnaces. The latter type of vessel was not the oared craft of more recent times but a decked sailing ship of a size which could vary between 40 and about 90 tons.

The orders were 'to impeach the joining together of the King of Spain's fleets out of their several ports, to keep victuals from them', and in particular 'to distress the ships within the havens themselves'. They could have been drafted by Drake himself, and their purpose was popularly noted as 'singeing the King of Spain's beard'. The effect was certainly that.

The foray showed with what ease well-armed and well-handled sailing ships could deal with galleys, which formed the chief defence of Cadiz other than the forts. If galleys could not be relied on to do their job in the confined and sheltered waters of their base, what prospects had they in the Atlantic? From 1587 onward not much is heard of their role in Armada preparations. Of the four which remained on the fleet list, none took part in the fighting, one being wrecked as far away as Bayonne. On the other hand, four galleasses from Naples were given important tasks.

Drake arrived in Cadiz Roads on 19 April, according to the old method of dating. Recently, Pope Gregory XIII had introduced a reformed calendar which was followed in Spain and elsewhere, but as England did not adopt it until 1752, her dating was ten days behind that of many countries.

The English remained three days within the perimeter of the port defences. It was an act of insolence completely justified. Drake said they were 'often times fought by twelve of the King's galleys', of which they sank two and drove off the rest. Having made havoc of shipping in the haven, and burnt a galleon which was being prepared as a flagship, Drake proceeded to secure a temporary land base at Cape Sagres, from which he could paralyse inshore traffic.

This disorganized the timetable for the provisioning and preparation of the Armada. It also had the effect, which Drake could scarcely have realized, of reducing the supply of wooden staves for the casks which were used on board for needs of every sort, fresh water included. This in turn led to difficulties when the Armada sailed.

The repercussions of the raid were various. Santa Cruz hastily re-equipped his squadron at Lisbon and sped to the Azores to protect the *flota*, the annual treasure fleet which was due at the islands. The Spaniards were also made to realize that they must increase the proportion of long-range guns in relation to those of the cannon type. Within the limits imposed by time and availability they did well in this respect, and they made sure of an additional supply of powder and shot. They took three times as many rounds per gun to sea as the English, with powder accordingly.

Finally (and it was characteristic of Drake's luck at this golden period of his life), while Borough went home in disgrace, Drake succeeded in capturing the *San Felipe*, a lumbering, old-fashioned Portuguese carrack from Goa. She was laden with spices, ivory, silk and gold.

III

In February 1588, at the outset of the year which was to see the Armada sail on its mission, Spain suffered the loss of Santa Cruz. The admiral had had to put up with many setbacks apart from interference by the enemy. He could not have been half so confident of success during the later months of his life as he had been when he first put forward a plan for the operation of which he was in charge. The conditions at Lisbon, the principal assembly base, were approaching chaos, for the marquis had always been happier at sea than at a desk.

Philip's choice of the Duke of Medina Sidonia as his replacement has been harshly criticized, particularly in view of the Duke's reluctance to accept the assignment. It would be equally reasonable to argue that it was the best in the circumstances, since there was only one Santa Cruz. Medina Sidonia, who was not yet forty, was loyal, dedicated, of the highest rank and standing, and an exceptionally good man of business. The coming months were to show his skill at administration, for he soon had Lisbon humming with well-directed activity. He attended to many details himself, particularly where the difficulties were unusual, such as in the stepping of masts for the bigger ships. There was also his ability to get on well with the touchy captains who were to sail with him, by whom he was respected. Every sign showed that he had as firm a grip as Howard, even if his private attitude was one of acceptance or resignation rather than enthusiasm. Certainly his discipline was good. Friend and foe were agreed about that, and no one doubted his courage. Philip gave him instructions which allowed him little scope for initiative. His primary task was a junction with Parma. After that, every move was to be made by agreement between the two leaders, and there was no officer of more experience than Parma.

The early summer of 1588 was notable for bad weather. This had the effect of delaying the start of the operation, for the Armada had to seek refuge for a time at Corunna, and English attempts to meet the Spaniards before they reached the entrance to the Channel had no success. Instead, the force at Plymouth was kept at readiness so long that there was anxiety about victuals, and a serious amount of sickness, not to speak of desertion. Moreover, payments from the Exchequer were delayed. Howard, and Drake, who was given the post of Vice-Admiral, had to disburse much private wealth to meet expenses. There was, in fact, more than one reason to rejoice when the Armada was at last sighted, even though Medina Sidonia achieved a measure of surprise.

Towards evening on Friday, 19 July, Captain Thomas Flemyng, a kinsman of Hawkins, sailed into Plymouth Sound with news that he had sighted the enemy off the Lizard. Tradition has it that Drake was playing bowls, and exclaimed that there was time to finish the game and beat the Spaniards too. The truth is anyone's guess, for the story did not appear in print until the following century. What is certain is that from three o'clock in the afternoon until nine in the evening the flood stream was making into the Sound, and it was not before darkness that the English could warp their ships out against the south-westerly breeze.

The night was made memorable by the blaze from beacons on southern headlands. In Macaulay's words:

> For swift to east and swift to west the
> ghastly war-flame spread,
> High on St Michael's Mount it shone: it shone
> on Beachy Head.
> Far on the deep the Spaniard saw, along each
> southern shire,
> Cape beyond cape, in endless range, those
> twinkling points of fire.

Not for three centuries and a half was England in greater danger; and then the invading hordes of German aircraft were met in the same way—by men well-equipped, possessed of skill and valour. The issue each time was decided not by patriotic flame by by discipline, gunfire and the elements.

Many reports of the Spanish formation spoke of it as being in the shape of a moon or crescent: even one of Shakespeare's sonnets alludes to 'the mortal moon'. It was not quite that, being disposed like a box, with what fighting men of a later generation would have called the 'soft' material protected by a rough shell. There was a total of 130 ships and 27,000 seamen and soldiers. This sight of this compact, slowly moving mass, the ships with painted sides and decorated sails, blessed by the Church as for a crusade, was awe-inspiring to those on the cliffs of Cornwall and Devon.

Leading and in the centre was the flagship *San Martin*, guarded by galleasses from Naples, two on each quarter. On the port side of the first formation was the Squadron of Castile, including galleons of the Indian Guard. Flores de Valdes was nominally in command. He was a cousin of Pedro, disliked for his jealous disposition. As he acted as the Duke's Chief of Staff his place was in the *San Martin*. To starboard was the Squadron of Portugal, including many of the finest ships. This was under the Commander-in-Chief's personal direction.

Behind came the troop- and store-carrying urcas and light craft. The urcas or hulks, often hired ships from Hanseatic sources, were unable to sail fast. They dictated the speed of the rest. The immediate escort was the Squadron of Guipuzcoa, commanded by Oquendo, and the Squadron of Andalusia, under Pedro de Valdes.

On the port wing, at the rear, was the Squadron of Biscay. This was nominally commanded by Recalde, who was in fact on board the galleon *San Juan* and close to Medina Sidonia throughout the campaign. To starboard was the Squadron of the Levant. It consisted mainly of merchant ships commandeered from Venice and Genoa, armed according to their capacity. The officer in charge was Martin de Bertendona.

The Duke considered an attack on Plymouth, which would have caught the English embayed, but decided that the risks were unjustified when he was still so distant from Parma. As it was, by fine seamanship, Howard managed to get most of his fleet to sea and across the line of the Spanish advance during the night of 20 July. His course was to the east of the Eddystone, which was then unlighted. He left an inshore detachment of eight ships to guard against a coastal raid, his main force being eighty ships, of which nine were royal. The rest were armed merchantmen, good for show but not for the stiffest fighting.

Howard began his approach early in the morning on 21 July. Both sides had a shock. The Duke was astonished by the swiftness and ease of handling of the English galleons, which could leave his own ships standing. For his part, Howard was disconcerted to find how many longer-range guns the Spaniards carried. He 'durst not venture to put in among them', as had been his hope. He was equally impressed by the way the enemy kept formation. A cannonade which started about nine o'clock lasted four hours and had no effect except to reduce Howard's tenuous supply of shot. His intention was now 'so to course the enemy as they shall have no leisure to land'. Honours were even. The Duke proceeded on his stately way towards the Isle of Wight. Howard and Drake were left with much to consider, one of their problems being that their fleet was too unwieldy and needed to be organized into manageable squadrons. They were engaged in a new kind of warfare, on a scale hitherto unprecedented, and must learn tactical lessons as they went along. It was one advantage of the slow pace of the Spanish advance that it gave the English time to plan within sight of the enemy. They were also in contact with the shore; and while Medina Sidonia continued steadily towards Parma, there was a further English force waiting for him in the Downs and off the approaches to the Thames with whom he would have to reckon.

Meanwhile, two Spanish galleons were lost, not in action but through misadventure. The *Nuestra Señora del Rosario* of 1,150 tons, flagship of the Squadron of Andalusia, collided with another ship, lost her bowsprit and had other damage. She fell behind the fleet, and was seen during the night by Drake in the *Revenge*. Drake doused his light in order to approach her, putting his squadron into disorder, and challenged her to surrender as soon as he saw her state. In view of the status of his opponent, Pedro de Valdes considered it no dishonour to submit. Drake took the Spaniard on board the *Revenge*, treating him with great courtesy, and de Valdes was thereupon able to observe the English tactics closer to.

The other casualty, the *San Salvador*, of the Squadron of Guipuzcoa, was slightly smaller than the *Rosario*. By accident or, as some said, through the treachery of a Flemish gunner, there was an explosion in her magazine. Two hundred men were killed, and thereafter the ship was in no state to fight. She too surrendered, was brought into Weymouth, but sank later.

These events took place on Monday, 21 July, and helped to put the English in good heart. Howard had divided his fleet into four squadrons, commanded by himself, Drake, Frobisher and Hawkins. Frobisher, in the *Triumph*, the largest ship in the English fleet, 1,100 tons, was detached towards Portland Bill. It is thought that Howard hoped to lure the Spaniards into the tide-race. What in fact happened was that early on the morning of 23 July the Duke sent in his galleasses to attack. The result was another noisy bombardment, but with no serious damage done. The same day Howard, further out to sea, and the Duke had another slogging match, the *Ark Royal* and other ships shooting at the *San Martin* 'ship by ship, whilst she on her part fired her ordnance very well and fast.' The upshot was again nothing more serious than an expenditure of ammunition. This was by now more worrying for the Spaniards than the English, who could look for replenishments from ashore. They were some time coming, and it was to Howard's advantage that at this stage there was a lull.

This was partly due to the wind failing. After a Council of War, held off the Isle of Wight, Howard took the opportunity to knight Hawkins, who sailed in the *Victory* of 800 tons, and Martin Frobisher, the Queen having given her Lord Admiral delegated authority to do so. It was here, on 25 July, not far from St Catherine's Point, that the *San Luis* of the Squadron of Portugal and the Castilian *Santa Aña,* which had fallen astern, were attacked by Hawkins. They were rescued by the galleasses, the calm being to the advantage of their oarsmen.

It was the last incident before Medina Sidonia brought his convoy to anchor off Calais, still in good order. All the same, his position was far from enviable. He had not beaten or dispersed the English fleet, which was now reinforced. He was without news of Parma, who was at Bruges. He was in an exposed and tide-swept roadstead, under the lee of the enemy fleet, and the best he could look for from Calais itself was benevolent neutrality. Actually, the Governor sent him victuals and fresh water, for which famine prices were exacted. The date was 27 July, English style, and only the first part of his mission was accomplished. Messengers went off post-haste to Parma, with urgent requests for immediate liaison and ammunition.

Parma was blockaded. Troops were ready, and barges too, for the crossing to England. Extra lengths of canal had been cut near the coast to facilitate movement, but Parma could mount no invasion unless protected by a powerful force at sea, otherwise his troops would be massacred before they landed. The light vessels of Justin of Nassau, the natural son of the Dutch hero, William the Silent, and now Admiral of Zeeland, kept watch on the Flemish banks. He sealed the Spanish army on shore as firmly as any well-organized larger fleet.

The Dutch 'fly boats' of shallow draft were ideal for use inshore and, although not heavily armed, were adequate for the purpose they served. Unfortunately, there was poor liaison between Justin and the English. It may well have been that Elizabeth's favourite, the grandee Earl of Leicester, whose arrogance had given offence as the Queen's representative in the Netherlands during a brief spell there, had been one reason why communication slackened. But, whatever the English view—and Howard actually heard that no Hollanders or Zeelanders were stirring—they were active. Parma knew that unless Medina Sidonia had already defeated the English fleet, and was in a position to deal with the 'fly boats', there was nothing he could do to further Philip's plans against England. Margate had been spoken of by the Spanish king as a possible landing-place, but, as Ralegh later observed: 'To invade by sea upon a perilous coast, being neither in possession of any port, nor succoured by any party, may better fit a prince presuming on his fortune than enriched with understanding.' Far from being able to secure him the use of a port, Parma, although he had retaken Antwerp from the rebels, found it useless for his purposes while Justin was at sea.

Sights From Ship to Shore

This picture shows a sailor
in the tops of a carrack-type
vessel measuring the distance
from ship to shore by use of a
quadrant, the forerunner of
the sextant. This instrument
was virtually the same as a
back-staff, the successor to the
cross-staff.

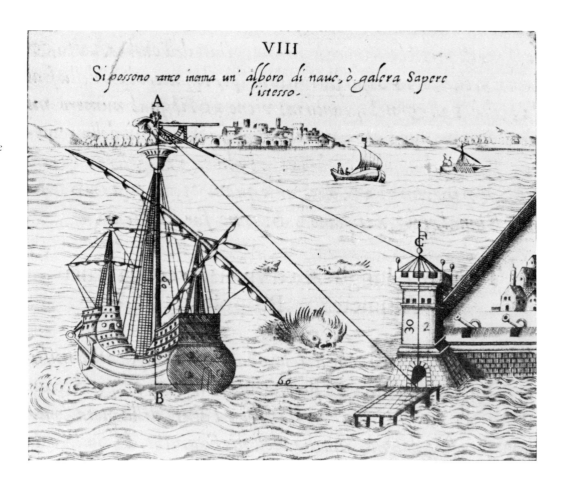

IV

Now that the English fleet was united and facing the Spaniards off Calais, it was the
moment for a decisive stroke, if Medina Sidonia was to be thwarted. The position
would never be more favourable.

At this stage the Queen wrote from London, as a very amateur tactician, to ask:
'What causes are they why the Spanish navy hath not been boarded by the Queen's
ships?' Her inquiry showed less knowledge of how her captains could best fight than
her equally chair-borne adversary at the Escorial. The immediate answer was that at
that stage Medina Sidonia's fleet might be disorganized by fire-ships. Then (but only
then), could a closer method of fighting be considered.

The Spanish Commander-in-Chief was well aware of the possibilities of danger from
this means, and had taken precautions against it by a line of patrol vessels constantly on
the alert. There was special reason for anxiety: fire-ship attack had a long history, but
within the last three years a new dimension had been added. At the siege of Antwerp,
an Italian in the service of the Dutch, one Federigo Giambelli, had invented an explosive vessel nicknamed a 'hell-burner', which had been used with enormous effect
and was credited with killing a thousand men when sent against a bridge of boats.
Giambelli was known to be in England where, although actually engaged on the
defences of London, he was thought to be hatching even more lethal methods of

20

destruction. Fire-ships were bad enough. The explosive variety, launched in Calais roadstead, could mean panic.

On Sunday, 28 July, the day after the Duke had anchored his fleet, a Council of War held on board the *Ark Royal* concluded that just such an attack, with the guns of the fire-ships shotted, should be set in motion. The ships themselves were already prepared. The wind was south-south-west, the ideal quarter. In the darkness, the blazing ships, guns going off as the heat exploded the charges, crews abandoning them at the last minute, aided by a flood of nearly three knots and the set of the current, bore down upon the Armada.

The move had the effect intended. Cables were cut, and a huddle of disorganized shipping was soon in danger of running ashore on the shoals of Gravelines, if it escaped the English.

It was then, in the early hours of 29 July, that Medina Sidonia showed his best, and Howard his worst. It had been agreed that the Lord Admiral should lead the follow-up attack after the fire-ships had done their work. Had he done so, the result could have been decisive. Instead he left the matter to Drake, who was always an individualist, while he gave his attention to the *San Lorenzo*, flagship of the galleasses, with Hugo de Moncado in command.

The galleass had run aground in the confusion. Howard sent a boat party to attack her, although the *San Lorenzo* was now useless to the Duke. Perhaps the Lord Admiral wished to get even with Drake for the capture of the *Rosario*. Whatever the motive, the delay was serious and fruitless. Although Moncado was killed and the galleass boarded, the intervention of the Governor of Calais, who claimed rights in the stranding and enforced them with gunfire, made Howard's party withdraw. Belatedly, the *Ark Royal* joined the fighting off Gravelines.

Howard's action had given Medina Sidonia the priceless chance to rally his galleons. He did so to such effect that although in the fighting which followed one of them was sunk and two others, the *San Felipe* and the *San Mateo*, taken by the Dutch, after much battering, one to the east and the other to the west of Ostend, he kept his main force together, and was prepared for every attack. His own courage was such that at critical stages in the fighting he would climb into one of the fighting tops of the *San Martin*, there to observe the behaviour of his captains, for this was the crunch.

Howard might boast 'we pluck their feathers by little and little', and Drake say he thought Medina Sidonia would be glad enough to be back among his orange groves, but the fact of the matter was that with almost everything in their favour, including replenished magazines, and the elation of knowing that any immediate idea of invasion could be dismissed, any English ships which ventured close to the galleons, as many did, got bloody noses. The *Revenge* tried it, and was 'riddled with every kind of shot.' Drake's cabin suffered, and people using it had narrow escapes.

Fighting continued from nine in the morning of 29 July until six in the evening. About five o'clock there was a sudden squall and the wind veered to north-west, putting the Spaniards on a dead lee shore, with the ebb stream adding to the leeward drift. The English held off. They could only watch wind and tide take effect, for the continuous bombardment had once more reduced their powder and shot.

The issue hung on Spanish seamanship. It did not fail; and on 30 July the wind suddenly backed to south-south-west, its old quarter, and saved the Duke from the Flemish banks. He himself would have liked to turn on the English and try to batter his way home down Channel, but everything was against this. Although, to Hawkins's way of thinking, his fleet still seemed 'very forcible . . . the greatest and strongest combination, to my understanding, that ever was gathered in Christendom', the Duke was forced to return by the long and dangerous route north-about. Howard shadowed him as far as the mouth of the Tyne, and then broke off.

Research into Spanish ironfounding, together with the results of recent underwater investigation and the recovery of artefacts from sunken Armada ships, has led to one firm conclusion. Although Spanish ordnance, short and medium range, was of a weight comparable with that of the English, in action their shot fragmented against stout oak sides. That was the reason why the English loss was so light. Every ship returned. Structural damage was easily reparable, and only one hundred men were killed in action. The number included one rash sailor who, in the *mêlée* off Gravelines, actually boarded a Spanish ship and was instantly cut down.

Of the Spanish ships which set out about seventy returned, though some were unfit for any further service. The fate of a few vessels will never be known, and there was a high proportion of galleons among the survivors. This is not to be wondered at, for they were the best equipped, and well manned. Sixteen ships were wrecked on the coast of Ireland and two in Scottish waters. One hulk foundered somewhere at sea, and another, the *San Pedro Mayor*, was lost on the coast of Devon. This was particularly sad, for she was acting as a hospital ship and had actually completed the passage north-about. Most of her crew were saved. Justin of Nassau's men had accounted for two galleons, and another ship, additional to the pair taken during the run up-Channel, surrendered to the English on her way back to the northern port from which she had been hired. Only one ship had actually been sunk by English gunfire, off Gravelines. She was the Biscayan *La Maria Juan*, of 665 tons.

The English fleet could have been ready for further action almost at once, but some of the ships were paid off to save money, the crews being turned away to beg or starve. There was terrible hardship once the excitement was over, and hundreds died of typhus. Spanish casualties, although not known exactly, were high, and must be reckoned in thousands, perhaps as many as half of those who set sail. Many, as with the English, died from sickness. Recalde barely survived the journey home, dying almost at once after his return.

The Duke's tactics could have been summed up in five words: 'Keep station for mutual support.' English standing instructions, dating back to the time of Henry VIII, stressed the value of holding the windward position. Signals were almost entirely restricted to hailing, with the use of speaking trumpets, and to the simplest flag signals, not shown according to a regular code, but by arrangement with the Admiral. If Howard's orders could have been compressed into a sentence, it would have been: 'Keep the wind—and your distance.'

Queen Elizabeth composed a song which was sung at a service of thanksgiving held at St Paul's Cathedral in the November following the deliverance:

> My soul ascend to holy place,
> Ascribe Him strength and sing Him praise,
> For He refraineth Prince's spirits
> And hath done wonders in my days.
> He made the winds and waters rise
> To scatter all mine enemies.

AN·DNI·1571·
ÆTATIS·SVÆ·
·29·

Sir Richard Granville killed
in a sea-fight near the Azores
1591

Sir Richard Grenville
unknown

Famous for his stubborn but foolhardy defence of the *Revenge* against fifty-three Spanish ships, Richard Grenville was a member of an old Cornish family, and was an MP in two Parliaments. Twice he sailed to Roanoke to colonize that place on Ralegh's behalf. On the news of an expected Spanish treasure fleet, he was sent, as second-in-command to Sir Thomas Howard, to the Azores to intercept it. The Spaniards, hearing of this, sent a large fleet to protect it, and Howard, greatly outnumbered and with many men sick, wisely made off; but Grenville did not follow, and for fifteen hours his 120 men held out against 5,000 Spaniards. Not until only twenty men were left did the *Revenge* yield. Grenville died of his wounds in the Spanish admiral's flagship not long after. The story is immortalized in Tennyson's poem 'The *Revenge*: A Ballad of the Fleet'.

Philip was not the only one who believed that God was on his side. He attributed the reverse to sins and shortcomings, and never reproached Medina Sidonia, who served him well for the rest of his life, ashore.

V

During the years which followed the Armada, England was given frequent cause for alarm. Undeterred by his losses Philip mounted other expeditions against Elizabeth. He could make use of her back door, Ireland, which had never submitted tamely to conquest, and whose chieftains were as Catholic as himself. Some of his attempts came to grief through stress of weather, some through bad management, but there were successes, even though on a small scale, such as landings in Cornwall which led to the burning of Mousehole and Penzance, and Spanish swagger on a coast from which many of her opponents had come.

Some idea of the scale on which such operations were conceived may be obtained from the list of provisions shipped for one of the smallest expeditions: 12,837 barrels of biscuits; 696 skins of wine; 1,498 barrels of salt pork; 1,031 barrels of fish; 6,082 barrels of cheese; 2,858 barrels of vegetables; 2,900 barrels of oil; 850 barrels of vinegar; 2,274 barrels of water; and 631 barrels of rice. With variations and omissions, such supplies would have been found in an English fleet, one of the main differences being that beer would have been carried instead of wine. This native beverage did not keep well at sea; complaints about this fact were incessant. Oil would have been in smaller quantities; rice omitted; and 'vegetables' would have been dried peas and beans. There was no appreciable difference between what sailors and soldiers ate on campaigning. Biscuit and cheese were the staples. The sailors could supplement dried victuals with fresh fish, caught at sea, and soldiers could rob the farmer of cattle and sheep.

One of the ideas which attracted Elizabethan maritime strategists was a watch on the Azores such as amounted at times to a blockade. The prize would not be the islands themselves, where water and provisions could be had through *force majeur*, but the annual treasure fleet, that magnet of hope. Philip took increasingly effective measures against depredations. Among them, for the area of the Caribbean, was the construction of vessels known as gallizabras. Like the galleass, these were a variation of the galley, heavily armed and making good use of sail. Gallizabras could hold their own against anything but a large man-of-war, and they were fast. For the ocean crossing, the 'Indian Guard' was strengthened.

The watch on the Azores led to the best-known single ship action of the era, the defiance of a Spanish fleet by Sir Richard Grenville, an account of which, written by Ralegh, was to become the basis of Tennyson's 'Ballad of the Fleet'.

The year was 1591, and Grenville sailed in Drake's Armada flagship, the *Revenge*. The force to which she belonged was commanded by Thomas Howard, a young cousin of the Lord Admiral. The ships had been nearly four months at sea, with poor results. Many men had gone sick and been sent ashore to recover, when suddenly there came news of the approach of a large Spanish fleet. It was in charge of Alonzo de Bezan, a younger brother of the dead Santa Cruz. It included thirty galleons, six of them of the latest build, nicknamed the Apostles by the English.

Howard, who was at Flores, barely had time to re-embark his shore parties and slip his cables when the Spaniards were on him. He ran before the wind, like a man of sense, for de Bezan was in overwhelming strength. Grenville, an obstinate firebrand, preferred to try to force his way through the galleons, for which he felt contempt. One of Howard's squadron, an armed victualler called the *George Noble*, actually turned back to help Grenville. Her captain was told to save himself before it was too late.

Grenville fought for sixteen hours, sank two galleons, and gravely damaged others before the upper works of the *Revenge* were a complete wreck. With powder expended, not a hand weapon unbroken, and himself badly wounded, he ordered his Gunner to 'split the ship'—scuttle her—rather than surrender. But the Master, and a handful of surviving seamen prevented this, 'it being no hard matter to dissuade men from death to life', as Ralegh said. The *Revenge* was surrendered to Martin de Bertendona, on honourable terms. The Spaniard was a most able officer. His father, years before, had escorted Philip to England on his way to marry Queen Mary. He himself had commanded the Squadron of the Levant in the Armada.

Apart from the expensive heroism, much of the interest in the action lies in the undoubted fact, which Grenville would have realized from accounts of the Armada actions, of the ineffectiveness of Spanish shot. At Flores, the range was point-blank, for the ships were grappled. A survivor told Ralegh that the *Revenge* survived 800 hits. As her own armament contained nothing larger than demi-cannon firing 32-pound shot, the superiority of English weapons, which had inflicted damage out of all proportion to that received, could not have been shown more effectively.

Capture of Cadiz 1596
Contemporary

Following rumours of a second Spanish attempt on England, a combined fleet was sent to Cadiz in 1596. The Earl of Nottingham, lately Lord Howard of Effingham, was in command at sea, with the Earl of Essex, Queen Elizabeth's favourite of the moment, leading the army. Because of the antipathy of the two commanders, as in Vernon's expedition 150 years later, little was achieved, although Cadiz was taken. The Navy burnt several ships, but land fighting was negligible.

Gun Founding c. *1600*
Jan van der Straet (also
known as Stradanus)

A scene in a gun foundry.
Early guns were usually cast-
iron, as bronze was too
expensive. Development was
continuous during the
fifteenth and sixteenth centuries, and guns, with a
multitude of names, ranged in
their shot from 70 lb weight
(cannon) to $\frac{1}{2}$–1 lb weight
(robinet). The culverin was
the most popular type of gun
at this time, but it was
eventually superseded by
longer-range guns of heavier
calibre.

When the *Revenge* was at last given up she was completely dismasted. Her decks were littered with corpses and she had no more powder. Even so, she was not in a sinking state. A few days later, under jury rig and with a Spanish prize crew, she was lost in a hurricane, close by the cliffs of Terceira. This was a fate shared by ships far less badly damaged.

Grenville himself died on board the galleon *San Pablo*, bitterly regretting that he had been prevented by his own men from killing himself rather than be taken by the enemy. His ship was the only royal galleon surrendered by England during the war with Spain. The action, though heroic, was an unnecessary gesture of bravado: but at least it showed that even the newer Spanish ships were highly vulnerable, and that their ironfounders had a lot to learn.

Five years after Flores came Ralegh's finest hour as a sea commander. In company with Howard of Effingham and the Earl of Essex he took part in a second raid on Cadiz. It was as devastating as Drake's, and this time landings were made and the town taken. No galleys disputed the passage of the English fleet though, oddly enough, their use was revived at about this time by the Genoese, Federico Spinola, who made a nuisance of himself on the coasts of France and Flanders. At Cadiz, Philip's galleons were attacked in harbour, but the treasure they contained was sacrificed, for the Spaniards fired their own fleet.

To some degree, Cadiz made up for the lack of success of an earlier descent on Portugal, where it was hoped that Dom Antonio, who had found refuge in England, would have a large following. It was not so. An expedition organized in his favour proved abortive.

Cadiz was the chief ray of splendour in years of anti-climax. At the time it took place Hawkins and Drake, those veteran campaigners who had shared so many adventures, had gone off once more to the Spanish Main. They found the scene transformed. There was no possibility of surprise in any area of importance, and the commanders themselves were failing. Hawkins was over sixty and a sick man before ever he set out. He died at sea off Puerto Rico. Drake, cast down by the news, died off Porto Bello not long after his kinsman. Drake had lost favour with the Queen to the extent that although she allowed him to sail on this final mission, she was too shrewd a judge of men not to know that, although not advanced in years, he had lost his old touch and that overflowing measure of luck which had attended him earlier in life.

Philip II died in 1598; Queen Elizabeth five years later. James I came down from Scotland to rule at Whitehall and to work for peace with Spain. He clapped Ralegh into the Tower, which enabled that indomitable man to embark on a history of the world. This contained wise passages based on his own experience, and observation of the scenes in which he had taken part. He composed the work for the benefit of Prince Henry, heir to the throne, who was among his admirers. Unfortunately, the prince died young, his inheritance devolving upon his brother Charles, to the ultimate misfortune of man and nation. But at least Henry was spared learning of the sad failure of Ralegh's last expedition to Guiana, and shock at the death on the scaffold of a towering Elizabethan.

THREE

THE RISE OF
THE DUTCH

The Sea Beggars — Victory at Gibraltar — The Prince Royal
Loss of the Vasa — Tromp at the Downs — The Sovereign of the Seas
War with England — The 'Fighting Instructions' — Blake's successes
The battle of the Sound

THE ENGLISH APART, no people in Europe had been more elated at the repulse of the Armada than the Dutch. They had suffered the rule of Philip II since 1555. They had endured the terrible measures of suppression taken by Alva. They knew that the sea was their salvation. Privateers, nicknamed the Sea Beggars, were encouraged by French Protestants to use the Huguenot port of Rochelle as an Atlantic base. Moreover, possession of the sovereign principality of Orange gave the leader of Dutch resistance, William the Silent, who was Prince of Orange and Count of Nassau, the right to his own flag on the high seas. He authorized the more responsible captains to fly the Lion of Nassau on a flag of three longitudinal stripes, orange, white and blue. From this procedure, in time, arose a great Navy.

In 1572 the Beggars, led by Guillaume de la Marck, took the port of Brill, with five and twenty sail and seven or eight hundred fighting men. When the Orange flag was planted on the walls, it was the first time it had flown on dry land in the Netherlands. Ironically, it happened the year after the victory over the Turks at Lepanto, for the Dutch had a saying '*Liever Turcx dan Paape*'—better Turk than Pope—so fervid was their Protestantism—which would have shocked deeply those who stemmed the tide of Islam. The phrase emphasized the gulf between one sort of Christian and another.

Dutch qualities included resolute courage allied with sturdy independence of spirit. They had a huge, well-regulated fishery which harvested the North Sea and areas further from home. This, and their cargo-carrying trade, was their nursery of seamen. With a small population—that of the province of Holland, 670,000, was only about twice the size of London—a high proportion were at sea, either full-time or seasonally. They were splendid navigators, used to the storms, shoals and treacheries of one of the more difficult coastlines of Europe. They encouraged invention. They were skilled at maps and charts. Their climate inured them to hard winter conditions. In sum, they had the necessary qualities to make for successful expansion. Philip, by repressive rule, gave them the needed stimulus. They resisted him, his viceroys and successors for close on a century. Although they paid in blood for what they did, few Dutchmen doubted victory.

The nation's chief handicap was that, although dependent on wood-built shipping of every kind, it had no forests. The best source of timber, and of naval stores in general, was the Baltic, the countries of which engaged in what the Dutch called their Eastland or Mother Trade. For generations the history of Holland cannot be understood without reference to that of Denmark, Sweden and Russia. The Dutch were inured to fighting by land and sea, but alliances varied, and at first their fortunes were linked with those of the Protestant states.

Various types of ship, for coastal and ocean-going traffic, were developed and built in Dutch yards. The term 'fly boat' covered several sorts of hull and rig. By the end of the sixteenth century, the fluyt was evolved, a cargo carrier which became familiar in every harbour of western Europe. A peculiarity was the stern, which was rounded near the water. Fluyts were narrow, and with flat bottoms. The Dutch came to the specialized man-of-war later than some maritime nations. When their galleons first appeared they were of a modest size, well adapted to home waters.

The year after the capture of Brill, and nearly a decade before the assassination of William the Silent at Delft, the nascent Dutch navy achieved a major success at sea. A small flotilla outmanoeuvred a Spanish squadron off Enkhuysen, on the waters of the Zuider Zee. The Spaniards, fighting in less handy ships, were all scattered, sunk or captured. The Dutch took seven prizes, among them a ship armed with thirty-two fine bronze guns. They also captured the Count of Bossu, who made a useful hostage, helping to ensure better treatment for Dutch prisoners of war. It was one of the last important incidents before the recall of Alva.

Although it was many years before the Dutch won another victory comparable in prestige, their commerce flowed. Philip played into their hands by barring them from Iberian ports. This forced them to quest further afield. An East India Company was established in 1602, following the example of England, which had given a Charter to a Company of a similar kind two years earlier, when Queen Elizabeth was still alive.

The Dutch were intent on ousting the Portuguese from primacy in the lucrative Eastern spice trade, and they soon adopted the policy of excluding all rivals, even Protestants and allies. It was an Eastern voyage begun in Holland in 1595 by four ships of the galleon type, three of which returned the following year, which laid the foundation of Dutch imperialism, long before their national independence had been recognized by treaty.

The earliest significant clash between Spanish and Dutch in which fleets rather than squadrons or detachments were involved arose directly from the need to protect Dutch traffic overseas. In April 1607, Jacob van Heemskerk was sent with about thirty fighting ships to cover homeward-bound shipping on the passage from the Straits of Gibraltar along the Atlantic coasts of Spain, Portugal and France.

Van Heemskerk received news that there were ten Spanish galleons assembled near the Rock. When he reached the Straits he summoned a council of war at which his captains, after much deliberation, seconded his wish to attack. The Spaniards, although warned, scorned the Dutchmen, smaller in size than themselves, and allowed van Heemskerk to come down upon them when they were still at anchor.

The Dutch withheld their fire until they were well in among the enemy. Then, since they were mobile and the Spaniards were not, they concentrated two or three ships against a single opponent, a move which in later phases of sail warfare came to be known as 'doubling'. At the end of four hours, the result was the same as at Enkhuysen—complete victory, with every Spaniard driven ashore or burnt. Dutch loss

Boy Using a Back-staff
From *A newe systeme of the Mathematicks* by Jonas Moore

The back-staff was an early navigational instrument measuring the altitude of the sun, as opposed to the cross-staff, which measured the altitude of heavenly bodies. The user of the back-staff had the sun behind him, hence its name. It was more or less the same as the quadrant invented by John Davis, the Elizabethan explorer.

was small by comparison, but as it included van Heemskerk himself, rejoicing was muted.

One result of the encounter was that Hendrik Vroom, a pioneer in marine painting, was commissioned to commemorate the battle, which he did with sensational effect, showing the destruction of the Spanish flagship. He had already worked on tapestry designs illustrating the defeat of the Armada, at the behest of Lord Howard of Effingham.

Being democratic, down-to-earth and not much interested in show, the Dutch did not waste money on prestige shipbuilding for themselves as to some extent England and other countries continued to do. James I, although not noted for his interest in the Navy, did at least authorize the construction, by Phineas Pett, best-known of a long line of shipbuilders, of what became a famous vessel. She was the *Prince Royal*, launched in 1610 and named in honour of Prince Henry, who lived only two years after her advent before he succumbed to typhoid. Vroom was commissioned to paint her. His work shows that she was fitted with three complete rows of gun-ports, and that the lateen topsail which would have been expected on her mizen and bonaventure had been replaced by a square sail. The vessel had an active life of more than half a century, and has claims to have been the precursor of the three-decked ship of the line.

The *Prince Royal* appeared during a twelve-year truce between Spain and Holland. War was resumed in 1621, the event being signalized in Holland by the inauguration of a West India Company, one of the clearest indications that Spanish rights overseas would be disregarded. England also suffered insult, although she was at peace with the Dutch. Pursuing their policy of exclusion, the Dutch massacred English traders at the spice island of Amboina, since they considered the English were encroaching on their own preserves. It was an injury deeply felt. Although for years it went unrevenged, it was never forgotten. The English said that the Dutch had no business to behave to others exactly as the Spanish were behaving to them when they trespassed, as they had long done, in forbidden areas.

The continuing war with Spain led to a series of Dutch successes. Their most rewarding triumph was the capture of the annual treasure fleet by Piet Hein when it was assembling at Matanzas, off the north coast of Cuba, in 1628. It made him a national hero, and brought Holland an influx of fifteen million florins. There had been nothing like it in all the years that ships from England, France and Holland had roved the Caribbean.

The year of Piet Hein's jubilant return to Holland saw an event in the Baltic of a very different kind, but significant for the future as symbolizing the limitations of Scandinavian power at sea. This was the loss of the galleon *Vasa*, belonging to King Gustavus Adolphus of Sweden.

At the time of the tragedy the Dutch were recognized as the most forward-looking shipbuilders in northern Europe, the introduction of wind-driven sawmills adding to their efficiency. Although there was plenty of work at home, their leading shipwrights were glad to go where still more lucrative employment was to be had. Among such places was Stockholm, where Henrik Hybertson designed the *Vasa*, built near the site of the present royal palace.

Since the Middle Ages the Baltic had seen a protracted struggle between Sweden and Denmark (which then included Norway), to decide whether or not Sweden had the capability of becoming a European as opposed to a purely Scandinavian power—a

Baltic prisoner. There was also need to decide whether Denmark had the strength to retain the key to the Sound, guarded by Kronborg Castle at Elsinore, the scene of *Hamlet*. The alternative entrance, by way of the Belt, was beset with difficulties and could be barred by forts.

Naval wars in the Baltic were incessant, King Christian IV of Denmark having the distinction of leading fleets in person, as well as being the only monarch to lose an eye in a sea battle. Feuding was so fierce that between 1563 and 1570 there were times when the Sound was closed, supplies of naval stores and grain interrupted, ocean trade at a standstill. Once Holland had built up a navy strong enough, she was to make it her business to ensure that neither Sweden nor Denmark dominated the Baltic so completely as to hold other nations to ransom. Only to that extent did Baltic maritime struggles concern other countries. As their historian, Dr R. C. Anderson, observed: 'The principal feature of these wars was their exclusiveness.'

In the 1630s Gustavus Adolphus, pre-eminent as a soldier, considered the time ripe to build a prestige ship, and ordered one from Hybertson. Unfortunately, the *Vasa* was badly handled on her maiden voyage and sank before she was clear of Stockholm harbour. The salvage of her hull and fittings has been one of the more dramatic

The Sea Beggars
H. C. Vroom

In this picture, the Sea Beggars have the Spaniards penned up in Haarlem Lake. Privateers receiving Letters of Marque from William of Orange, leader of Dutch resistance to the Spaniards, they were encouraged to use the French Protestant port of La Rochelle. Led by Guillaume de la Marck, they unexpectedly captured the harbour of Brill in 1572. Twice more the Sea Beggars defeated Spanish squadrons, and, although piratical by nature, they were the fore-runners of the efficient Dutch fleet of the next century.

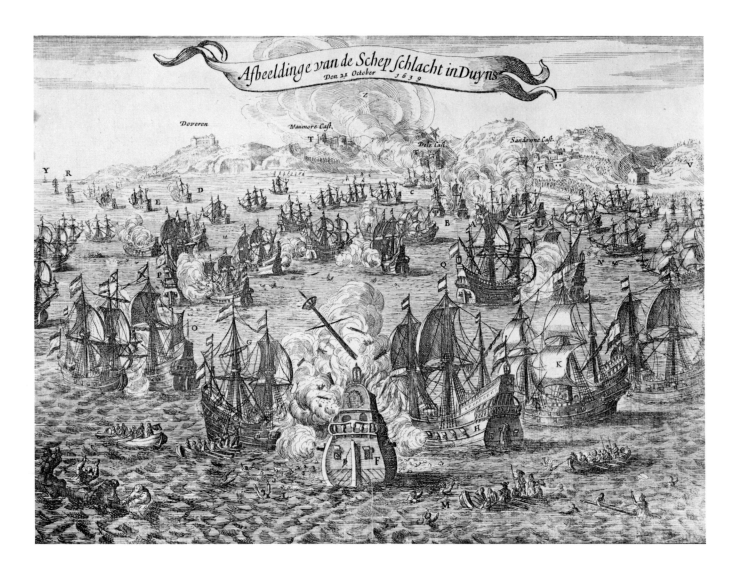

episodes of modern times, and she is the survivor among big sailing ships of war most comparable in interest to the *Victory* at Portsmouth. Gustavus's intervention in the Thirty Years War in Germany, which was covered by a fleet, took place two years after the loss of the galleon, and laid the foundations of Sweden's brief empire. He himself did not disrupt trade with Holland, but his shipbuilding activities helped towards a clash between his successors and the Dutch, which led to an alliance with Denmark, and to more than one important naval battle. Meanwhile, the Dutch were occupied elsewhere, continuing their triumphs against Spain.

II

An important success was won off Dover on 21 October 1639, English time, and became known as the battle of the Downs. In one way it was an echo of the Armada; in another, a mark of humiliation not only on Spain but to some extent on England.

The circumstances were as follows. Martin Harpetzoon Tromp, son of one of van Heemskerk's frigate captains, who was to become a Dutch sea commander second

32

The Battle of the Downs, 1639
Chrispyn van de Passe the
Younger.

This was the battle in
which the Spaniards, under
Oquendo, son of one of the
commanders of the Armada,
tried finally to wrest the
mastery of the seas from the
Dutch. Stalemate developed
over weeks and it was not
until that fateful date, 21
October, that Maarten
Tromp, leader of the Dutch,
attacked. Not many victories
can have been more complete,
and Oquendo, a broken
man like his father, returned
to Spain. Humiliatingly, the
English, under Sir John
Pennington, had to stand by,
watched by the Dutch
Admiral Witte de With,
unable to take part in a battle
in their own English Channel.

in fame only to de Ruyter, defeated a Spanish squadron near Gravelines and then proceeded to blockade Spanish-held Dunkirk. In order to relieve the port the Spaniards assembled a fleet of 77 ships, of which Admiral Oquendo was given charge. He was a son of the officer who had commanded the Squadron of Guipuzcoa in the Armada and his task was not unlike that of Medina Sidonia. He was to convoy 24,000 men in fifty transports to join Spanish forces in the Low Countries, liberating Dunkirk as he did so.

Spanish planning assumed that Oquendo, in spite of the existence of a state of war with France, would meet with no serious opposition on his way up Channel; indeed, at the time, the French fleet available in northern waters was negligible. But it was also assumed, with excessive rashness, that the fleet would be able to brush Tromp aside. No tactical plan had been worked out for anything but a straightforward progress from Spain to Dunkirk.

Tromp was not only alert, but full of confidence. He had light forces on the watch between Dunkirk and the westerly approaches to the Channel. The Spaniards were sighted in September off Selsey Bill. They were in the compact order which had been a feature of the Armada, and for the same reason—the protection of transports.

When the initial clash took place the Dutch had only seventeen ships in company, their main force being concentrated off Dunkirk. But Tromp had inherited van Heemskerk's faith in attack, and when he ordered a concentration of fire on the flagship *Santiago*, Oquendo retreated towards Dover. He knew he could not hope to fulfil his mission without a serious battle, and needed time to consider. His view was that at the worst he would be protected by English neutrality. His misfortune was that the English had not the strength necessary to prevent a clash in their own waters.

Oquendo anchored close to a squadron under Sir John Pennington, a friend of Ralegh in earlier days, who promptly removed the Spaniards from nine transports which had been hired from England, thus adding to a tense situation.

English sympathies were divided: the general population favoured the Dutch, but the Court inclined to Spain. Oquendo was allowed to send ashore for fresh water and victuals, for which he was charged a high rate. Tromp was reinforced, but slowly. Weeks passed; and at last some of the bolder Spaniards, under cover of night, got away by ones and twos to ports of Flanders.

At last, Tromp, with an insolence perhaps arising from the known ineffectiveness of Spanish shot, offered to send Oquendo 500 barrels of gunpowder if he would fight it out. The Dutchman had to deal with five Admiralties, those of Rotterdam, Amsterdam, North Quarter, Middleberg and Friesland; all were asked to strain every nerve to send him more ships. At last he had a hundred ships under his orders. Most were small, but fire-ships were included. He told an Englishman that his King would soon have Oquendo's guns, his countrymen their ships, sunk or afloat, and the devil their men.

On the day of battle Tromp sent a subordinate flag officer, de With, to watch Pennington, in case the English should interfere. Then he bore down on the enemy with the pick of his fleet. Oquendo and some of his captains fought stubbornly, but many ships were burnt, and seven thousand men perished. The *Santiago* and thirteen other ships escaped, much battered, and made for Dunkirk, the blockade of which Tromp had to relinquish in order to make sure of victory. By the end of the winter Oquendo was back in Spain and the Dutch dominant in northern waters. The long struggle with Spain ended at last in 1648, when the independence of the United Provinces was formally recognized at the Treaty of Münster.

33

By a strange chance, the settlement between Holland and Spain almost coincided with the publication, in three magnificent volumes, of a maritime treatise, in many respects in advance of its time, by one of the survivors of the raid on Cadiz of 1596, bringing echoes of an earlier epoch. This was *Dell Arcano del Mare*. It was issued in Florence by Robert Dudley, a son of the Earl of Leicester, who had been knighted for his part in the attack on the Spanish port.

Dudley had left England under a cloud, taken employment with the Grand Duke of Tuscany, and on the Duke's behalf had drained a morass which then existed between Pisa and the sea. It was a feat of engineering to which Leghorn owed its future prosperity. Dudley's knowledge of navigation, charting, astronomical observations, military and naval theory was exceptional, and his work was so much admired in Italy that a new edition was called for after his death, at a ripe age, in 1649. In one respect he was misguided. He foresaw a future for the gallizabras as a general type of fighting ship, for which he suggested an armament of 50 guns, which would have turned the vessel into a ship of the line with oars as an auxiliary. His work was much studied, particularly in Mediterranean countries, where the oared vessel was still being built, but it had no effect in his native country, to which he did not return, nor in Holland, whose navy would soon be occupied with a more formidable opponent than Spain.

III

A little before the battle of the Downs, both England and France indulged in prestige ships. Charles I asked the designer of the *Prince Royal*, Phineas Pett, to engage on another master work. This was the *Sovereign of the Seas*, later known as the *Royal Sovereign*. She was completed in 1637, a year earlier than the French *Couronne*, which, though much the same size, about 2,000 tons, carried 72 guns on two decks, whereas the *Sovereign* mounted 100 guns on three.

Charles took close interest in every detail of the vessel, which was an advance on anything which had yet appeared in England. Her overall length was 232 feet; 128 feet on the keel; she was 48 feet at her greatest breadth, and had a draught of 23½ feet. Costly as she was, at £65,586. 16s. 9½d., she lasted nearly half a century before being accidentally burnt. Rebuilt and cut down, she took a notable part in many actions, and in spite of a protest by Trinity House that her size would raise difficulties, this did not occur.

The *Sovereign* had no bonaventure, but she carried an extra sail at the top of her other three masts, 'royals' on the fore and main, and a top-gallant sail on the mizen. She was the most richly decorated vessel afloat. Her carving was begun by Gerard Christmas and continued, after his death, by his sons and assistants from drawings by van Dyck. Her stern was rounded, flattening out about ten feet from the waterline. The Dutch themselves praised her, calling her the 'Golden Devil', and on one occasion she is said to have 'sailed through and through the Holland fleet, and played hard upon them'. Charles's subjects protested at his expenditure on 'Ship Money', fearing it would lead to 'Soldier Money', to which they would have objected more strongly still. As it was, 'Ship Money' was one of the many causes of the English Civil War, which was won by Parliament largely because, at critical times, the party at Westminster secured control of the fleet.

The Jesus *of Lübeck*
From the Anthony Roll

Lübeck was one of the first two ports of the Hanseatic League, a north German trading confederacy, the other being Hamburg. The merchants of the Hansa towns held a virtual monopoly and their seaborne trade was phenomenal. The *Jesus* of Lübeck had been bought by Henry VIII and was lent by his daughter, Elizabeth, to Sir John Hawkins for the slave trade. While at San Juan de Uloa, Hawkins and Drake were surprised by a Spanish squadron and, through treachery, attacked by them. The *Jesus* was lost. This illustration appears in the Anthony Roll at Cambridge, part of which was given to Pepys by Charles II.

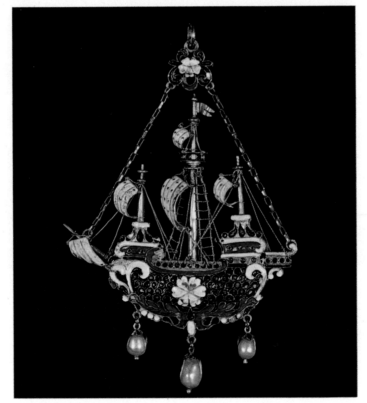

Three-Masted Venetian Ship in the form of a Pendant

This pendant of gold and pearls shows a typical three-masted ship of the fifteenth century, when Venice was at the zenith of her power as a trading nation, in spite of continual wars with neighbouring Genoa. After Lepanto in 1571 Venetian power began to decline through the Oriental explorations of the Portuguese and Spanish, although the Republic's demise did not occur until 1797 when she was absorbed into the Napoleonic Empire.

Portuguese Carracks off a
Rocky Coast, c. *1530*
Attributed to Cornelius
Anthoniszoon

The carrack was a large
trading vessel of the four-
teenth to the seventeenth
centuries until superseded by
the galleon, and was a com-
promise between square and
lateen rig. They were broad-
beamed, stout vessels carrying
high castles fore and aft.
Some of the largest were of
over 1,000 tons. Most of the
early exploration undertaken
by the Spanish and
Portuguese was in this type of
ship.

Charles, Lord Howard of Effingham, later Earl of Nottingham
Daniel Mytens

This portrait was painted thirty years after the Armada, showing Charles Howard, by then Earl of Nottingham. The Queen was of the belief that her Lord High Admiral, as a nobleman, apart from showing some efficiency, should be in command of the fleet against the Armada, if only to keep her buccaneers, such as Drake and his fellows, in some sort of order. Drake and his superior saw eye to eye, which can also be said of Howard's portrait in Queen Anne's House at Greenwich. From whichever direction one looks at his portrait, the eyes are met at every point.

Howard's masterly management of his motley fleet, aided by weather adverse for Spanish hopes, foiled the invasion of England.

The Great Michael
(Model)

Built by James IV of Scotland, the *Great Michael* was one of the 'prestige ships' of the day, and resulted in the King's brother-in-law, Henry VIII, building the *Henry Grâce à Dieu*, or *Great Harry*. The *Great Michael*, having 'wasted all the woods of Fife' in her building, had only a short life – six years – and was lost on her way to France. She was said to have been **240** feet in length, with ten-foot thick sides.

Not only the last battle of the Third Dutch War, it was also the most fiercely contested. Prince Rupert and d'Estrées made contact with de Ruyter on 11 August. D'Estrées' division took little part in the ensuing action, but finally Rupert, in the centre, broke free. The rear divisions of both fleets fought an extraordinary battle, the commanders of both, Cornelis Tromp and Spragge, transferring to three different flagships each, though eventually Spragge was drowned. Although the battle was indecisive, the moral victory was de Ruyter's.

Whereas the Thirty Years War had devastated much of Germany, setting the country back for generations, in England the case was different. There had indeed been division, suffering and loss; yet after the King's execution in 1649, and the later assumption of power by Oliver Cromwell, the Commonwealth was seen by foreigners to be formidable, with a Navy which increased yearly. Nowhere was this of more significance than in Holland.

The Civil War had been won, after several false starts, by organization and discipline, and some of the spirit of Cromwell's 'Ironside' cavalry began to be shown at sea. Parliament found in Robert Blake an officer of outstanding quality, who took to command afloat as readily as he had done ashore. Blake's first service to his masters was to contain and then to scatter a small Royalist force which at first roved in Ireland, in Portugal, on the coast of Africa, and even in the Caribbean. The leaders were the Palatine princes, Rupert and Maurice. Rupert had made a name as a soldier, and although he was no match for Blake, and his brother was lost in a West Indian hurricane, he managed to preserve some of his ships, returned with them to France, and was heard of again when his cousin, Charles II, regained the throne of England.

Meanwhile, war came about between England and Holland, two countries which should have continued as allies. Trade was the difficulty. Rivalry in commerce was continuous, with the Dutch coming off best. The situation was aggravated by the passing of a Navigation Act in 1651, with the idea of encouraging home merchant shipping. It ordained that goods were to be imported into England either in English ships or in those of the country where they were produced. It was an undisguised threat to the Dutch carriers.

The English also wished to uphold the principle of a right of search for contraband of war, when engaged with an enemy by sea. The Dutch, with an eye to prosperity for neutral carriers in such a conflict, insisted that 'the flag covered the goods'. The two ideas could not be reconciled.

Another frequent cause of friction arose from what was known as the 'English Claim to the Salute.' In times when punctilio counted for much, the 'Honour of the Flag' could cause the utmost trouble. This had been shown when in 1637 Captain Henry Stradling, commanding the *Dreadnought* off the Lizard, had actually fired on a Dutch commodore on his way back from Brazil with a convoy, because he would not 'strike for the King of England' until forced to do so. Two years later, after he had beaten Oquendo, partly in English territorial waters, Tromp had added insult to injury by an ironical salute to Pennington's flag.

It was in furtherance of Charles's claim to the Salute, from all foreigners met with in what were vaguely termed 'British seas', that the *Sovereign* had been embellished with national emblems of every sort. They were intended to make known a right to maritime dominion which certainly did not always have a basis in fact. Not unnaturally, this was a cause of longstanding grievance with the Dutch. Besides all this, there was a fear in England that their rivals across the North Sea, with closer access to the Baltic, might take all the proceeds from the tax known as the Sound Dues at Elsinore. English trade with Scandinavia was growing. In 1618, no fewer than 1179 Dutch ships had paid Sound dues, as against only 90 English; but the English proportion was rising, and the northern trade was becoming vital.

Blake found when he began to cross swords with Tromp in 1652, on an element which Tromp had known since boyhood, that it was a very different matter from

35

harassing Prince Rupert. At first, he got the worst of encounters, but there were two factors working in his favour. The first was that the Dutch had far more merchant convoys to protect than he had, which limited their freedom. The second was that the five Dutch Admiralties, well as they had worked together against the Spanish, became progressively more difficult. At one stage, conflicting directives, and acid post-mortems, so handicapped the Dutch admiral that he wrote: 'My trouble arises from this, that after I have given all that is in me to the service of my country, I may be molested on my return home with subtle questions.' How many commanders, before and since Tromp's time, have echoed his words! Blake was luckier. Cromwell, who knew the perplexities that beset a field commander, wrote to his friend: 'You must handle the reins as you shall find your opportunity, and the ability of the fleet to be.' Blake could be sure of backing, even when things went wrong. By 1653 two other 'Generals-at-Sea' were giving him support. One was George Monck, who had campaigned since his youth and was professional in the fullest sense of the word; the other was Richard Deane, noted as an artillerist. The war would be won by superior gunfire and regular tactics.

On 29 March 1653, the triumvirate issued Instructions, under their joint signatures 'for the Better Ordering of the Fleet.' This was because, the year before, Blake had been worsted by Tromp off Dungeness partly owing to some of his captains not supporting him. The Instructions, which were the forerunners of a succession of such documents, were the most important issued to any sailing fleet up to that time. They enjoined the line ahead formation as the one to be taken up at the start of an action, and they provided for its application not merely to individual squadrons, but to the whole fleet.

When once the instructions had been understood, and put into practice by signals from a simple code of flags, the least intelligent captain could see that they enabled ships to develop their maximum force. Tactics being dependent on seamanship, the adoption of the line ahead in a satisfactory manner would scarcely have been possible had not Commonwealth ships had much practice in cruising together.

Captains were ordered particularly to guard against a concentrated attack on the flagship, which occurred so often in sea battles. In such an event, ran the sixth article of the Instructions, 'The ships of the fleet or of the respective squadron are to endeavour to keep up in a line as close they can betwixt him and the enemy, having always one eye to defend him in case the enemy should come to annoy him.'

It is notable that Ralegh, in this as in so many ways an exemplar of seamanlike knowledge, had issued standing orders on rather similar lines on his expedition to the Orinoco in 1617. From this it is arguable that his Elizabethan contemporaries had also come to the conclusion that there must be a well understood and regular battle formation. Ideally, there should be no more 'charges' and partial engagements, though, of course, there were.

Even before the issue of Fighting Instructions, the English were beginning to take the measure of their more experienced opponents. Tromp had the worst of a struggle which began off Portland on 18 February 1653 and lasted three days, but he saved many of the valuable convoy he was guarding, which included richly-laden ships from the East Indies, at the cost of twelve warships. Deane was killed off the Gabbard in June, but not before the Dutch had been beaten. Monck, who shared the same flagship as Deane, covered his colleague's body with his cloak so that the sailors should not be discouraged. Tromp himself was mortally wounded near Scheveningen in July, his last

Copenhagen 1658
C. J. Visscher

Charles X Gustavus of Sweden wished to extend possessions in the Baltic, and to this end invaded Denmark in 1657. There was a renewal of war the following year when Charles besieged Copenhagen, but he was repulsed by the Dutch, who, wishing to keep the Sound open for their trade, now intervened. Wrangel met his Dutch opponent, Obdam, at the entrance to the Sound; the ensuing battle was a *mêlée* at the end of which the Dutch retreated on Copenhagen, an event the Swedes claimed as a victory; however, as they were in no condition to follow, and the Dutch mission was to relieve Copenhagen, which they did, this theory held no water.

PRÆLIUM NAVALE INTER BELGAS ET SUECOS. A° 1658.

words being: 'I have finished my course—be of good courage.' He had set a fine example of valour all his life. The monument which his nation erected to him in the Nieuwe Kerk at Delft, not far from that of William the Silent, moved Pepys to admiration when he saw it.

Although the war ended in England's favour, with her flag respected throughout Europe, it settled nothing. The Dutch were unlikely to accept second place as carriers, and their race of outstanding sea commanders did not cease with Tromp: but, at least, the humiliation of Amboina had been avenged.

By his incursions into the Mediterranean, first in pursuit of Rupert and later in an expedition against the pirates of the Barbary Coast, when he won an important success at Porto Farina on the coast of Tunisia, Blake made his Government felt abroad in a way which had not been known since the days of Drake and Hawkins. More was to come, for when he had settled with Holland, Cromwell turned upon Spain, and stumbled to success in the West Indies. He sent William Penn, father of the founder of Pennsylvania, with an amphibious force to attack Hispaniola, the modern Haiti. Penn and the general, Venables, were driven off but, rather than achieve nothing, they seized and held Jamaica. The island became of increasing importance in an area where England already had a flourishing settlement at Barbados.

Blake's own final service was a blockade of Cadiz, in the style of his predecessors. Later, he destroyed a Spanish West India fleet at Santa Cruz, Teneriffe, but died on the way home.

Clarendon, a political opponent, paid him a lasting tribute in his *History of the Rebellion*:

> He was the first that infused that perfection of courage into the seamen, by making them see by experience, what mighty things they could do, if they were resolved; and taught them to fight in fire as well as upon water; and though he hath been very well imitated and followed, he was the first that gave the example of that kind of naval courage and bold and resolute achievements.

IV

Only four years after peace had been made with England, a serious crisis arose in the Baltic. It was left to the Dutch to resolve it, for, after the death of Cromwell, England's energies were mainly directed to trying to settle her internal affairs without bloodshed. Cromwell's son and successor, Richard, proved to be a man of straw, factions were rife, and it was nearly two years before the monarchy was restored with the return of Charles II. This was largely through the firmness of Monck, who saw the trend of public opinion. In the meantime there occurred a struggle for control of the Sound which resulted in a battle of much consequence for the future.

Gustavus Adolphus, after his death in battle at Lützen, had been succeeded on the throne of Sweden by his eccentric daughter, Christina, who abdicated after making known her conversion to Catholicism. The reins of government were taken over by her kinsman, who became King Charles X Gustavus. He proved to be one of the most restless and ambitious soldiers who ever disturbed the northern countries. He laid siege to Danzig, the centre of the grain trade, thus disrupting a traffic of great importance to Holland, whose ships carried most of the cargoes. Charles's long-term aim was to enlarge the gains made by Gustavus Adolphus, and to turn the Baltic into a Swedish lake.

The Dutch won the first round in 1656 when, under pressure from the Amsterdam merchants, they sent a fleet under Obdam and Cornelis Tromp, the lesser son of a great father, to relieve the city. Although the Swedes had a strong navy and capable admirals such as Karl Gustaf Wrangel, the King did not at that stage wish to challenge a fleet with sea experience more extensive than his own, particularly when it was reinforced by a Danish squadron.

When Charles, thwarted at Danzig, which was declared a neutral port, turned on Denmark and began to carry all before him, matters altered. The Danish king, Frederick III, appealed to the Dutch for all help in their power. He was reassured by the words of van Bueningen, the Dutch representative at his Court, who said: 'the oaken keys of the Sound lie in the docks of Amsterdam.'

The boast may have been true enough in a long-term sense, but for the moment the Dutch were up against a difficult proposition. Obdam left the Vlie on 7 October 1658 with a large fleet, and anchored two weeks later in the Kattegat. There he heard that Kronborg, overlooking the Sound on the Danish side, had already fallen to Charles who had removed some of the biggest guns to help in an attack on Copenhagen. Thus, both

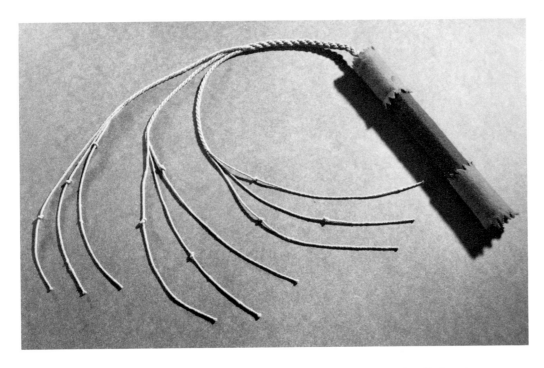

Cat O' Nine Tails

The infamous instrument
of punishment in the Royal
Navy, the 'cat', was not
officially abolished until 1879,
but had fallen into disuse long
before. Consisting of a thick
rope handle and nine knotted
lengths of cord, it was used
for flogging seamen for various misdemeanours, ranging
from drunkenness to insubor-
dination. Flogging round the
fleet usually ended in death
for the miserable miscreant.
The expression 'letting the
cat out of the bag' refers to
the bag in which the whip
was kept.

Baltic shores were in the same hands, the very event Obdam had sailed to prevent.

At first, head-winds prevented the Dutch from proceeding towards the Danish capital, where Wrangel had his fleet in readiness to help the Swedes ashore. Hearing of the Dutch approach, he sailed to meet the enemy.

Obdam's force was in three squadrons. His van was under de With in the *Brederode*, the centre under his own direction in the *Eendracht*, and the rear under Floriszoon in the *Joshua*. There were a few Danish ships in support, but Frederick's main fleet was in Copenhagen harbour, concerned with the defence of the city, which was to be saved by the heroic efforts of the citizens, led by their King.

The opening shots were fired at about nine o'clock in the morning, and the battle continued for several hours. The Dutch had the advantage of the wind and advanced without regular order, as was often their way. The action thus developed into a series of ship-to-ship duels, in which concerted tactics played scarcely any part, and where squadronal and fleet flagships, as always, were the object of particular attack.

This was well instanced when de With, a veteran of many sea campaigns, in the smaller *Brederode* of 59 guns, made bold to attack Wrangel himself in the *Viktoria*, 74. However, when Obdam came up, who, according to etiquette, was Wrangel's proper opponent, de With drew off and engaged the *Drake* and the *Leopard*, which were ships nearer his own weight of metal. The *Leopard* was soon so badly damaged by the Dutchman's fire that she had to be run ashore on the islet of Hven, where she burnt out. Shortly afterwards, the *Drake* and the *Brederode* both grounded on the Danish side of the channel. The Swedes managed to get the *Drake* off, but the *Brederode* stuck fast, and was attacked by the *Wismar* of 44 guns. After two hours' cannonading, a party from the *Wismar* boarded, de With was killed and his flagship taken. Almost immediately afterwards she slipped into deeper water and sank. She was the subject of more than one study by the Dutch artist, William van de Velde the Elder, who was with the fleet. He and his son became prototypes of official war artists. Their work, based on

39

innumerable sketches, often made under fire, has never been exceeded in accuracy and beauty, and is one of the most valuable sources of information about the ships of their day.

The next movement on the part of the *Drake* was to go to the relief of the Swedish flagship, which was being hard pressed by Obdam in the *Eendracht* and other ships. The *Viktoria* had, in fact, been so much damaged that when at last she shook off her assailants, Wrangel had to take her out of action to near Kronborg Castle on the Danish shore, where she anchored for repairs.

It was now Obdam's turn to be hard pressed. He was soon engaged by four Swedish ships, one of which, the *Cesar*, had just beaten off the Dutch *Joshua*, killing Admiral Floriszoon in so doing. The Dutch captains rallied to Obdam's support, the *Cesar* was driven off, and the *Pelikan* captured. The *Morgonstjerna* also struck, but foundered almost at once.

In further duels the advantage lay with the Dutch. Two more Swedish ships surrendered, and although the Dutch *Breda* of 28 guns was at one time lost, the enemy abandoned her when she caught fire and she was recovered later.

During the early afternoon, with the wind freshening, the Dutch fleet broke clear of the Swedes and ran down to Copenhagen, very few of Wrangel's ships being in any state to follow. Because of this move by the enemy, Wrangel claimed a victory, but, since Obdam's immediate object was to help the defence of the Danish capital, a feat which he achieved, it was hard for Wrangel to support his claim, even to Charles X. The Dutch losses had certainly been less than those of their opponents. The *Brederode* had been captured and sunk, together with a few vessels not large enough to lie in a regular line of battle. They had also lost two flag officers, de With and Floriszoon. This was a more important matter, since ships can be replaced, while notable leaders are uncommon. Wrangel, on the other hand, had lost five big ships—three taken, one taken and sunk, one run ashore and burnt.

The war itself did not end until the following year, when Michel de Ruyter, who shares with the elder Tromp the leading place in Dutch naval history, sailed for the Baltic with a fleet and 12,000 troops to reinforce the advantage gained by Obdam. Such a measure prevented Charles X from fulfilling his aim of a northern hegemony, with himself in the leading place. He died early in 1660, and although the peace terms which were agreed at Copenhagen were on the whole favourable to Sweden, the Dutch made sure of the old right of passage for foreign shipping through the Sound, subject to tolls. It was a matter over which they had active support from England which, at one time, had aimed at an alliance with Sweden.

The fight between Wrangel and Obdam, typical of many stern battles which have taken place between fleets of northern Europe, was mainly significant as showing the lengths to which maritime Powers were prepared to go and the sacrifices they would make to maintain free access to the Baltic. It was not the last contest in which the same principle was involved, but it was the most celebrated.

It was fortunate for Europe in general that, over the course of time, the Scandinavian countries could never consistently combine to make the Baltic a sea over which they could exercise undisputed control. The enmity between Sweden and Denmark continued, and it was only by making sure of some balance of strength between them that supplies upon which, throughout the era of sail, so many others were dependent, could be brought to them by sea.

40

FOUR

ENGLAND, HOLLAND AND FRANCE

―――――――――――――――――――

England and Holland renew warfare — The attack on Bergen
The Four Days' Battle — Holmes's 'Bonfire' — The Dutch in the Medway
Louis XIV invades the United Provinces — Anglo-French activity
De Ruyter's last campaign

DURING THE CENTURY following the battle of the Sound, Swedish acquisitions on the eastern and southern shores of the Baltic contracted under repeated reverses. Dutch naval power declined relative to that of England, although Holland remained one of the foremost maritime countries. France emerged as an aspirant to sea supremacy, but not a strong one, since her Continental interests and ambitions were paramount. Spain continued to provide inexpensive victories for other nations.

Tension between England and Holland had subsided during the negotiations with Sweden and Denmark over the future of the Sound. It turned to something warmer when Charles II, after a sojourn in the Low Countries immediately before his return to England, was given an enthusiastic send-off at Scheveningen to the land from which he had had to flee in disguise nine years earlier. Yet trouble recurred within a few years, chiefly owing to continued Dutch expansion as traders and carriers. This led to serious clashes overseas, in Africa particularly, where both England and Holland had 'factories' or trading-posts. As Monck put it: 'One of us must down.'

England was not in as strong a position as she had been under Cromwell. France was obliged to help Holland by the terms of an existing treaty originally aimed at Spain, though it was unlikely that her efforts would be strenuous. Wise heads suggested caution, but there was a strong party in London of what a later age would term 'hawks'. They included the King's brother, James, Duke of York, whose stubborn character was not matched by an intelligence comparable with that of the King. James was intent on extending his experience of war, and the 'hawks' had their way.

There were problems. Money was short, and many ships were in a bad state. According to Pepys, who had become a member of the Navy Board as Clerk of the Acts, and was making himself familiar with every side of the administration of the fleet, little was right. If his moans were to have been taken at their face value England should have made a poor showing. Men had to be pressed, and when pressed were not paid. Corruption was rife in the dockyards. Personal feuds erupted continually, yet nearly all the principal officers who had served the Commonwealth so well gave loyal service to Charles II.

Fleets continued to be assembled, supplied and manned, however inefficiently,

41

ATACCO FATTO DALLI VASCELLI INGLESI A QVELLI DEGLI OLANDESI NEL PORTO DI BERGE IN NORVEGIA IL DI 12 DI AGOSTO 1665

throughout the times of which Pepys wrote. In the case of this new Dutch war it seemed at first as if events might go in England's favour despite all shortcomings. An encounter which had started in the approaches to the Thames and reached its climax off Lowestoft on 3 June 1665 seemed a good omen. The Dutch had over a hundred ships at sea, the English rather more. The English fleet was commanded by the Duke of York in person. His two senior admirals were Prince Rupert, whose practical talents were valued by his royal cousins, and the Earl of Sandwich, Pepys's patron. The Dutch Commander-in-Chief was the veteran Obdam, hero of the Sound, flying his flag in the *Eendracht* which, like himself, had survived many battles.

According to an anonymous account written from afloat, and now among the Harleian manuscripts at the British Museum, the fleets first engaged at long shot, the English in line, as required by the Fighting Instructions. The distance appears to have been too great, so James bore down on the Dutch and, according to the narrative, cut through Obdam's formation, which was ragged. 'About three of the clock,' runs the

42

account, 'Obdam's ship was blown up, as we suppose by a lucky shot, which amazed their whole fleet as it encouraged ours. So we fell in Pell Mell with them. After which it will be hard, till Stories be compared, to give a particular account of what happened.'

The writer, whoever he was, put his finger on the difficulty of describing sea battles accurately, then and always. He also made the point that it was a 'Pell Mell' battle that the English would favour. They were not always able to bring it about, but at Lowestoft they succeeded.

Unfortunately, when the various 'Stories' were collated, it appeared that a great opportunity had been missed. The Dutch, after the loss of the *Eendracht*, were in full flight, and the Duke of York ordered a pursuit to be continued throughout the night following the battle. He then went below to get some sleep. Henry Brouncker, his gentleman-in-waiting, later went to Harman, the flag captain of the *Royal Charles*, with an order to shorten sail. Believing the message came from the Duke, Harman did this. His example was followed by the rest of the fleet, and the Dutch escaped. The Duke was furious, but the harm had been done. Brouncker's friends believed that the act arose from concern for the safety of the royal person, not from faint-heartedness. Whatever the motive, it was misguided.

In spite of disappointment, there was public enthusiasm over the battle. Medals were struck; and in the opening of his *Essay On Dramatic Poesy* (1668), Dryden referred to it in a passage which showed the impression the event had made on a man of letters in his middle thirties.

> It was that memorable day, in the first summer of the late war, when our navy engaged the Dutch; a day wherein the two most mighty and best appointed fleets which any age had ever seen, disputed the command of the greater half of the globe, the commerce of nations, and the riches of the universe. While these vast floating bodies, on either side, moved against each other in parallel lines, and our countrymen, under the happy conduct of his Royal Highness, went breaking, by little and little, into the line of the enemies; the noise of the cannon from both navies reached our ears about the City, so that all men being alarmed with it, and in a dreadful suspense of the event which they knew was then deciding, every one went following the sound as his fancy led him; and leaving the town almost empty, some took towards the park, some cross the river, others down it; all seeking the noise in the depth of silence.

Repercussions in Holland were violent. Jan Evertsen, who had been second in command to Obdam, was thrown into a river by an excited mob. As he was later exonerated from blame and lived to do his country notable service it was as well that he was fished out little the worse. One or two captains were shot; others were degraded or dismissed. In fact, on both sides, the battle resulted in a pattern of behaviour which was often to be repeated when sailing fleets were in action—confusion; limited vision owing to gunsmoke; suspicion of lack of support; accusation; recrimination; distrust.

Cornelis Tromp was chosen to replace Obdam, but before he could take the fleet to sea de Ruyter arrived from the West Indies, where he had noted, from their dispositions in that area, how ineffective French help was likely to be. The States of Holland, knowing de Ruyter to be their best commander, superseded Tromp, and it says much for his willingness to serve that, although furious at such a humiliation, Tromp agreed to second place.

The Medway: Capture and Burning of HMS Royal Charles 1667
D. Langendyck

During the Second Dutch War, de Ruyter led a Dutch fleet up the River Medway, breaking a boom at Sheerness and burning five ships, including the *Royal Charles*, and capturing two others, while Monck sank two more. The presence of the Dutch blockading London caused such panic that even Samuel Pepys made two wills and sent his family out of the city with directions to bury as much of his money as they could in his father's garden. De Ruyter left after what amounted to a month's siege.

Just two months after Lowestoft an untoward episode occurred at Bergen in Norway, an account of which does not always find its way into history books. The United Provinces were then, owing to a series of deaths, and the minority of the reigning Prince of Orange, lacking an august figurehead. In consequence, they were not highly regarded in monarchical countries, even though they were nominally supported by Louis XIV of France, the most absolute ruler living. The attitude applied to Frederick III of Denmark, in spite of the benefits he had received from Dutch help.

Although Denmark was neutral at the outset of the Anglo-Dutch war, Frederick inclined towards England, to whose royal house he was related. He made a secret arrangement that an English fleet should be allowed to enter Bergen to attack a convoy of Dutch merchantmen, some of them from the East Indies, which were awaiting escort into their own home waters. The consideration was that Frederick was to receive half the value of the plunder.

The scheme failed ignominiously. Sandwich sent Sir Thomas Teddemans to Norway with fourteen small ships of the line, but either by accident or design, the attack was set in train before the Governor of Bergen had been told by his King to allow it. As a result, the English were met by heavy fire, not only from the Dutch ships, some of

which were armed, but from the landward forts. After four hours, Teddemans had to retreat, with loss. A month later, Pepys noted in his diary that the Dutch had got home safe '. . . which,' he commented, 'will make us all ridiculous.'

The affair made an official breach between England and Denmark inevitable. The following year Frederick signed an agreement whereby the Dutch were to pay him a subsidy of 600,000 dollars towards the expenses of a Danish fleet, provided Frederick kept at least forty ships in commission to prevent English ships entering Danish waters.

In this same year of 1666 there occurred two considerable sea battles and two devastating fires. The battles were in the normal course of the war. The first of the fires was a deliberate act which followed a landing on the Dutch coast. The second, which was fortuitous, is famous as the Great Fire of London.

The first battle extended from the 1st to the 4th of June, and became known as the Four Days' fight. It provided various object lessons. Among them was that it was unwise to divide the fleet. The English did so on this occasion because they anticipated the advent of a French force from Toulon in support of the Dutch. This did not in fact take place until all was over.

As the King decided that his brother should not risk his life again at sea so soon after Lowestoft, where he had had many narrow shaves, Rupert and Monck were appointed joint Commanders-in-Chief. Monck had recently enhanced his high reputation by administering the affairs of the capital when the plague was at its height. Although he was then nearing sixty, his age, so far from damping his ardour, had, if anything,

Sir Robert Holmes, his Bonfire
William van de Velde the Elder

First coming into prominence in an attempt to regain English factories in Africa from the Dutch, the next year (1664) Sir Robert Holmes occupied New Amsterdam, renaming it New York after his patron, the Lord High Admiral. Commanding the *Revenge* at Lowestoft, he played a large part during the Four Days' Battle. In 1666, he operated off the Dutch coast, his most famous exploit being the burning of some of the Dutch fleet and 170 merchantmen in the River Vlie, the resulting conflagration being known as 'Holmes's bonfire'. Fighting at Solebay, he survived for another twenty years.

45

increased it. Rupert, eleven years younger, had always been known for dash, and the two were well matched. Monck was phlegmatic in temper, Rupert explosive. They had fought together years before against the Spaniards, and they now worked tirelessly to get the fleet into good shape.

Rupert went off down Channel on what turned out to be a wild goose chase, and on 1 June Monck sighted the Dutch in thick weather off the North Foreland. Although heavily outnumbered, he had the wind in his favour and decided to attack. At first all went well. Cornelis Tromp and his squadron were chased towards the French coast and de Ruyter, with the main body, was unable to get into action until noon. Then real trouble started for the English. As the shoals of Dunkirk drew near Monck was forced to turn about, and he was badly mauled by the Dutch centre and rear. The *Swiftsure* surrendered when her admiral, Sir William Berkeley, was killed after a gallant fight, and another flagship, the *Henry*, just escaped being overwhelmed by Jan Evertsen.

Action was resumed next day, and once again Monck chose to attack, in spite of his battered state. He pressed the Dutch hard, but after hours of fighting against heavy odds he withdrew slowly towards the English coast. The retreat continued, in good order, on 3 June, on which day three disabled ships had to be burnt to prevent capture. Then followed another blow. Sir George Ayscue's flagship, the *Royal Prince* of 90 guns, one of the finest vessels afloat, grounded on the Galloper Sand, where she was surrounded and burnt, Ayscue becoming a prisoner of war. However, during the early afternoon Rupert, warned and brought back by the sound of gunfire, came up in time to save Monck from total destruction.

The English admirals conferred, and decided to fight on. The result was a *mêlée* in which both fleets fought to a standstill. The *Royal Charles*, which flew Monck's flag, and the *Royal James*, with Rupert's, were badly damaged. Yet another admiral, Sir Christopher Myngs, who had commanded the van, was mortally wounded on board the *Victory*, but by then de Ruyter had had enough, and the Dutch withdrew.

The English lost 8,000 men and seventeen ships, with two admirals killed and one a prisoner, but Dutch loss was also heavy, and de Ruyter, so familiar with every aspect of war, was astonished at the spirit of his opponents. Dutch admiration went so far as to cause the body of Sir William Berkeley to be embalmed. In a most gracious gesture, it was returned to England for burial.

Pepys's friend and fellow diarist, John Evelyn, saw the fleet a few days after its return, noting:

> I beheld that sad spectacle, namely more than half of that gallant bulwark of the Kingdom miserably shattered, hardly a vessel entire, but appearing rather so many wrecks and hulls, so cruelly had the Dutch mangled us.

Even so, the general spirit (as has so often been the case after a serious English reverse) was buoyant. Pepys himself, in an Admiralty coach, was witness to a scene which occurred at Myngs's funeral.

> About a dozen able, lusty proper men came to the coach-side with tears in their eyes and one of them . . . spoke for the rest . . . 'We are here a dozen of us that have long known and loved and served our dead commander . . . and have now done the last office of laying him in the ground. We should be glad we had any other to offer after him, and in revenge of him. All we have is our lives; if you will

please to get His Royal Highness to give us a fire-ship among us all, here are a dozen of us, out of all which choose you one to be commander, and the rest of us, whoever he is, will serve him; and if possible do that which shall show our memory of the dead commander, and our revenge!'

Pepys remarked that the offer was 'one of the most romantique that I ever heard, and could not have been believed, but that I did see it.' The value of this incident is as showing how, throughout the age of sail, and however hard their conditions, sailors were capable of the utmost devotion to those they trusted.

Astonishing energy was generated during the weeks following the battle. Ships were patched up and provisioned. Men were got together by every means, fair and foul, and at the end of July, Rupert and Monck, and no doubt Myngs's lusty sailors, had their reward.

The Dutch, who were ready for action by 15 July, reached the coast of England a week later. They found the English anchored off the Gunfleet, the sandbank to the south of Harwich. After two days' manoeuvring, action was joined at about ten o'clock on 25 July, St James's Day, not far from Orfordness. Jan Evertsen was killed early in the fight, and so were two other senior Dutch officers. De Ruyter's flagship was dismasted and, after about six hours' fierce fighting, the Dutch gave way. De Ruyter conducted his retreat with the same masterly skill that Monck had shown when similarly beset.

On this occasion Tromp's rarely suppressed desire to act independently got the better of him. Without authority, he took his squadron out of the line to attack the English rear. Although he managed to destroy one ship, the *Resolution*, of 74 guns, he was badly worsted. He was hotly pursued to the Dutch coast, along which Rupert and Monck were soon parading. De Ruyter was furious at Tromp's behaviour and he was sent ashore.

An immediate result of the success was a massive raid by Sir Robert Holmes on Westerschelling. Holmes was a swashbuckling type, a favourite with Rupert and a survivor of his forlorn cruise after the English Civil War. A landing was made, aided by treachery, and about 160 merchant ships were burnt in the Vlie in what became known as 'Holmes's Bonfire'.

To the Dutch way of thinking, it was by God's judgement that, after such massive destruction of their property, much of London should be destroyed within a few weeks. Fire raged in the City between 2nd and 6th September, when most of the mediaeval buildings were consumed, and thousands of people made homeless.

Worse was to follow. During the following year Charles laid up his large ships, with the result that de Ruyter, in the course of a skilfully conducted raid on the Thames and Medway, put London in a panic, destroyed many vessels, and actually towed the *Royal Charles* back to Holland. Treachery was not all on one side, and Dutch success was made easier by English deserters acting as pilots. The *Royal Charles* lay long at Hellevoetsluis. The stern-piece with the royal arms was taken ashore, where it remains to this day.

After such humiliation, England was fortunate to make a tolerable peace. This was partly owing to the work of the outlying squadrons, which had done well. In North America, the Dutch settlement at New Amsterdam had been captured. It was retained by the British for over a century under the name of New York. In the area of the

Cornelis Tromp (1629–91)
Nicolaas Maes

Son of a famous father—
Maarten Tromp—he com-
manded an expedition to
Morocco in 1650 and served
in the Mediterranean. Losing
his command, he regained it
in 1673, distinguishing himself at Schooneveld and causing panic in London when the
English were driven back up
the Thames. Having fought
for the Danes in one of their
many wars against Sweden,
he became a noble of
Denmark. He died at
Amsterdam in 1691, while in
command of an expedition
against France.

Abraham Duquesne (1610–88)
Alexandre Steuben

Duquesne, the son of a
Dieppois merchant, saw
much sea service in the war
against Spain. Joining the
Swedish navy as a vice-
admiral in 1643, he led them
to victory over the Danes at
the battle of Gothenburg.
Back in France, he compelled
the surrender of Bordeaux in
1650 during the revolution of
the Fronde. For twice defeating the Dutch fleet in 1676, at
Stromboli and at Augusta, he
was granted a patent of
nobility, a rare occurrence.
The famous Dutch admiral,
de Ruyter, died of his wounds
shortly after the latter battle.

48

Caribbean and South America, the redoubtable Harman, once a leading captain under Blake, and later the Duke of York's loyal subordinate, had success. He destroyed a French squadron at Martinique and raided settlements at Surinam and Cayenne. But the real reason why Holland made peace was more dramatic. Louis XIV declared war on Spain, with the aim of acquiring the Spanish Netherlands. The Dutch were soon in mortal danger from their ally.

II

The crisis for Holland was averted, though only for a time, by a makeshift alliance with England and Sweden. This caused Louis to pause, and to make an equally temporary peace with Spain, through which he strengthened his northern frontiers. Charles II, who was to be his pensioner, secretly promised to re-engage in war with Holland as soon as Louis was prepared to renew his drive towards a frontier on the Rhine.

The blow fell in 1672. French armies marched north, and the Dutch cut their dykes to defend their country. At this time of emergency, the nation turned once more to the House of Orange, as it had done when facing Philip II. The young Prince William, later to become William III of England, whose minority had been darkened by the annexation of his southern principality by Louis, was appointed Captain General at the age of twenty-two. He was to dedicate the rest of his life to opposing the man who had robbed him of his patrimony.

Louis welcomed alliance with England because it gave him the use of a navy more experienced than his own. He himself was land-bound, the idea of the Roi Soleil at sea being almost comical. However, he knew the care that Charles II and his brother had for their fleet, and may even have heard of a remark by Bishop Burnet that Charles had rather too *much* sea science for a prince.

The French produced a line of privateering captains second to none, but as a national service their navy had persisting limitations. Richelieu was the first statesman to build it up, and he used it mainly in the Mediterranean, in war with Spain. After the Cardinal's death came a period of neglect, rebuilding being left to Jean-Baptiste Colbert. Unfortunately, at the time of the assault on Holland, Colbert's influence was diminishing because his taxes made him unpopular, and the toy fleet which he had assembled for the King's amusement on the lake at Versailles ceased to interest his master. Louis is only once recorded to have visited his ships of war. Although he was impressed by what he saw, the actions of his fleet, as opposed to that of his armies, make no great show among the spread of grandiloquent commemorations which awe or tire the visitor to his principal palace.

Colbert worked well. He solved the manning problem, at least in theory, by a system of enrolment, the *Inscription Maritime*, a register of seamen. There was provision for a *Caisse des Invalides*, to look after the wounded. Pay could be made direct to a seaman's family. A corps of marine artillery was formed; and if he had established the officer class on a more satisfactory basis, he might have made the French navy a model armament. Unfortunately, he looked to the aristocracy for leadership, much as was done in Spain, and this at a time when other navies were encouraging, though with limited success, promotion of the 'tarpaulin', the man bred to the sea, as opposed to the well-connected amateur.

*Battle between Duquesne and
de Ruyter*
Engraved by Voyez

In 1674 Sicily rebelled
against Spain and requested
help from France. Spain
enlisted their allies, the
Dutch, and thus it was that
de Ruyter and Duquesne,
both Protestants, found themselves fighting for Catholic
countries in alien waters.
January 1676 saw a first
inconclusive encounter,
although de Ruyter enforced
the blockade of Messina for
four months. In April they
met again off Augusta, where
the Spanish did not support
the Dutch effectively, and de
Ruyter received his mortal
wound. Two months later,
the Dutch were defeated off
Palermo.

In shipbuilding, Colbert had at first relied on the Dutch, as did so many nations, and he also employed the services of a Neapolitan, Biagio Pangallo, who became known as Maître Blaise. He taught shipwrights that by undercutting the hull they could produce some of the fastest ships afloat, as had been the case at the time of the Armada. Artistically, Pierre Puget was employed to decorate sterns in an elaborate way—what was known as 'ginger-bread work'. So glorious were his designs that he actually suggested that they were the most important part of the ship. Louis, with his love of display, would probably have agreed, but no fighting seaman could have been expected to do so.

Critical and expert eyes looked closely at the newest French ships when they came to join forces with the English fleet. They were impressive. None was more approved than the *Superbe*, which wore the pendant of the Chevalier de Rabesnières-Treillebois. King Charles himself visited her, and so did the Duke of York. So did Sir Anthony Deane, a leading ship designer, who noted:

This ship was greatly commended both by the French and English that went on board her. She was 40 foot broad, carried 74 guns and six months provisions, and but 2½ decks; ours, being narrower, could not store so much provisions nor carry their guns so far from the water. Which Sir Anthony Deane observing measured the ship and gave his Majesty an account hereof, who was pleased to command A.D. to build the *Harwich* as near as he could to the *Superbe*'s dimensions; which was done accordingly with such satisfaction as to be the pattern for the 2nd and 3rd rates built by the late Act of Parliament, which is generally agreed to be without exception, and the highest improvement that is known to this day.

French tactical notions were another matter, and it is significant that, when his treatise on the subject appeared later on in the century, Paul Hoste, the father of naval tactical studies, called it *L'Art des Armées Navales.* A military emphasis appeared throughout, not just in the title.

Although Hoste, a Jesuit and a teacher of mathematics, had experience at sea, he thought of naval actions in terms of outmanoeuvring an enemy fleet rather than of destroying it. This was the theory of the primacy of the Ulterior Object. Plans should be aimed at securing the success of a mission without undue loss. Anything more rational or more different from the English idea of searching out and attacking the enemy fleet could hardly be imagined. It is not surprising that Hoste's majestic folio of 1697, the result of many years' cogitation, was not translated into English until 1762, and then only partially.

The new war was not popular in England, and not likely to be. Had the secret negotiations which brought it about become generally known most Englishmen would have wished Charles II back in exile, and a man at the helm more concerned with the nation's long-term interests, less with those of the monarchy.

Louis sent a fleet of thirty ships of war to serve under the Duke of York, who returned to sea service so that there should be no question over chief command. Even Louis was unlikely to dispute the claim of the Lord High Admiral of England. His own representative was the Comte d'Estrées, who flew his flag in the *Saint-Philippe* of 78 guns, the largest French ship. Among the more notable officers were Abraham Duquesne, commanding the van squadron in the *Terrible,* 70 guns, and the Chevalier de Tourville in the 50-gun *Sage.*

For the Dutch, much depended on de Ruyter, and he was equal to every demand. Ordered to protect an up-Channel convoy of great importance, his hope was also to prevent the junction of the French and English fleets. This he could not do, and the Allies, concluding that he felt himself outmatched, proceeded in leisurely fashion to Solebay, off Southwold, to revictual. There, they were attacked at anchor, in much the same way as Monck had attacked Cornelis Tromp six years earlier.

The battle took place on 28 May 1672. De Ruyter's tactics were to send a small force forward to mask or, as he put it, to 'amuse' the French, from whom he expected little opposition. He himself attacked the Duke of York in the centre, and he sent a force under van Ghent against the Blue Squadron, commanded by Lord Sandwich in the *Royal James.*

Boldness succeeded. The Allies were taken by surprise, and were in some disorder. The fire-ships on which the Dutch relied to make up for lack of preponderance in artillery were never used to better effect. The Duke of York was forced to change flagships more than once and, although stoutly supported, held his own with difficulty.

As for Sandwich, he was to leeward of the enemy. Having fought for several hours, and expended all her powder, the *Royal James* was set ablaze by fire-ships, and burnt steadily down to the waterline. The admiral tried to get away in a boat, but it sank, and all were drowned. His body was found floating many miles from the scene of the battle, recognizable by the Star of the Garter and some splendid rings.

The Dutch lost three ships, all much smaller than the *Royal James,* which was a cheap price for such a success as they had gained. De Ruyter had disrupted allied plans for an invasion of Holland from the sea, at least for the first campaigning season.

There was much criticism of the lack of zeal shown by the French, for whom de Ruyter had shown such obvious contempt. It was said in England that Louis had sent d'Estrées to sea merely to make sure that he got his money's-worth out of the English. Duquesne came in for special blame, and he refused ever again to serve with d'Estrées.

The passing of the Test Act by the English Parliament in 1673, under the provisions of which Catholics could not hold office under the Crown, precluded the Duke of York from flying his flag at sea for the campaign of that year. Monck being dead, the choice of a successor fell upon Prince Rupert who, by then, was beset by recurrent illnesses, and was no strong partisan for the war. D'Estrées was again appointed to command the French fleet, and Sir Edward Spragge sailed as second to the Prince, in spite of Rupert's repeated requests that his old comrade-in-arms, Sir Robert Holmes, should be given a flag in his fleet.

Spragge had distinguished himself two years earlier at Bugia Bay, in the Mediterranean, where he had defeated a force of Algerines, and made a satisfactory local settlement, but, although a good leader for independent missions, he was less satisfactory in a fleet. He had a particular feud with Cornelis Tromp, who once again had a command under de Ruyter; and once again showed less than the discipline which the Dutch Commander-in-Chief could have looked for.

Exactly a year after the fight at Solebay there began the first of two separate actions in the Schooneveld, the long, narrow basin which guards the estuary of the Scheldt. Once again the object of the Allies was to prepare the way for a landing in Holland, and once again de Ruyter, with inferior numbers, got the better of the engagements, in that the purpose of his enemies was thwarted.

The total allied strength was eighty-one ships of the line, to which de Ruyter could oppose only fifty-five. But the Dutch admiral had placed himself with great skill amid a maze of shoals and sandbanks. In the circumstances, and allowing for French ineptitude at manoeuvring, Rupert hesitated for some time before making an attack. Before he could do so de Ruyter suddenly emerged, with the wind in his favour, and a running fight followed for some nine hours. The Allies extricated themselves with difficulty and anchored to repair their damage off the Oster Bank. The 70-gun Dutch *Deventer*, much battered by gunfire, foundered during the course of the night.

On 4 June, de Ruyter once more attacked from the windward position. Again the fighting was inconclusive, but it had the effect of forcing the Allies to leave the Dutch coast to replenish. It also led to a duel between Tromp and Spragge of a kind which, when the fleets met for the third and last time, was to have sad consequences.

The struggle was renewed on 11 August 1673 off the Texel. The French, who were in the van, were 'amused', as at Solebay, by Bankert, the Dutch Vice-Admiral, who had taken their measure. De Ruyter made for Rupert in the centre. Unaided by the French, who engaged at a distance and did not acknowledge signals, and by Spragge, who drifted to leeward and became absorbed in another round with what he called his 'consort', Tromp, the Prince had to forgo any advantage which superior numbers might have given him by the need to bear down to rescue Spragge's flagship, the newly-built *Royal Prince* of 100 guns. The feat was achieved, but nothing could moderate the exuberance of Spragge, who decided to transfer to a less badly damaged vessel and was drowned in so doing when a shot struck his boat.

Battle of Palermo 1676
After Petrus Schotel

Towards nightfall the two fleets drew apart exhausted, de Ruyter seeking the shelter of his intricate home coast. No ships had been lost on either side, but once more the prospect of a seaborne invasion of Holland had been blighted.

French efforts had been so feeble throughout that d'Estrées' second-in-command, the Marquis de Martel, was sent to the Bastille for charging his chief with having dishonoured the French flag by refusing to fight, except half-heartedly. 'Instead,' Martel reported, 'he kept the wind and contented himself to give his ships leave to shoot at more than cannon and a half distance from the enemy . . . The English sustained all the enemy attacks with an incomparable resolution.' It was no wonder that such stark truth generated fury.

The immediate naval war ended after the battle of the Texel, to the relief of most Englishmen and all Dutchmen. De Ruyter and the young Prince of Orange had, by their leadership on sea and land, preserved their country. For, although the struggle with France continued for five years more, the most acute danger for the United Provinces had passed.

De Ruyter received many tributes from his countrymen, and lived to serve them further. To the Dutch sailors he and the elder Tromp were always *Bestevaer* (Grandad). Alfred Mahan, the classic exponent of sea power, wrote fitting words about him.

Under Abraham Duquesne, who received a marquisate afterwards, the French won a signal victory over the Dutch off Palermo in June 1676, less than two months after de Ruyter had died of wounds after Augusta. His successor, Haan, was not strong enough to prevent the French relieving Messina, which led to the battle and the retreat of the Dutch in defeat.

He went to this final strife of the two great sea-peoples in the fullness of his own genius, with an admirably tempered instrument in his hands, and with the glorious disadvantage of numbers, to save his country. The mission was fulfilled not by courage alone, but by courage, forethought and skill.

III

Strained as their resources had been by the trials brought on them by Louis, now at the zenith of his power, there was little rest for de Ruyter or Cornelis Tromp. They were next called upon to act not in the Channel or the North Sea, but the Baltic and the Mediterranean. The United Provinces were drawn into renewed alliance with Denmark, and they had also put a force at the disposal of Spain, which had become engaged in the war with Louis. The Spaniards were concerned to subdue rebellious subjects in Sicily, where the French established a garrison.

De Ruyter found himself campaigning against Duquesne. Tromp became for a time the colleague of the Norwegian-born Niels Juel, a national hero in Denmark through his prowess at sea.

After an indecisive winter battle off Stromboli, a combined Spanish and Dutch force made an unsuccessful attack on the French position at Messina. Sailing south, the Allies hoped to draw Duquesne into open water, and they succeeded. Unfortunately, de Ruyter was not in chief command and, when battle was joined near Augusta, the Dutchman, leading the van, was as badly supported by the chief commander, Don Francisco de la Cerda, who fought at long range, as Rupert had been by d'Estrées, preventing the rear getting into action until the evening. Duquesne was allowed to retreat to leeward with his fleet intact, and the night of 22 April 1676 saw an end to the action. In the course of the engagement de Ruyter received a mortal wound, from which he died at Syracuse a week later.

It was bitter irony that the Dutch admiral should lose his life through the incompetence of the former oppressors of his country. He was by then sixty-eight, and should have been enjoying retirement and acclaim at home. Astonishingly, it was the first time he had ever been wounded in battle, and it was Colbert himself who said of the event that he saw no real comparison between the head and heart of Duquesne and that of his opponent.

Cornelis Tromp's day of glory in the north came off the isle of Öland on 1 June, when he and Niels Juel defeated the Swedes under Admiral Creuz. The Swedish flagship, *Krona*, sank in a sudden squall, with her gun-ports open, and three of their ships were taken.

FIVE

DYNASTIC STRUGGLES

Pepys and the fleet — The Comte de Tourville — James II and William III
Battles of Beachy Head, Barfleur and La Hogue — Rooke at Vigo
The capture of Gibraltar — The battle of Malaga — The Treaty of Utrecht
Byng at Cape Passaro — Affairs in the Baltic

IN 1677, the year after the death of de Ruyter, an event took place which altered the aspect of affairs between England and Holland. Mary Stuart, the seventeen-year-old daughter of the Duke of York, later James II, married William of Orange. The bride and bridegroom were first cousins—William's mother, Mary, was, like the Duke, a child of Charles I, and thus his father-in-law was also his uncle. Although the marriage proved childless, the fact of its existence played an essential part in the disturbances of the next decades.

Charles II had no legitimate children. His heir, the Duke of York, being a Catholic, was not acceptable to a large proportion of his future subjects. If the Protestant population were to challenge his position once he had ascended the throne, as it had already done when he was merely Duke of York, the attitude of William of Orange could prove decisive.

In the years following the Fire of London, which by some was ascribed to Catholic machination, there was a witch-hunt against the Duke's co-religionists. Among victims was Pepys, not by reason of his personal beliefs, but through his attachment to the Duke. As a consequence, the Service to which both men were devoted suffered, for Charles, with deliberate cynicism, allowed Commissioners, for whose capacity he had nothing but contempt, to govern its affairs. Pepys was actually committed to the Tower of London for a short time, but although released, and reinstated later as Secretary of the Admiralty, he had too little time to repair the damage before being dismissed for ever. This was a consequence of the flight of James II from England in 1688, after a reign of three years following the death of his brother.

During his various tenures of office, Pepys had made himself a master of naval business in a way which was recognized at the time as exceptional, and has been a source of wonder ever since. He established the officer structure; the ratings of ships; the contractual side of provisioning; the surveying of home waters, during the course of which Captain Grenville Collins's charts set a high standard of accuracy. He was no mere office man, for he went on voyages, once to Tangiers. He took pains to understand the entire business of shipbuilding, absorbing much from his friend, Sir Anthony Deane.

Nothing would satisfy him but personal examination of the neglect into which some of the ships had been allowed to fall during the time of his eclipse: 'Their holds not cleaned nor aired,' he wrote, 'but suffered to heat and moulder, till I have with my own hands gathered toadstools in the most considerable of them, as big as my fists.' He

Samuel Pepys
John Hayls

Samuel Pepys, familiar to posterity for his famous Diary, was a well-known character of his time. An able civil servant, he was rarely without employment, the exceptions being when he was imprisoned on suspicion of supporting James II. His work for the Navy was exceptional, and in his reorganization he swept away many abuses. His Diary, a lively document ending in 1669, unfortunately notes none of his activity in that sphere.

became in due time Master of Trinity House, the Corporation established by Henry VIII to care for the safety of navigation and the licensing of pilots. He was a Baron of the Cinque Ports, that antique south coast federation, and President of the Royal Society. In fact, apart from the ever-fascinating Diary, which only extends from 1660 to 1669, he is important as the principal permanent figure in his country's main armed service at a critical stage of its evolution.

It was well that Pepys worked to such effect, for when a 'Protestant wind' brought an unopposed invasion from Holland under William of Orange, resulting in James's exile to St Germain-en-Laye, there was need of a fleet to defend the new order of things, and of commanders to lead it. The fleet was there, and the commanders too, but the margin of superiority over the forces of France, which took James's side in the dynastic dispute, was for some time narrow or uncertain.

The effectiveness of the French navy had improved since the battles off the Dutch coast, and if Deane and others had profited from copying some of the best points of foreign ships during the Anglo-French combination, the benefit was not all on one side. The French adopted English methods of signalling and tactical instructions. Although, as was their way, they systematized well, they did not at first carry matters further than had the Duke of York. He had used nine flags and one pendant to make his commands known, the basis being the relationship of the message to the position at which the flag appeared.

The signals and instructions issued in 1689 by the Comte de Tourville as French Commander-in-Chief, at the outset of what became known as the War of the English Succession, showed no advance in tactical thought. Yet within four years they had been transformed for the better, from which it must be concluded that the experience of the exiled James II had been put at Tourville's disposal.

James's attempt to defeat the Dutch usurper was of necessity based on the use of the French fleet and French resources. He landed an army in Ireland, which had so often been the object of the attentions of those who looked after the strategy of Philip II. For some time he was a considerable threat to the security of England and Scotland.

The first regular naval battle, which took place in Bantry Bay on 1 May 1689, was an indecisive cannonade, but as the English, under Arthur Herbert, were in decidedly inferior force—they had only twenty-two ships as against thirty-nine opposing them— William decided to turn it into a propaganda victory. He visited the fleet at Spithead, made Herbert an earl, knighted two of his captains, and then, leaving English affairs in the hands of Mary, his consort, gave his attention to the land campaigning, where he felt at home.

During the summer of 1690 Tourville had command of one of the most formidable fleets his country ever assembled. William was committed to what was known as a Grand Alliance against Louis. It included, besides England, Holland and Austria; thus, owing to necessary dispersals brought about by the campaign in Ireland, and obligations to the Mediterranean, Admiral Herbert (now Lord Torrington) had at his disposal only thirty-four English and twenty-two Dutch ships to oppose Tourville's seventy-five. Even so, the English admiral had orders to fight, for it was considered that an invasion of England was a serious possibility. This had actually been suggested by one of the most distinguished of Tourville's captains, Jean Bart. It so happened that Bart had been present as a very youthful volunteer in de Ruyter's flagship when the Dutch made their raid on the Medway in 1667.

The French officers included Victor-Marie d'Estrées, son of the Commander-in-Chief in the previous war; Château-Renault in the great *Dauphin Royal*, and the Chevalier de Forbin. The whole appearance of the fleet ships brilliantly painted, bands marking the lines of the gun-ports, gilded carving glittering in the summer light, should have spread alarm in the allied squadrons when the opposing fleets met off Beachy Head on 30 June 1690. Unfortunately, it had the opposite effect on the Dutch,

who were in the van. They thought nothing of the French, either in point of numbers or efficiency, and with headstrong courage sailed into the attack, with the wind in their favour.

It was the tactics of contempt, and in the circumstances it was wrong. The French, with the advantage of numbers, were very different from those who had shown up so badly in the previous war, and they retained their advantage. One of the Dutch admirals, Schey, giving evidence later, stated: 'It was asked me if I saw it likely to beat so great a number with so few. I answered that this would not be the first time we fought the French with half the number.' The result was unfortunate. When reports of the battle were received in London, Torrington was dismissed. William was furious at the loss of four of the Dutch ships and sympathized with the fury of the Dutch officers that the English had not engaged 'Pell Mell', in the tradition of Lowestoft and the Four Days' Battle.

When news became known that Torrington had retired to the Gunfleet, and that the French had command of the Channel, London had a moment of panic. Among those who were not alarmed was Torrington himself. He stated his reason for optimism in the course of a sentence which has been remembered. 'Most men were in fear that the

Battle of La Hogue 1692
Benjamin West the Elder

The second of two battles in the War of the English Succession (1688–97)—Barfleur, fought a few days before, being the first—La Hogue finally settled the aspirations of James II of regaining his throne. A group of twelve ships, escaping from Barfleur, were destroyed by Sir George Rooke off La Hogue, watched from the beach by the dispossessed English king and his natural son, the Duke of Berwick. Rooke's boats went into the bay, where the French thought themselves safe under the guns of two forts. After severe hand-to-hand fighting, the French were defeated.

Battle of Malaga: First Part 1704
Unknown

In an attempt to capture Gibraltar, taken three weeks earlier by Rooke and Prince George of Hesse, Louis XIV sent his natural son, the Comte de Toulouse, to retake it. The English had the support of the Dutch, and the French that of Spain. Both fleets were large; no initiative was shown on either side, and the battle developed into a steady cannonade, with virtually no manoeuvring. Although much shot had been expended at Gibraltar by the English and their ammunition was low, the French took no account of this and did not renew the action the following day, when Rooke was able to put in at Gibraltar with his shattered ships.

French would invade,' he wrote, 'but I was always of another opinion, for I always said that whilst we had a *fleet in being* they would not make the attempt.' He was right. Tourville failed to follow up his victory because his sailors were falling sick and his ships were short of supplies. Across in Ireland good news soon spread good cheer. Londonderry, which had been under siege, was relieved by sea, and the day after the encounter off Beachy Head, William won the battle of the Boyne.

The man who supplanted Torrington was Edward Russell, later Earl of Orford, who became the principal naval figure of the war. At a time when many wavered, and tried to re-insure themselves with James II, Russell had been staunch for William III. He was under forty years of age and had had eleven years service in or about the fleet. Although in length and variety of combat experience his record did not compare with that of Torrington, the 'cherry-cheeked Russell', as versifiers called him, inspired confidence in quarters which mattered, and he was never at a loss when consulted on matters of grand strategy. By comparison with the greater figures in naval history his stature is modest, but he did what was required of him, and he won a victory against Tourville which was decisive for the future course of events. Nevertheless, it is not the name 'Russell' or 'Orford' which is most often commemorated, but 'Barfleur', the scene of the battle where he had the better of the day.

When, in the summer of 1692, Tourville sailed from Brest for the Channel to resume the sea campaigning, he had orders expressed in terms which must have seemed risible to a veteran. 'His Majesty,' they ran, 'desires him to leave Brest even should he have information that the enemy is at sea with a force superior to that in readiness to sail with him . . . Should he meet with enemy ships, he is to chase them back to their ports, whatever number they may be.' Orders were seldom quite so unrealistic as these, and the result could have been foreseen. Tourville felt that his honour obliged him to fight whatever the odds.

On 19 May he came upon the Anglo-Dutch fleet, nearly a hundred strong, more than twice his own strength of forty-four. It was to leeward, near Cape Barfleur. He determined to concentrate what force he could on the English centre and rear, leaving the Dutch who, as usual, were in the van, at long shot. After some four hours' cannonading,

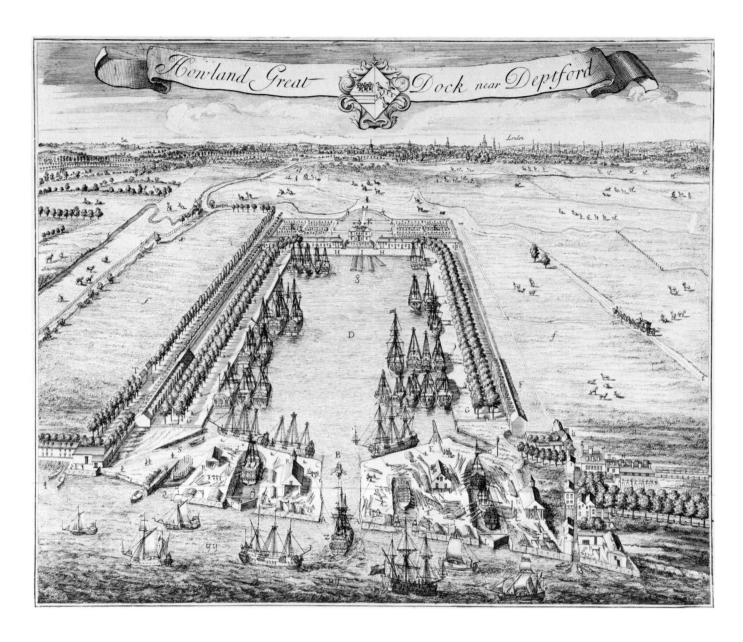

Howland Great Dock near Deptford

fog descended. Sir Cloudisley Shovell, in the English centre, then managed with a few ships to double the *Soleil Royal*, the pride of the French fleet, and Richard Carter, in the rear, also managed to put the French between two fires.

Tourville's formation held gallantly for some time, but at last his ships scattered in disorder, overwhelmed by numbers. A group of nine made for the North Sea and got home round the north of Scotland without further misadventure. A second, commanded by the Marquis d'Amfreville, pursued by the English, were piloted into the river Rance by the skill of Hervé Riel. A third, including the fleet flagship, made a stand near Cherbourg, but were overwhelmed and burnt. A last group, twelve in all, were destroyed by Sir George Rooke in an action at La Hogue nearly a week after the fleets had first made contact. This was the most dramatic episode of all. It was observed by James II himself, and his natural son, the Duke of Berwick.

60

Howland's Great Dock at Deptford
Engraving by Jan Kip

Deptford was one of the earliest naval dockyards in England and by the time of the Stuarts it was the most important shipbuilding yard in the country, and very much associated with the name of Pett, a shipwright dynasty. It was here that Peter the Great came to learn the techniques of shipbuilding. The Royal Navy vacated Deptford altogether in 1965, although old warehouses are still in evidence. Trinity House was founded here in 1517.

Towards evening on 23 May, Rooke's fire-ships and boats swept in towards six ships of the line which had anchored close under the guns of Fort Lisset, on the French coast. All these were destroyed. On the other side of the bay further French vessels had taken refuge under what they had hoped was the sure protection of Fort St Vaast. They perished next day. At one stage, when the French were in acute danger, James ordered cavalry to the water's edge to repel seamen who had landed. The men were dragged from their horses with boat-hooks.

As a measure of finality, when the vessels had been boarded and the crews driven off, the English sailors, before setting fire to their captures, turned their guns against the fort and silenced it. James is said to have remarked wryly to Berwick: 'None but my brave English tars could have done so gallant a deed!'

James's daughter Mary, who had made herself beloved in England, did not long survive the victory, dying at an early age in 1694. Her memorial is the Naval Hospital at Greenwich. This was established to provide for her sailors in the same way as Chelsea Hospital, the foundation which her uncle had already established for soldiers. Both places owe much to the architectural genius of Sir Christopher Wren.

By a happy coincidence, in the same year that it was decided to proceed with Greenwich Hospital, Charles Montagu, first Earl of Halifax, published his *Rough Draft of a New Model at Sea*. In it occurred a passage which soon became famous:

> It may be said now to England, Martha, Martha, thou art busy about many things, but one thing is necessary. To the question, What shall we do to be saved in this world there is no other answer but this, Look to your moat.
>
> The first article of an Englishman's political creed must be, that he believeth in the sea, without that there needeth no general council to pronounce him incapable of salvation here.

Admiral Benbow Exhorting His Men to Continue the Battle
Unknown

John Benbow was one of the few admirals who rose to flag rank from the lower deck. He started his career in the Navy, but soon engaged in his own trading exploits. Rejoining the Navy in 1689, he took part in the battles of Beachy Head and La Hogue, later becoming master attendant at Deptford Dockyard, where he rented John Evelyn's house, which he later sublet to Peter the Great. During the War of the Austrian Succession, his leg was shattered in an action against the French in the West Indies. This drawing shows him urging his subordinates to carry on the fight. He died of his wound in Jamaica.

We are in an island, confined to it by God Almighty, not as a penalty but a grace, and one of the greatest that can be given to mankind. Happy confinement, that hath made us free, rich and quiet; a fair portion in this world, and very well worth the preserving; a figure that ever hath been envied, and could never be imitated by our neighbours . . .

II

Although James II died in 1701 and William III in the following year, to be succeeded peacefully by James's second daughter, Anne, dynastic problems continued to vex Europe on an ever greater scale. While Louis XIV still lived, the danger of French domination of Europe threatened all other States. It was increased when he decided to uphold the cause of the Pretender, James's young son, who was in France, and to accept the reversion of the Spanish throne on behalf of his grandson, Philip, Duke of Anjou.

The essential counter was a new Alliance, which came to include, in addition to England, Holland and Austria, Savoy and Portugal. Savoy was to produce a military leader of the first order in Prince Eugene, and Anne had in her service a supreme soldier in Marlborough. With the eye of a master of strategy, Marlborough saw that one of the best uses for the English Navy was to make itself felt in the Mediterranean. There, the first essential was to acquire an adequate base, and it was with this need in mind that some of the earlier operations of the War of the Spanish Succession took place, including an attempt by Sir George Rooke on Cadiz.

This was made during the autumn of 1702, a large Anglo-Dutch fleet being involved —eighty ships of war and fifty transports. It was mismanaged. Rooke was sick, and rarely left his cot. He was also anxious to get back home before the winter storms, so that he was continually looking over his shoulder. The troops, when put ashore, did little but roister.

Rooke scarcely deserved the luck which came his way on the voyage back to England. A naval chaplain went ashore at Lagos, where his ship had put into water. He happened to meet the French consul, who told him, in a boastful way, that an 'invincible' French fleet was escorting a Spanish treasure fleet into Vigo Bay. It was the sort of item that should have been kept Top Secret. The chaplain hastened to tell his captain, who instantly put to sea, found the main fleet, and gave the news to the admiral.

However poorly he felt, Rooke was not the man to resist the lure of a treasure fleet, particularly when he was in such numerical strength, and had done so little. His captains agreed to an immediate attack on Vigo, which they found was defended by a boom across the harbour entrance, with a fort and guard-ships at either end.

The soldiers landed and took one of the forts, while the *Torbay*, flagship of Sir Thomas Hopsonn, the leading ship of the English line, charged the boom and broke it. Then the wind fell calm and the ships following the *Torbay* drifted into wreckage, leaving the *Torbay* at anchor between the guard-ships, engaging them both at once. When the wind freshened once again the next two ships, which were Dutch, got through the boom and boarded one of the guard-ships. Château-Renault, the French commander, then sent a fire-ship to attack the *Torbay*, whose rigging was set ablaze. After a while the fire-ship exploded and, as she had been hastily prepared, she still had cargo in her hold. This was snuff. It fell so thickly on the burning *Torbay* that it put out most of her fires, and her sneezing crew were able to save her.

Réné Duguay-Trouin (1673–1736)
Artist unknown, *c.* 1745

The Claude Duval of the Dunkirk privateers, Réné Duguay-Trouin rose quickly through their ranks to become a captain with a royal commission—and a patent of nobility—and with his fellow Dunkirkers, Jean Bart and the Chevalier de Forbin, was a thorn in the side of the English in particular, though also preying on the ships of other countries. It was mainly owing to their depredations that an Act of Parliament was passed in 1708 instituting the convoy system.

The Capture and Burning of HMS Devonshire
From H. S. Lecky, *The King's Ships,* 1913

HMS *Devonshire*, in a squadron of five, was detailed to escort a convoy of 130 sail bound for Lisbon with merchandise, which included weapons and horses. A day after leaving harbour they were engaged by Duguay-Trouin and de Forbin. The *Royal Oak* escaped, but the others struck, except for the *Devonshire*, which finally blew up, with only two survivors. Sixty merchantmen were also taken by the privateers.

Helsingborg Taken by Danes under Christian V

Christian V, who ruled Denmark from 1670 to 1699, saw in his own alliance with the Dutch, and that of Sweden with France, a chance to regain lost territory from the Swedes. His sole success was achieved by his navy with the capture of Helsingborg. This, however, was offset by Swedish victories on land, particularly that of Lund in 1676, and Christian left his country in worse case than before.

The destruction of the Franco-Spanish fleet thereafter proved a matter of no difficulty. The flagship and six others were burnt and the rest were either captured or driven aground. The treasure ships were treated with more circumspection since there was the prospect of rich salvage. Much silver was brought home, to be struck into coins marked 'Vigo', but a high proportion had been unloaded and moved inland for safety before the arrival of the English fleet.

Rooke had accomplished, almost by accident, the annihilation of the enemy's first-line Atlantic squadron. Partly as a result of this, but chiefly on the advice of Marshal Vauban, Louis decided to support a large-scale privateering war in northern waters, for which a series of ports were particularly suitable as bases. Some of the leading naval officers were allowed to serve in this *guerre de course*, and profited accordingly.

Anglo-Dutch trade suffered greatly as a result of the cruises conducted by a succession of men whose names are well remembered in France—Jean Bart and de Forbin, who operated mainly from Dunkirk; Réné Duguay-Trouin of Brest and St Mâlo; Jean Doublet of Honfleur; Jacques Cassard of Nantes and Marseilles; the d'Iberville brothers of La Rochelle. The results they achieved were sensational, and the cost was small. It was 1708 before an Act was passed in the English Parliament for the regulation of convoys, which were the only sound answer. The damage was not all one way, but by comparison with that of the Alliance, French overseas trade was modest.

Away in the West Indies, where a small squadron under Vice-Admiral Benbow had orders to protect British interests, an action took place which showed how sternly cowardice among captains was regarded in a service whose Fighting Instructions emphasized support for the flagship.

Benbow was a 'tarpaulin' who had risen by way of the merchant service and a Master's warrant. He was not a diplomatic or a popular character, but he was brave and determined. Between 19 and 24 August 1702, with his flag in the *Breda* of 70 guns, he pursued a French force under Admiral du Casse, which consisted of four ships of the line and several smaller vessels.

Four of the English captains, out of dislike of Benbow, deliberately kept out of action and, when summoned to a Council of War on board the flagship, advised against continuing the chase. Only the *Falmouth*, of the ships under his command, supported the admiral. On 24 August, according to Benbow's own report, he 'fired a broadside with double and round alow, and round and partridge [ball] aloft, which the enemy returned very heartily. At three o'clock by a chain shot my right leg was broke to pieces, and I was carried below.'

Benbow directed the final round with his injured limb in a cradle. When he made port at Jamaica he put the delinquent officers under arrest. He had not been long at Port Royal before he received the following note from his opponent, if an account of his life published in the *Naval Chronicle* is to be credited:

> Sir,
> I had little hopes on Monday last, but to have supped in your cabin: it pleased God to order it otherwise: I am thankful for it. As for those cowardly captains who deserted you, hang them up, for by – – – – – – they deserve it.
> Your's DU CASSE

Two of Benbow's captains were shot as the result of courts martial; one was cashiered; and the fourth died before his trial could take place. Unfortunately Benbow himself died of his wound before the winter.

III

Two years after their exploit at Vigo the Allies assembled a large fleet, fifty-three ships of the line, forty-one English and twelve Dutch, with ancillary vessels and a force of 2000 Marines, as a naval contribution to a combined operation with the object of taking Toulon, the main French base in the Mediterranean. To have any chance of success such an ambitious project needed support from the army commanded by Prince Eugene of Savoy. This was not forthcoming, so another use had to be found for Rooke's ships. He had good fortune over secondary objectives, for there was one near at hand— Gibraltar. This rock fortress had attracted English governments ever since the time of Oliver Cromwell, and it was believed not to be strongly defended.

The attack began on 23 July 1704. Sir John Leake, commanding the *Prince George*, wrote in his diary:

At 5 (a.m.) the Ships that was appointed to cannonade the Town began to fire, as likewise the Bomb Vessels to heave in their Bombs; which was continued till 9 o'clock, when they fired more leisurely by the Admiral's order, plying only their lower Tier. At 11 o'clock the Ships that lay against the new Mole, having beat the Spaniards from their guns, a signal was made for all the boats to attack it.

Everything went well. At 4 o'clock in the afternoon of 24 July the Prince of Hesse

summoned the Town from the North Gate, where the Marines were encamped, and soon after the Admiral did the same from the South Gate, where the seamen were, and received the answer from the Governor that at 8 o'clock he would capitulate.

Next day, the Marines marched in and took over garrison duties. Their Corps, which has served with distinction in every part of the world, wears 'Gibraltar' and a Globe on its badge to this day.

Leake's mention of bomb vessels indicates that the English had successfully adopted a type of vessel first used operationally by the French admiral Duquesne in an assault on an Algerine stronghold. The bomb ketch, as it came to be known, was a broad-beamed vessel with her foremast removed to make room for the mortars. Sturdy beam bridges supported the gun platform and distributed the shock of recoil when the mortars were fired. The projectiles weighed about 200 lb, and, as the heaviest ship's guns did not fire a ball of more than 48 lb, bomb ketches could be highly effective, given the right conditions.

Such an important conquest as Gibraltar, initially so easy, entailed holding it, and this without the advantage of an adequate harbour, which would take time to extend. In war, advantages are seldom won without pains, and it was soon clear that Rooke would have to defend what he had taken. A French fleet under the Comte de Toulouse, a son of Louis XIV by Madame de Montespan, was on its way from Toulon to dispute the matter. Rooke, seriously short of ammunition after his protracted bombardment of the fortress during which he had expended 15,000 cannon-balls, was faced with a formidable threat. It was from a force consisting of fifty-one ships of the line and twenty oared galleys which for the last time made their appearance in a major fleet. Rooke would need all his skill and experience if he were not to lose his prize and, lacking any other base, be forced to return to the Channel.

On 12 August the two fleets met off the Spanish coast near Malaga. During the preliminary manoeuvring, Toulouse gained a tactical advantage in getting between Rooke and Gibraltar. This was balanced, to some extent, by Rooke having the wind-gauge, which enabled him to attack at will.

There followed a typically indecisive cannonade by ships in rigid line of battle. Sir Cloudisley Shovell, in the Allied van, held his own well, as did the Dutch admiral, Gerard Kallenberg, in the rear, but Rooke was hard pressed in the centre, for it was in his ships that the shortage of ammunition was most acute.

Both sides spent the night following the battle repairing damage. By dawn the wind had changed in favour of the French, and Rooke prepared to receive an attack. None came. Toulouse held off, so Rooke made up his mind that at the first opportunity he would try to break through the French line and make for the Rock. Absence of wind on 14 August made any such attempt impossible and, at dawn next day, when Rooke was ready to make his attempt, he saw that the French had vanished.

Action at Vigo Bay, 12 October 1702
Ludolf Bakhuizen

Admiral Rooke, on his way home, had the fortune to hear of a Spanish treasure fleet, escorted by a strong French squadron, making its way to Vigo. After his ignominious failure at Cadiz it was a chance to redeem himself. Bursting the boom at Vigo he landed troops, who took the batteries, and fierce fighting ensued in the Bay. The French ships were taken or destroyed and much treasure acquired.

Peter the Great Inspecting a Ship
Studio of Abraham Storck

Peter the Great, Tsar of All the Russias, was essentially a savage living on the fringe of sophistication. An autocrat, he remained barbaric while forcing civilization upon his country. After various intrigues, he became sole Tsar at the age of twenty-four, and it was then that he undertook his trips to the West, his imagination being fired by the process of shipbuilding. He worked as a common labourer in both Amsterdam and the London dockyards, learning a great deal from the Pett family of shipbuilders. With a tremendous appetite for strong drink and a boisterous disposition, he and his suite soon reduced the house of John Evelyn, the famous diarist, where he was lodging, to a 'bear garden'. Evelyn was pleased to see him go. Although he died at a comparatively early age, no doubt because of his excesses, he had succeeded in bringing Russia to the forefront of the European nations.

Landing at Cape Breton Island, 1745
After J. W. Stevens

The New Englanders, incensed by raids from French and Indians based at the great fortress of Louisbourg on Cape Breton Island, and infuriated at the British Government's dilatoriness in dealing with the nuisance, took matters into their own hands and mounted an expedition against the place. From April to June 1745 Louisbourg was under siege from a force led by Sir William Pepperell and supported by some naval vessels under Sir Peter Warren. It surrendered on 16 June. This was one of the first occasions field artillery was used in North America. To the fury of the colonists, Louisbourg was exchanged for Madras at the Treaty of Aix-la-Chapelle in 1748.

Battle of Quiberon Bay, 1759
R. Wright

Hawke's victory over
Conflans in Quiberon Bay
was the crowning event of the
'Year of Victories'. Early in
November, by press of
weather, the British fleet
blockading Brest was forced
to run for Torbay and shelter.
Hawke left this port as
Conflans left Brest. The
French commander kept to-
wards the coast, ignoring
Commodore Duff's squadron,
left to watch Quiberon,
intending to keep amongst the
inshore rocks, never dreaming
Hawke would follow. As
Hawke's fleet came up 'Form
as you chase!' flew at the
Royal George's masthead. In
the ensuing mêlée amongst
the rocks and shoals the

French lost seven ships,
although another seven
escaped up the River Vilaine,
and a few more, having taken
little or no part in the
fighting, made for Rochefort.
The British lost only the
Essex and *Resolution*, both
being wrecked during the
night on the Four Shoal.

Toulouse, very much aware of his damaged ships, decided that he could not face another pounding, not realizing the condition of Rooke's powder and shot. As the Allied fleet was still between him and his base, he took advantage of wind and darkness to slip round during the night and make for home.

This meant a strategic victory for Rooke, who had saved Gibraltar, and never again did the French seek a major encounter to gain control of the Mediterranean. They and the Spaniards did indeed make two efforts to retake Gibraltar. Each time relief came by means of a squadron under Sir John Leake. Even so, Gibraltar was not in itself the satisfactory base the Allies required. It had no anchorage safe in all weathers, and the inadequacy of the existing water supply (which was soon enlarged, for the natural reserves were ample), severely limited its use for a large fleet.

As everyone expected, the galleys proved useless in battle. Toulouse admitted the loss of four, two French and two Spanish, when claiming, quite beyond hope of belief, to have destroyed most of Rooke's fleet and captured the Admiral. Such grand-scale propaganda, suitable for a king's son, deceived no one. In sober fact, no ships were lost on either side, although the casualty lists were heavy.

While Marlborough was conducting the great campaigns which weakened and in the end almost destroyed the armies of France, the contribution of the Allied navies was to disperse enemy strength by amphibious operations. In the summer of 1705 the Earl of Peterborough, supported by a fleet under Shovell, took Barcelona and advanced to Valencia in the name of the Archduke Charles, the claimant to the Spanish throne backed by the Alliance.

During the following year, an attempt was made by the French to recapture Barcelona. The fortifications had actually been breached when, on 26 April, just as the French were preparing to storm the walls, an approaching fleet was sighted. The French covering force out at sea immediately withdrew to Toulon, leaving the way open for Leake to sail in and land troop reinforcements sufficient to make the French raise the siege.

The failure in 1704 to capture Toulon did not imply that the idea was abandoned. A further plan with the same end in view was put into operation in 1707. Once again, lack of enthusiasm on the part of Eugene of Savoy, who advanced too slowly, enabled the French to reinforce and hold the base. Shovell, commanding at sea, moved in his bomb ketches and damaged the ships in the dockyard. To save them from complete destruction the French scuttled them in shallow water.

On his way home in the autumn Shovell, in his flagship, the *Association*, together with the *Eagle* and the *Romney*, was wrecked on the Isles of Scilly, only one man surviving. The weather had been overcast and no 'sights' had been possible for some days. The disaster, 2,000 men and five ships lost in all, for the smaller *Phoenix* and *Firebrand* also foundered, was partly due to the fact that the ships had been set too far north by the action of a current which was investigated later in the century by the geographer James Rennell, after whom it is now named. It also demonstrated, in the most emphatic way, the need for an adequate winter base in the Mediterranean.

The event, besides being a shock to the nation, was of general significance. Admiral Shovell was among the ablest of Queen Anne's sea officers, and with him were lost Sir John Narborough and his brother James, sons of Lady Shovell by her first marriage.

The significance for the seafaring world at large lay in the fact that a highly experienced Commander-in-Chief, who had ridden out what was known as the Great Storm

Captain Maurice Suckling
Thomas Bardwell

His greatest claims to fame are twofold: he was Nelson's uncle, and he took his nephew to sea for the first time on being asked to provide for him. 'What has poor Horace done . . . that he, above all the rest, should be sent to rough it at sea? . . . The first time we go into action, a cannon-ball may knock off his head and provide for him at once.' While in command of the *Dreadnought,* he and two other ships fought an action, coincidentally forty-eight years to the day before 'poor little Horace's' victory at Trafalgar. Later Comptroller of the Navy, Suckling died in 1778.

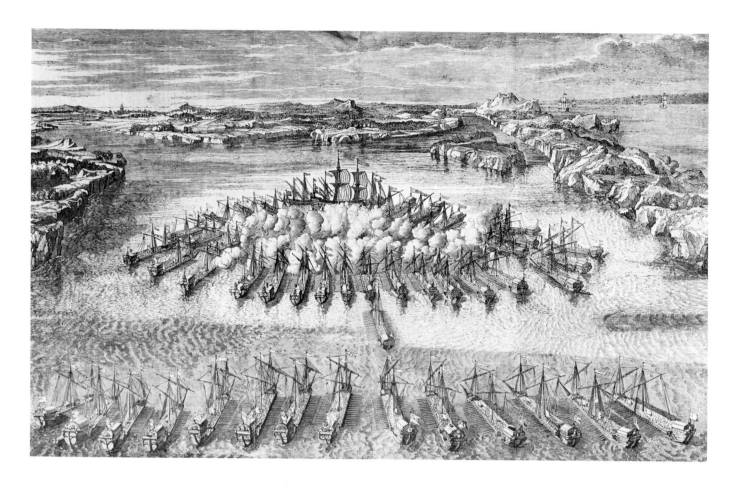

The Swedish Navy controlled the Baltic, but Peter the Great had designs over its sovereignty, and, with his newly-created navy, many ships officered by Scots, finally ended the claims of Charles XII that the Baltic was his own. The result of this battle also decided the fate of Finland, which thus became a Russian dependency, though returned to Sweden by the Treaty of Nystad in 1721. This treaty established Russia as an emerging European power.

of 27 November 1703 in which thirteen English men-of-war were lost, and as many French, and which destroyed the Eddystone lighthouse, with a fleet well equipped according to the standards of the time, simply did not know where he was although so close to home. The loss would have been still more serious but for the seamanship of officers of the *Royal Anne* and the *St George*, who at the very last minute managed to save their ships when almost on the rocks.

It was not for lack of effort that Shovell was lost. During the thick weather he had met with, the admiral signalled for the ships to lay-to, summoning the sailing masters to the *Association*. All but one were of the opinion that they were in the neighbourhood of Ushant. The master of the *Lennox* held that they were nearer Scilly. He was right, and he saved his ship. The sequence of events pointed to the wisdom of those who, in 1675, had established a Royal Observatory at Greenwich, 'for rectifying the tables of the motion of the heavens, and the places of the fixed stars, so as to find out the so much desired longitude of places for perfecting the art of navigation.' It was soon clear that the task would be protracted.

Seven years after the *Association* was lost with her men and her treasure, and not unconnected with the episode, an official Board of Longitude was set up. A reward of £20,000, an immense sum in those days, was offered to anyone who could devise a certain method of determining longitude to within half a degree, or thirty geographical miles, which one may think was a generous enough margin for error. The two methods

68

which were pursued with ultimate success were those of the calculation of 'lunar distances', and the construction of a highly accurate chronometer.

The Mediterranean winter base was acquired in 1708, at the expense of Spain. Sir John Leake crowned the manifold services which he, and his father before him as Master Gunner of England, had rendered to his country. A fleet under his charge, conveying an army under General Stanhope, took Minorca, after overcoming a very moderate resistance. This gave the British fleet the use of the splendid harbour and anchorage at Port Mahon. Moreover, the new base was well situated for masking Toulon, and for protecting the important Anglo-Dutch trade with the Levant. With Gibraltar and Minorca in her hands, Britain was established as the paramount naval power in the Middle Sea.

In spite of the near-bankruptcy of France, and the increasing war-weariness of the Allies, peace was not made until 1713. By the provisions of the Treaty of Utrecht it was ordained that France and Spain were never to be formally united, although Philip of Anjou was to reign as Philip V of the House of Bourbon for nearly half a century, and to introduce many French methods of government into Spain. Gibraltar and Minorca were to remain in British hands, and the privateer base at Dunkirk, which had been the means of so much loss, was to be demolished. Sea power, added to Marlborough's military genius, had given Britain the capability of attacking her enemies where and when she chose.

Battle of Cape Passaro 1718
Richard Paton

Although war between the Quadruple Alliance and Spain was not declared until December, George Byng brought a Spanish fleet, under de Gastañeta, who were intending to take Sicily from the French, to action in August 1718. The *San Isidoro*, 64, started the firing, which soon became general, and Byng achieved a complete victory, for which he was created Viscount Torrington. It was his son, Admiral John Byng, who met his death at the hands of a firing squad.

69

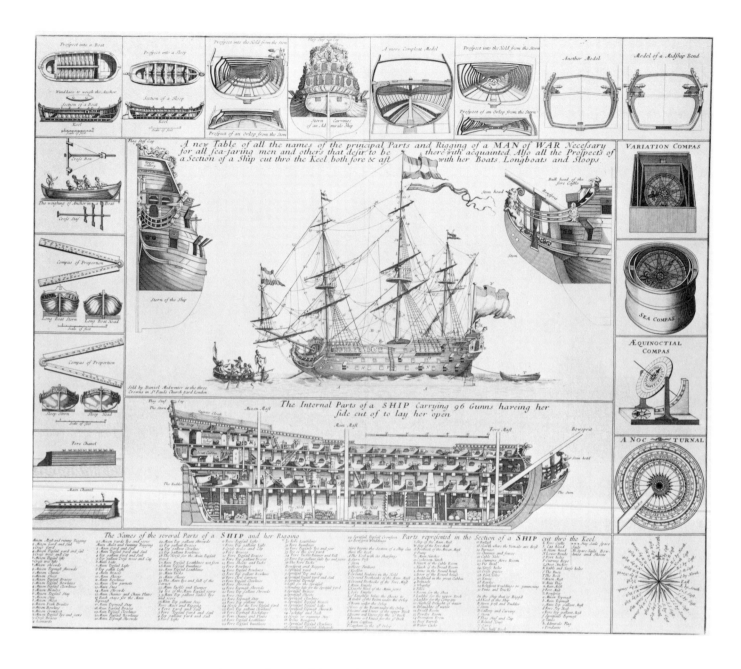

Among the provisions of the Treaty was the temporary cession of Sicily to the Duke of Savoy, once more at the expense of Spain. Naturally enough, being the principal loser by the war, Spain was anxious to abrogate the Treaty, the terms of which were, however, reaffirmed in a Triple Alliance between England, France and Holland, formed in 1717. Matters came to a head a year later, when Spain tried to reoccupy Messina.

Sir George Byng, who had served with distinction at the capture of Gibraltar and the battle of Malaga, was sent with a fleet to uphold the Alliance. He came upon a Spanish fleet off Cape Passaro on 11 August 1718, which was covering the landing of troops. An action developed which soon became a general chase, in the course of which the Spaniards were completely routed. Byng, in his flagship, the *Barfleur*, engaged the large

Cross-section of Ship and Rigging c. 1700

Remarkably clear and comprehensive, this print of about 1700 shows a ship of 96 guns, with a chart below delineating all the parts of the rigging, and a cross-section of the vessel to show compartments and the contents—note the 'Bedstead in the great Cabbin'—such as beef barrels, water casks, ballast, spare sails, etc., carried. Around the border are depicted various nautical instruments, and ships and their boats, cut through to enable examination of their construction.

San Luis, and the Spanish flagship, the *Real San Filipe*, after being raked by the *Superb*, hauled down her colours. Of the Spanish fleet, sixteen ships were taken and seven burnt.

It was one of the most complete victories on record, but apart from its interest as a 'chase' action, in which certain admirals would specialize, it was of no great merit, owing to the ineptitude of the Spaniards. It was a repetition of their behaviour in the same area forty-two years earlier, when they had de Ruyter on their side. They had learnt nothing, except in shipbuilding, where the beauty and merit of their designs equalled those of the French.

IV

In Great Britain, as the style of the realm now was, Anne had been succeeded on the throne by George the First, who was also Elector of Hanover. The King's vested interest in northern Europe led him to watch the affairs of the Baltic closely. There, much was stirring. Since 1699 matters had been complicated by a secret agreement between the Tsar of Russia, Peter the Great, and Augustus the Strong of Saxony, to conquer and divide the acquisitions of Gustavus Adolphus and Charles X of Sweden.

Unexpectedly, Peter found himself facing a military prodigy in the person of Charles XII, who beat him soundly at Narva in 1700. Later, the Swedish king over-reached himself in an invasion of the Russian interior. In his turn, he was beaten at Poltava, and forced to flee to Turkey. The interest of Britain and Holland was now to ensure that, as a result of Charles's misadventure, the balance of power in the Baltic did not alter too violently.

That this was possible was shown through Peter's interest in everything maritime. It had begun in his boyhood and was continued in working visits to the dockyards of Holland and England, where he toiled as a common shipwright. He established a new capital on the Neva, Petersburg, which he called his 'Window on the West'. There, the principal building was the Admiralty, to control his newly-built fleet.

George I, in consultation with the Dutch, more than once sent Admiral Sir John Norris into the Baltic, ostensibly to protect the interests of traders, but also to ensure that Sweden was not irrevocably crushed by her giant neighbour. The English and Dutch were not called upon to fight, though they would have done so had there been any serious question of interruption of the flow of sea traffic, or a too drastic redistribution of territory.

Charles XII was killed in 1718 near Frederikshald—

> His fall was destin'd to a barren strand,
> A petty fortress, and a dubious hand;
> He left the name, at which the world grew pale,
> To point a moral, or adorn a tale.

Johnson's well-known lines in *The Vanity of Human Wishes* were certainly appropriate, since, for all his qualities, Charles had left his kingdom bankrupt. After Peter the Great's death, seven years later, Baltic affairs resumed the sort of equilibrium in which merchants could conduct their business.

71

SIX

ENGLAND, SPAIN
AND FRANCE

*War between Britain and Spain — Vernon at Porto Bello and Cartagena
Anson's circumnavigation — Battles off Cape Finisterre and Ushant
Treatment of scurvy — The steering wheel — Rating of ships*

As FAR AS the principal naval Powers were concerned, twenty years of relative peace at sea followed the victory off Cape Passaro. In contrast with England, where the naval dockyards languished, as did theoretical investigation into better ways of ship construction—never an enthusiastic pursuit—there was much activity elsewhere, particularly in France. There, Pierre Bouguer, who was later to become Professor of Hydrography at Le Havre, discovered that a ship's stability when heeling depended upon whether a point called the metacentre, at which the righting force met the centre line of the ship, lay below or above her centre of gravity. If below, the ship would capsize. If above, the ship would right herself, but too high a metacentre caused violent movement, making the ship a bad gun-platform. The naval architect's problem was to design a hull which gave an adequate righting moment with reasonable steadiness. Bouguer's ideas were recognized as invaluable, but took time to percolate, and his own country was naturally the first to benefit. French shipbuilding, traditionally excellent and frequently copied, had a sound theoretical basis.

In Britain, the attention of the mercantile interest was increasingly drawn to the Spanish possessions in the New World which, so it was believed, were riper than ever for exploitation. It was an echo of feeling in the time of Hawkins and Drake. As early as 1711 a South Sea Company had been formed to carry on the trade which was expected to develop as a result of the Treaty of Utrecht. At first it prospered, though it never sent a single ship into the Pacific. A speculating mania then developed, the 'bubble' burst, and Sir Robert Walpole, who had opposed the South Sea Act, was left to restore public confidence. He was to rule as First Minister and was at last reluctantly forced into war with Spain as the result of atrocities alleged to have been perpetrated on English traders, in particular a certain Captain Jenkins, by the *garda costas* of the Caribbean. A provision in the Treaty of Utrecht whereby Britain was allowed to supply 4,800 negroes annually to Spanish America—the *Assiento*—and to send one ship annually to Porto Bello, had offered scope for plentiful abuse.

The chief naval figures of the war, Edward Vernon and George Anson, were contrasts in character. Vernon was an irrepressible chatterbox, but there was sense in what he said, and he had great practical ability. Anson's serene silences became as proverbial among his contemporaries as his courage in adversity.

Vernon was given command of an expedition to the Caribbean, partly as a result of a boast he made in the House of Commons that he could take Porto Bello, on the

72

Vernon at Cartagena
Contemporary

connecting link of land between North and South America, with six ships. He sailed in July 1739 to reinforce a squadron already in the West Indies, but his orders were to capture the galleons which brought the main South American trade to Spain each October. Nothing was said about the seizure of territory, although the Government knew well enough what was in the Admiral's mind.

Vernon arrived at Port Royal, Jamaica, in October, and found that the galleons had not yet assembled at Havana for the voyage to Europe. He thereupon decided to make good his boast.

The fortifications at Porto Bello consisted of three principal works: the so-called Iron Castle at the harbour entrance, and two others inside. Vernon realized that the only way for an attack to succeed was by a bombardment at point-blank range, followed up by landing parties when the defenders were still demoralized.

The attack was made on 21 November, the ships approaching to within 200 yards before opening fire. They towed boats filled with soldiers, who were to land as soon as Vernon gave the signal. A change in the wind prevented a simultaneous assault on all three forts, but the successful storming of the Iron Castle undermined what was at best not a very strong spirit of resistance. The Governor surrendered next day. It was a cheap success and not very important, but when the news reached England, Vernon's popularity rose to extravagant heights. This was the sort of item the public wanted to hear.

After a disappointing failure at Cartagena, Vernon achieved another modest success in March 1740 at Chagres, to the west of Porto Bello, which was the headquarters of the hated Coastguards. After a seven-hour bombardment of the castle, the port surrendered and its defences were slighted.

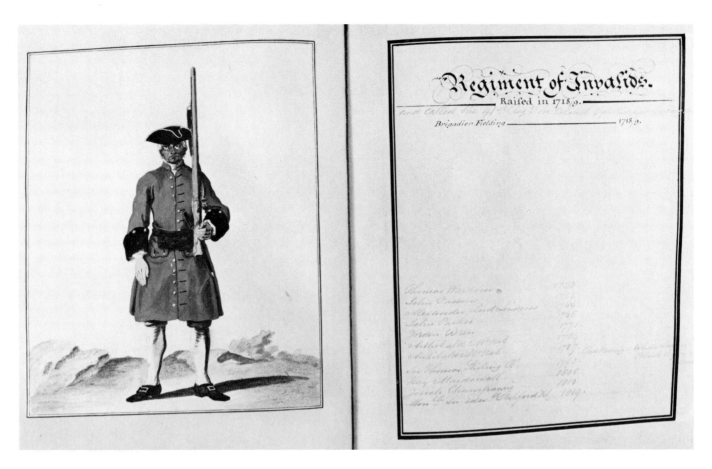

Soldier of Invalid Company of 1742

Soldier of Invalid Company of 1742

The 500 ancients who accompanied Anson on his circumnavigation of 1744, and of whom not one survived, would have come from an Invalid Company. All pensions were, until as late as 1954, administered from the Royal Chelsea Hospital, and Out-Pensioners (those not accommodated there) were required, when the regular army was stretched, to assist in garrison duties. In 1740 there were sixteen such Invalid Companies, and it would be from one of these that Anson's unfortunates would have been selected.

Encouraged by Porto Bello, and still more by Chagres, the home Government decided on a larger-scale attempt on Cartagena. By this time, Vernon had become sceptical of easy successes, owing to Spanish reinforcements, his own failure before the chosen place, and the sickness which was rapidly depleting his crews. He was appalled when, in January 1741, a force of 8,000 troops arrived at Jamaica, but without the general, Lord Cathcart, who had died during the voyage out. The senior soldier, Major-General Thomas Wentworth, soon proved to be an uncongenial ally, but with an addition of twenty ships of the line under an able officer in Sir Chaloner Ogle, he decided to make the attempt.

Ogle had in his squadron a young Scots surgeon, Tobias Smollett of the *Chichester*, and the events of the next few months provided him, as a future novelist, with material for some mordant pages in *Roderick Random*. Smollett would also have observed early instances of the serving of 'grog' to ship's companies. Vernon had written from his flagship, the *Burford*, to Josiah Burchett, who, many years before, had been Pepys's clerk and was now Secretary of the Admiralty, to say that: 'Whereas the Pernicious Custom of Seamen drinking their Allowance of Rum in Drams, and often at once, is attended with many Fatal Effects,' he had ordered that, as from August 1740, the daily allowance of half a pint per man was to be diluted with a quart of water, 'to be mixed in one Scuttle Butt kept for the purpose and to be done on Deck, and in the presence of the Lieutenant of the Watch.' Such was the beginning of a ceremony which obtained for over two centuries, the name 'grog' being derived from a grogram cloak which

74

Vernon habitually wore, and which led to his nickname of 'Old Grog'. Many a man has become groggy without the faintest idea of the origin of the term.

On 4 March 1741, the Admiral duly arrived off Cartagena with twenty-nine ships of the line, twenty-four smaller vessels, and eighty-five transports and store ships. Such a large fleet should have been capable of anything, since there was likely to be little or no opposition afloat. At first all went well. The inner harbour was penetrated, and Vernon was so confident that a bold attack would result in the capture of the town that he tempted Providence by sending dispatches home announcing its fall.

He had reckoned without Wentworth. Instead of going in at once the general waited until 9 April, by which time the Spaniards had had ample time to prepare. He was then repulsed with heavy loss—forty-three officers and 600 men. The following week he told Vernon that of his original 8,000 soldiers, less than half that number were effective. Vernon had no choice but to return to Jamaica. There, another attempt, this time against Cuba, was organized, but by that time Vernon and Wentworth were so estranged that they could only communicate by letter. It would have been miraculous had a combined operation conducted by two such men succeeded. There was never any chance that it would.

Vernon returned home in October 1742 and was furious when he was given no further immediate employment by the Admiralty, to whom the tone of his remarks had been astringent. In 1745, when danger arose owing to the attempt of Prince Charles Edward Stuart to regain the throne which his grandfather, James II, had abandoned nearly sixty years before, it became imperative to employ the ablest officers at sea. Vernon was recalled. After the crisis had passed, and the Prince was once more in exile, he had no further service. His dispositions had helped to ensure the failure of the Stuart adventure, and he is entitled to consideration for his stress on the importance of a strong Channel squadron, stationed as far west as possible when not actively watching the French Atlantic ports, as being the most effective means of Britain's security.

One matter was not learnt in Vernon's time or, indeed, throughout the era of sail. This was how to master what later admirals would refer to as 'the contagion of the climate' in the Caribbean. Neither the appropriate seasons for campaigning, nor alleviation of the fevers and other sicknesses which became all too well known, were studied to any purpose. The losses which Vernon experienced were to be repeated, in equally distressing terms, throughout the eighteenth century.

II

Vernon had started off well, and ended sadly. Anson's fate was the reverse. He was authorized to fly a Commodore's pendant in command of a small squadron—six King's ships and two supply ships—whose destination was the Pacific. The idea behind the expedition was that the Spanish empire in South America might be subverted, and the area opened up to British trade.

No operation was ever worse mounted. Manning difficulties were so acute, almost all available men having been sent to Vernon's fleet, that 500 pensioners from Chelsea, many limbless and all decrepit, were drafted to the ships, as well as two hundred raw recruits to serve as Marines. Not a single pensioner survived the voyage; many deserted before it began, in September 1740. To make matters worse, there was so little security

3rd-Rate HMS Intrepid
J. Mynde, pub. J. Boydell

Intrepid, a famous name in
the Royal Navy, is here
shown as a third rate, i.e.
carrying, before 1810 when
the rating system was
changed, from 70 to 84 guns,
and after 1810, 80 to 90 guns.

The *Intrepid* shown here is
almost certainly the ship
which took part in actions at
Minorca, Lagos, Quiberon
and Havana. In this picture it
appears that she is being
inspected by the King in the
royal barge, the rigging being
manned. The present
Intrepid, a landing assault
ship, is one of the Dartmouth
Training Squadron.

that the Spaniards had ample opportunity not only to learn the plans, but to send a
superior force under Don Jose Pizarro to thwart them.

Anson and Pizarro never met. Pizarro encountered appalling weather in the South
Atlantic, and so did Anson, particularly rounding Cape Horn. Only three of the original
British squadron arrived at the Pacific rendezvous, the island of Juan Fernandez, by
which time 600 men had been lost through sickness, mainly scurvy. It was with the
greatest difficulty that the ships could be worked at all, so depleted were the crews.

Thus reduced, Anson could only carry out raids on local Spanish shipping and on
smaller ports, where he had some success. Then his second most important ship, the
Gloucester, had to be abandoned for lack of sufficient men to work her, and after an
adventure at Tinian, where the *Centurion* herself was driven out to sea by a storm and
only with difficulty regained the island, the Commodore arrived at Macao in November
1742. He had only his flagship by now, and a total of two hundred and ten men out of
the 1,500 or so with whom he had set out.

After a five-month stay, beset with difficulties from the mandarins, Anson set sail for
the Philippines in the hope of recouping his losses by capturing the galleon which sailed
annually from Acapulco in Mexico to Manila. The ship would be loaded with silver
with which to pay for Oriental goods which the Spaniards transported to Europe.

The great moment of the voyage, the result of intense preparation and infinite
patience, came on 20 June 1743, when the *Nuestra Señora de Cavadonga* was sighted off
Cape Espiritu Santo, and one of the most famous single-ship actions began.

It lasted less than two hours, by which time the galleon was in no state to do

anything but surrender. She was smaller than the *Centurion*, in spite of the painters who commemorated the occasion, who liked to regard it as a David and Goliath affair. She was less well armed, and was encumbered with passengers. Her commander, Don Gerónimo Montero, was wounded in the chest, and a high proportion of his fighting men became casualties.

The *Centurion* escaped lightly because of the skill with which she was fought, the result of three years' training under every condition. One seaman was killed, another died of wounds, a third died after an amputation, and there were sixteen wounded, including a lieutenant.

Although Anson had won his prize, which was literally stuffed with treasure—1,313,843 'pieces of eight', a coin of the value of eight *reales*, equivalent to a Spanish dollar, and 35,682 ounces of virgin silver—his difficulties were by no means over. He had 492 prisoners, of whom 170 were wounded. He had a badly damaged prize. He had to face the problems involved in getting the two ships back to Macao, and of transferring the treasure safely to the *Centurion*. He surmounted every trial, as was his way, and sailed for home in December, six months after the engagement.

On reaching the Channel, with his hold as full of treasure as Drake's *Golden Hind* in 1580, a final episode could have led to disaster. Unknown to Anson, England had been at war with France since 1741. His ship ran clean through a French fleet, shrouded by fog, when in the chops of the Channel.

Naturally enough, Anson had a great affection for the *Centurion*, the means of his fame and fortune. In 1736, before he took her over, she had carried the first experimental marine timekeeper designed by John Harrison (1693–1776), the genius who eventually, with his fourth instrument, solved the problem of keeping accurate time at sea,

First Battle of Finisterre 1747
Samuel Scott

Two battles took place off Finisterre in 1747, the first being in May and the second in October. De la Jonquière and St Georges left Rochefort with two convoys for India and North America. Anson, in the *Prince George*, 90, was sent in pursuit. Sighting the enemy, a running fight ensued, ending in the entire French fleet—twelve ships in all—being captured. Six of the ships in the convoy were also taken.

and thus of finding longitude other than by the astronomical method of 'lunar distances'. There, the principle was that the position of the moon in relation to the sun and stars could be predicted and used to discover time at a standard meridian. Unfortunately, Harrison's chronometer was not included in Anson's equipment, or it might have spared him much distress.

Anson was given his flag a year after the completion of his voyage. Henceforward, and until the end of his life, he was at or near the centre of events. He was as zealous and efficient as Pepys had been in his care for the Navy. Among much else, he established the Marines on a permanent instead of a temporary basis. The two hundred recruits he had embarked in 1740 became the forerunners of a notable force, successors to the men who had taken part in the capture of Gibraltar.

In May 1747, when in charge of the Western Squadron so favoured by Vernon, the circumnavigator won a decisive naval battle in what had become known as the War of the Austrian Succession. He had followed Vernon's example in practising aggressive and flexible tactics, and when French ships under La Jonquière were seen to be trying to avoid action off Cape Finisterre, he hoisted the signal for a 'General Chase'. This gave freedom to every captain to attack the first enemy ship he could catch. It resulted in thirteen prizes, six men-of-war and seven merchantmen, and a nice accession to Anson's wealth. A peerage followed, and then marriage to the daughter of Lord Chancellor Hardwicke. Anson's was a success story on a grand scale, and it is good to think he deserved such a fate.

Similar good fortune, in an action much on the pattern of Anson's, attended the first battle in which Edward Hawke held command. He had made his name in 1744 when captain of the *Berwick*, in a clash near Toulon which was bungled owing to the non-co-operation of two admirals, Thomas Mathews and Richard Lestock. Both were explosive characters, and they were on the worst of terms. The unsatisfactory nature of the battle led to courts martial, and to the dismissal of Mathews, whose courage no one questioned, for not obeying the strict letter of the Fighting Instructions, and engaging ship to ship. The official inquiries led to much ill-feeling, with every reason. In this affair, Hawke had boldly taken the *Berwick* out of the line, and as a result the *Poder*, the only enemy ship to be lost, surrendered. Three years later, as a Rear-Admiral, Hawke succeeded Anson in the Channel command. It was a profitable instance of placing vital posts in vigorous hands.

One of Hawke's tasks was to intercept a large French convoy bound for the West Indies from La Rochelle under l'Étanduère. Sighting the enemy far into the Atlantic, he repeated the tactics of his predecessor and hoisted the General Chase. Action continued from 11 a.m. until nightfall on 14 October 1747. Hawke's own flagship, the *Devonshire*, had a large share in accounting for three of the six ships taken. To complete his success, the admiral detached a sloop which raced to the Caribbean to alert the local commander, George Pocock, who was able to capture thirty merchantmen. The battle, sometimes known as the second of Finisterre, and sometimes as Ushant, nearer which the chase ended, was notable not only for the rise of Hawke, who was knighted, but for the fact that it was the first in which Rodney played an important part. A sadness was that it led to the death of Philip Saumarez, who had been one of the ablest officers on Anson's world voyage, as a result of one of the last shots fired.

The war proved to be only an interlude in a world-wide maritime struggle in which, for much of the eighteenth century, Britain was opposed to France and Spain. It had extended to North America, where the great French fortress of Louisbourg, on Cape Breton Island, had fallen in 1745 to a fleet under Sir Peter Warren and troops under William Pepperell. To the indignation of British colonists, the fortress was handed back to France under the terms of the Treaty of Aix-la-Chapelle, the provisions of which left most of the larger problems unsolved. They did not so much as mention the Spanish *garda costas* who had been the original cause of trouble.

In peaceful and thus more profitable directions, the period of the war and the years preceding it saw valuable advances. A reflecting quadrant had been invented by John Hadley in 1731 which soon replaced Davis's back-staff as a convenient means of taking sights, an almost equally useful instrument being devised four years later by Thomas Godfrey in Philadelphia. Johann Tobias Mayer, a German mathematician, made tables of the moon's motion which were incorporated into *Nautical Almanacks*. These began to be published in Britain in 1767 and have continued ever since.

One scourge of life at sea, scurvy, had been highlighted by the events of Anson's voyage, in the course of which he had lost 1,300 men from disease as against a total of four by enemy action. The figures moved Dr James Lind (1716–94) to conduct the first series of dietetic experiments afloat. He rediscovered that among the best anti-scorbutics were oranges and lemons. The fact had been known to Sir James Lancaster, who, as a youth, had fought against the Spanish Armada and had risen to command the first fleet owned by the East India Company. It had actually been published by James Woodall of St Bartholomew's Hospital in 1639, in an account of the instruments and medicines used by naval surgeons.

Oranges and lemons were at least twice as effective as the lime juice which, generations later, became an official issue by reason of cheapness. Although the cause of the disease, a deficiency of vitamin C, was not understood until recently, Lind gave the remedy in a *Treatise of the Scurvy* which appeared in 1753. Yet, even with the evidence before them, scurvy was allowed by the victualling authorities to decimate the fleet throughout most of the remainder of the century. It was only after Lind's death that his abler pupils induced the Admiralty to issue lemon juice after crews had been six weeks on salt provisions.

For convenience in ship-handling, a notable advance of the period was the gradual replacement of the whipstaff by the steering wheel. In earlier times the rudder had been controlled by a pin on the end of the tiller, over which fitted a ring at the end of a long thin pole. The pole passed through a pivot in the deck above the tiller, fitting so that it could slide up and down as well as sideways. The helmsman held the upper end of the pole, and by pushing or pulling he could move the tiller and thus steer the ship, but the rudder could not be put over very far, and much had to be done by altering the trim of the sails. When it blew hard, the whipstaff had to be disconnected altogether, and steering done by means of tackles.

The Venetians adopted the wheel as early as 1719, but it took several decades before it became a regular fitting elsewhere. In *The Naval Expositor* of 1750, for instance, wheel and whipstaff were described side by side. There were no regrets on the part of helmsmen when the wheel at last became standard.

From the mid-eighteenth century dated a regulation uniform for British naval officers, the first patterns for which appeared in 1748. This was the result of a submission by members of the original Navy Club, which had been founded in Charles II's time by senior officers, most of whom had served with Prince Rupert. The colours, blue and

Mr Patrick 'Purser' Gibson (1720–1829)
Luke Macartan

Little is known about 'Purser' Gibson, apart from the fact that he was apparently 109 when he died. At one time he thought he was 116 but 'couldn't be sure'. He certainly served with Sir John Colpoys (1742–1821), and could well have been at Quebec in 1759, as a sailor named Pat Gibson is mentioned. The purser was the warrant officer responsible for clothing and provisions. His salary was part paid, part (12½ per cent) commission, and this last was one cause of unrest among the men he was supposed to serve. Most pursers became rich men, as the victualling of ships was not closely checked for many years.

white, are supposed to have been chosen by George II, who had admired a habit worn by the Duchess of Bedford when riding in the Park. Although there was laxity and even eccentricity in the way in which the regulations were applied, the idea itself found favour elsewhere. There are few navies in the world in which uniforms show no reflection of British practice. The lower deck had to wait more than a century before a general pattern of dress was ordained.

As with dress, so with ships. Steps towards uniformity were taken when Anson became First Lord of the Admiralty in 1751. One of his aims was to reform the dockyards, by then notorious for the conservatism which kept the Royal Navy behind the navies of France, Spain and Holland in point of design as well as for corruption. Anson's reclassification of ships helped in standardization of parts, and was soon copied elsewhere.

'Rating' of ships dated back to the time of Charles I, the object then being to regulate pay, which, so far as officers and warrant officers were concerned, varied according to the size of a ship's company. Anson's system was according to the number of guns carried. Speaking in general terms, and allowing for small variations, first-rates carried 100 guns; second-rates, 90 guns: both types were three-decked ships, usually equipped for an admiral. Third-rates of 74 or 64 guns were actually the backbone of the fleet, and it is unfortunate that, in other spheres, the term 'third rate' should have become derogatory. There was everything to be admired in a smart third-rate ship-of-the-line, and she was easier to handle than her larger sisters. Moreover, 74s often carried a Flag. From now on, ships carrying fewer than 50 guns were not seen in the line of battle. They were confined to scouting and escort duties, and they included frigates, the 'eyes of the fleet' upon which so much depended.

SEVEN

THE SEVEN YEARS WAR

War in the New World — Byng at Minorca
Combined operations: Rochefort; Louisbourg; Quebec
Victories by Boscawen and Hawke — India — Spanish losses — Coppering

IN ONE MATTER AT LEAST, the British government, which had concluded the Treaty of Aix-la-Chapelle, had done wisely. In 1749 it laid the foundation of a military stronghold and naval base at Halifax, Nova Scotia. This was at the instigation of Lord Halifax, President of the Board of Trade and Plantations, after whom it was named. He was a member of the family whose plea, that the first article of an Englishman's creed must be that he 'believeth in the sea', had been reinforced by the words: 'Formerly our force of shipping contributed greatly to our trade and safety; now it is become indispensably necessary to our very being.' Halifax was a counter to the French fortress at Louisbourg. It was to play an important part in the Seven Years War (1756–63) which began in America before it extended to Europe.

Apart from the matter of Halifax, the colonists in the eastern States of North America found themselves indifferently supported by the mother country against incursions by the French in Canada, which was then called New France. They and their Indian allies aimed to prevent British expansion to the west. As George II was Elector of Hanover as well as King of England, the principal matter with which he tried to concern his ministers was French influence in Europe, not in North America. It was William Pitt who changed that outlook. 'The present war,' he declared in a great speech, made when called to office much against the King's inclination, 'was undertaken for the long-injured, long-neglected, long-forgotten people of America.' This was a rhetorical overstatement, but it made the point. Pitt, the foremost strategist of his age, intended to support Frederick the Great of Prussia, Britain's European ally, by means of subsidies, not great armed forces, and to concentrate the energies of his own countrymen on overseas enterprises, and amphibious operations designed to disperse French strength. In this course, he had in mind the advantages of power by sea. At his side, Anson was available as First Lord of the Admiralty. Afloat, a galaxy of flag officers included Hawke, Boscawen and Saunders, all of whom had proved themselves in action.

Both in North America and in Europe the war began inauspiciously. The Americans fared badly against the French, and in the Mediterranean the first naval encounter ended in tragedy. Minorca, the precious base captured in an earlier war, came under siege, with a depleted garrison, and with the only prospect of relief being by means of a powerful fleet. Unfortunately, the man sent to the Mediterranean, Admiral John Byng, a son of the victor of Passaro, lacked the force of character equal to an important mission at the outset of war.

Rum Ration Equipment

The rum ration ('grog')
became general in the Royal
Navy after the subjugation of
Jamaica in the seventeenth
century. To reduce drunkenness, Vernon added a quart
of water to the ration, which
was issued at noon and at 6
p.m. The evening issue was
abolished in 1824 and the
ration reduced from a pint to
a gill in 1850. The rum issue
was abolished altogether in
1970 when Sir Michael
'Ginger' Le Fanu was First
Sea Lord. Not unnaturally,
his nickname was changed to
'Dry Ginger'.

*Jonas Hanway and the Marine
Society*
Edward Edwards

Reputedly the first man in
England to carry an umbrella,
Hanway was a noted traveller
and philanthropist. He
founded the Marine Society
in 1756 both to care for
destitute boys and to man the
Royal Navy by means other
than the press-gang, provid-
ing his charges with clothes
and bedding. Later
Commissioner for Victualling
the Navy, he was also famous
in his time for an acrimonious
correspondence with Dr
Johnson as to the merits of
tea-drinking.

When Byng reached the area of dispute, the French had already landed on the island, and the garrison was confined to a perimeter based on Port Mahon. Byng had command of thirteen ships of the line, and found a French fleet of comparable force in support of the army ashore. There was never a better instance of the differing attitudes taken by French and English towards naval operations. The French idea was to safeguard the island, and avoid battle if possible. The British tradition was the opposite. The object that mattered was destruction of the enemy fleet, or, at the very least, the infliction of such damage that it was in no position to pursue its aims.

Byng's opponent happened to be the Marquis de la Galissonière, a hump-backed, dropsical little man who, after many years' service in the Navy, had been made Governor of New France, where he had proved himself a thorn in the side of the colonists of New England.

The fleets met on 20 May 1756. Byng, after some manoeuvring, gained the advantage of the wind, and made an attack on Galissonière on a line of bearing, that is, at an angle—'lasking' was the term sometimes used. His hope was to strike the French line a little ahead of its centre, so that the van would be out of action for some time, and he could concentrate on centre and rear.

Galissonière, seeing the danger, backed topsails, and awaited the attack under little more than steerage way. Thus Byng's plan was foiled at the outset. Its ruin was completed by the leading captains, who, misunderstanding the admiral's intentions, as so often happened before the invention of a more efficient system of signals, made sail to stretch ahead, in order that the van ships should oppose one another.

In the battle which followed no ships were lost on either side, but the British received more damage than their opponents, whose gunnery was good. Both fleets remained in the area and it was up to Byng whether to renew an attack or retire to Gibraltar. He summoned a Council of War, after which he decided to retreat, otherwise Gibraltar itself might be in danger. This cost him his life. Minorca surrendered a few weeks after the battle and when Byng returned home the Government wanted a scapegoat. Byng, rigorously confined, was court martialled. Although he had to be condemned to death under the ruling Articles of War for 'Neglect of Duty' in that he did not do his utmost to destroy the enemy, the Court expressly stated:

> We cannot help laying the Distresses of our Minds . . . on this occasion, in finding ourselves under a Necessity of condemning a Man to Death, from the great Severity of the . . . Article of War . . . he falls under; and which admits of no Mitigation, *even if the Crime should be committed by an Error in Judgement only* . . .

In returning their verdict, the Court, which acquitted Byng of cowardice or disaffection, emphasized the words italicized, and George II deserves execration in that he did not exercise his prerogative of mercy. Voltaire's stinging words: '*dans ce pays-ci il est bon de tuer de temps en temps un amiral pour encourager les autres*' were deserved, although it was not many years later that his own countrymen, as the result of the loss of Pondicherry, executed Lally after a trial which all admitted was a travesty of justice.

The amphibious operations did not always go well, but those who had direction of affairs were generally able to learn from failure. For instance, against Louisbourg, where Pitt had hoped for success in 1757, it was found that the French had been so strongly reinforced that no attempt was possible. But, as a result, the blockade was tightened, and it became increasingly hard for the French to get reinforcements across the Atlantic.

In the same year an effort at Rochefort failed. Here, the fault was lack of spirit in the general, Mordaunt, who was too old and pessimistic for the business. However, it led to a friendship which Horace Walpole likened to the union of cannon and gunpowder. This was between Captain Lord Howe of the Navy, and Lieutenant-Colonel James Wolfe. Both men distinguished themselves at Rochefort, Howe by a close bombardment of one of the forts, which surrendered; Wolfe by a tactical plan for a landing which was shelved. 'We have lost the lucky moment in war,' he wrote despondently to a friend, 'and are not able to recover it.'

The remark was true of Rochefort, but Wolfe was given an opportunity the year following, when a full-scale attempt was to be made on Louisbourg. Hawke had spoken in such high terms of this eager young officer belonging to the sister Service that the King promoted him to full colonel, and he was offered command of a brigade on the expedition to Cape Breton Island.

Knowing the importance of the capture of Louisbourg to the success of his strategy for Canada, Pitt made no mistake this time in his choice of the chief commanders. Amherst, an experienced Guardsman, was given charge of the troops. He had once been on the staff of Field Marshal Ligonier, who was to the Army what Anson was to the Fleet. Amherst proved slow but sure throughout his New World campaigning, and with Wolfe to provide brilliance, matters augured well. Pitt chose Edward Boscawen for the naval command. 'Wry-necked Dick', as the sailors called him from a peculiar tilt of the head, was in his middle forties, had much war experience and was beloved by all who knew him.

As Boscawen sailed from England with his fleet, Hawke descended on the Basque Roads and destroyed a French squadron preparing to take out reinforcements and stores to Canada. Further south, in the Mediterranean, Admirals Osborne and Saunders broke up a concentration from Toulon which had sailed with the same object. During the course of this operation the Marquis Duquesne was captured. He was a great-nephew of de Ruyter's famous opponent and, like Galissonière, had once been Governor of Canada. With the Marquis, the *Foudroyant* was taken. She was a splendidly built ship of 80 guns, and she fell to the much smaller *Monmouth*, 64, after a gruelling battle in which the *Monmouth*'s captain, Arthur Gardiner, was killed. The action was completed by the ship's first lieutenant, Robert Carkett, who had risen from the lower deck. As the *Foudroyant* had carried Galissonière's flag at Minorca this was a signal victory, made possible by the fact that some of the *Foudroyant*'s seamen deserted their guns in the face of close-range fire. Taken into the British service, the ship had a notable career under her new flag.

Boscawen had able subordinates. They included Sir Charles Hardy, son and grandson of distinguished sea officers, with his flag in the *Royal William*, and John Simcoe, captain of the *Pembroke*, who had as his sailing master James Cook. Within a few years Cook would make his name as the greatest hydrographer, explorer and circumnavigator his Navy ever produced. At Louisbourg he began to learn surveying, taking instruction from military experts who were with the expedition.

Wolfe made his reputation during the siege, and Boscawen increased his stature as Pitt's favourite admiral. Wolfe had rousing words to say about the Navy, remarking that Boscawen had 'given all and even more than we could ask of him. He is . . . no bad *fantassin* [foot soldier] and an excellent backhand at a siege.' As for Hardy, 'I have often been at pains for Sir Charles's squadron at an anchor off the harbour's mouth. They rid out some very hard gales of wind rather than leave an opening for the French to escape.'

What Wolfe meant by his last remark was that there were five enemy ships of the line

Action between HMS Monmouth *and* Foudroyant *Francis Swaine 1758*

One of the great single-ship actions, that between HMS *Monmouth* and the French *Foudroyant*, took place early in 1758. Admiral Duquesne, with his flag in *Foudroyant*, 80, with three other ships, was sent to join de la Clue at Cartagena, but soon found himself in the midst of a British fleet. One of his ships was taken, the other two escaped. *Foudroyant* was now chased by *Monmouth*, *Swiftsure* and *Hampton Court*, and she and *Monmouth* started firing at each other at 7 a.m., having outdistanced the rest. Both ships were dismasted, and Captain Gardiner was shot through the head. *Foudroyant* struck at 1 o'clock and Duquesne was taken prisoner. Captain Gardiner died the following day.

at anchor under the guns of the fortress, which could have done considerable mischief had not many of the seamen been drafted for duty ashore. Their end was dramatic. On 21 July 1758 three of them were set on fire by batteries bombarding the town. Four nights later, Captains Laforey and Balfour, with 600 seamen, stole into the harbour under cover of darkness and seized the two remaining vessels. One, the *Bienfaisant*, grounded as soon as her cable was cut, and was promptly set ablaze. The other, the *Prudent*, was towed by ships' boats across the harbour and anchored near Amherst's batteries. The humiliation was more than the French could bear, and within a day or two the capitulation was signed.

The siege had taken longer than expected, and by the time matters were settled it was too late for anything more than a limited reconnaissance up the St Lawrence. News came of a British reverse at Fort Ticonderoga, near the foot of Lake Champlain, whereupon the commanders decided to send six battalions to reinforce the army. An attack on Quebec would have to wait until the following year.

Even so, 1758 ended well. To set against the defeat at Ticonderoga, General Forbes captured Fort Duquesne, in the head waters of the river Ohio, renaming the place Pittsburg in honour of the statesman. Another success was by Colonel Bradstreet, who made a lightning advance on Frontenac, on the southern tip of Lake Ontario, capturing the entire flotilla of six French ships which had dominated the inland waters. If the fall of Louisbourg left the front door of Canada ajar, Bradstreet made certain that the back door was open too.

II

Boscawen was not available for the expedition to Quebec, being given the still more important post of Commander-in-Chief, Mediterranean. Admiral Saunders was appointed, and this left an aggrieved officer in Sir Charles Hardy. Although this was regrettable, Hardy would have his recompense in due course, and Saunders, who had been with Anson on his world voyage, was one of the best, as well as one of the luckiest, officers in the fleet.

Amherst was given overall command in Canada. Wolfe was appointed major-general at the age of thirty-two, and put in charge of the military side of the foray to Quebec. It was no rash promotion, for Wolfe's battle experience had begun at the age of sixteen. He had already proved himself in regimental and brigade command, and Pitt believed in youth when he found it joined to ability.

Matters started badly. The crossing to Halifax was protracted by bad weather, and when Saunders reached Nova Scotia he found to his consternation that Rear-Admiral Philip Durell, who should have known better, was still in harbour. His excuse was that the ice had been severe that year, and he did not believe that the French could have got ships up the St Lawrence before being intercepted.

He was wrong. Louis-Antoine de Bougainville, one day to become Cook's rival as circumnavigator, but then a colonel in the French army, had evaded the blockade and was now in the approaches to the river. With him were three frigates and nearly a score of supply ships. Montcalm, who commanded the troops in French Canada, rejoiced at the return of this able young officer, who had served with him before against the British. He brought the latest news from home. Equally welcome in a country where every trained man counted, there were four hundred engineers, gunners and other technicians to add to his strength.

There now took place one of the more memorable feats in the annals of warfare under sail. Wholly against the expectations of the soldiers, but to their delight, Saunders proposed to take the greater part of his fleet, and all the transports, which were mainly American, the entire distance of nearly seven hundred miles from the open Atlantic to the basin of Quebec. This would be in the face of powerful currents, rapids, a tortuous course, and winds which were mainly adverse. The decision was unparalleled, for the St Lawrence had never been properly charted, and the French considered the passage to Quebec and beyond impracticable for anything bigger than a frigate. But Saunders had not been Anson's pupil for nothing, and he knew the quality of his sailing masters.

The passage was completed without mishap, and a camp was established on the Isle of Orleans, north-east of the city. Quebec was soon under fire from batteries mounted on the opposite bank, manned by Marines.

At first, French light craft, with the advantage of local knowledge, were aggressive and caused annoyance, but a fire-ship attack mounted on the night of 28 June 1759 failed completely, except as a spectacle. It was the same with a similar attempt a month later, during which time Saunders suffered from one of those sudden storms, familiar in the area, which caused damage to the transports.

The investment of Quebec grew closer and closer, until the time came when Wolfe considered it possible to make an assault on Montcalm's lines east of the city. Saunders made a reconnaissance in the *Centurion*, Anson's old flagship. She was moved close inshore, with other vessels, to give the troops the support of her guns. Even with the fullest naval backing a frontal attack on a strong and prepared position was likely to fail, and Wolfe's men were repulsed with heavy loss. If Montcalm were to be defeated, it would be by less obvious means.

Wolfe, who was ailing, was by this time on bad terms with his three brigadiers and, when at last he sought their advice as to the next move, they were careful to consult Saunders before they made their report. The unanimous opinion was that the best chance was by means of an attack from up-river of the city. The plan was made easier by the fact that Saunders had already got ships, and flat-bottomed boats, past the defences. They were under the command of Rear-Admiral Charles Holmes, who flew his flag in the line-of-battleship *Sutherland*.

The general agreed, and on the night of 12–13 September Commander James Chads, who had served under Howe at Rochefort, conducted a hazardous boat journey to the Anse du Foulon. There, a path led to the Heights of Abraham, south-west of the city. The battle fought on the morning after the landing was a tactical masterpiece, won by Wolfe, who died in the hour of victory.

The part played by the fleet in the final stages was essential. Saunders made a convincing feint on the Beauport Lines, on the opposite side of Quebec, where the July assault had failed, and where the French now had most of their troops. Detachments of seamen manhandled guns up the steep path to the battlefield, and it may well have been a shot from one of them which gave Montcalm the wound which killed him. When it became possible, parties landed close under the battlements of Quebec, and the flow of supplies from the fleet to the soldiers never ceased.

This was flawless co-operation. It was completed the following year, when the British

86

frigate *Lowestoft* was first up the St Lawrence, to find a garrison afflicted by scurvy, by shortage of victuals, and by a serious repulse after a sortie beyond the walls of the city.

The conquest of Canada was completed by Amherst, but it was 1759, not 1760, which was known in Britain as 'Wonderful'. Wolfe and Saunders had assured the fall of Quebec; the army had fought gloriously at Minden; there had been sea victories by Boscawen and Hawke; the French, under Thomas, Baron Lally, had been forced to abandon their attempt to take Madras owing to lack of naval support; and in the West Indies, Guadeloupe had fallen. 'We have not had more conquest than fine weather,' wrote Horace Walpole, basking in the glow of a protracted summer. 'One would think we had plundered the East and West Indies of sunshine.'

III

While so much was happening outside Europe, in France the idea was revived of an invasion of the British Isles. The scheme had original features: 20,000 men, embarked at Ostend, were to be landed on the coast of Essex, a threat which was to be heralded by an attempt on the Firth of Clyde by an army of similar size, embarked in Brittany. There would be a diversionary attack on Northern Ireland, led by Thurot, a successful privateer commander.

The covering fleet was to be formed from those at Brest and Toulon which, when combined, would escort the army of Brittany to Scotland. The ships would then sail round the north of Scotland and by the North Sea, to Ostend, to bring over the second force. This would be put ashore in the estuary of the Blackwater.

Away in the Mediterranean, Boscawen's duty was to watch the Toulon fleet, and to

Fire-ship Attack on the British Fleet Before Quebec 1759
Samuel Scott

Quebec was besieged in the summer and autumn of 1759 by British forces under General Wolfe and Admiral Saunders. To the consternation of the French, Saunders managed to bring his fleet as far up the St Lawrence as the Île d'Orléans, a magnificent feat of navigation. To counter this threat, the French sent seven ships down river towards the British, but they fired the ships too soon and, although the *Centurion* had to run for it, boats soon appeared, grappled the blazing ships and drew them ashore, where they burnt out harmlessly.

Battle of Lagos 1759
Thomas Luny

Admiral Boscawen, on hearing that de la Clue and a French squadron were on passage from Toulon to Brest, immediately left Gibraltar in pursuit. He found his quarry off Portugal, and action began early in the afternoon, carrying on throughout the night, Boscawen having changed from his disabled *Namur* to the *Newark*. One of the French ships had already been taken, but during the night one escaped, while the four others were driven into Lagos Bay, where two more were captured and a further two burnt. De la Clue died of his wounds.

prevent any such combination. Early in August 1759, after an unsuccessful effort to force the French admiral, de la Clue, to put to sea, by attacking two frigates lying offshore of the base, Boscawen withdrew his fleet to Gibraltar. Most of his ships were in urgent need of attention. Water and victuals were also running low.

De la Clue took the chance to slip out of Toulon, hoping to get through the Straits while the British were in dockyard hands. Unfortunately for him, the alertness of a frigate captain gave Boscawen a few hours' notice to get his ships to sea, in whatever condition they may have been. He sailed with the signal flying for a chase, captains to engage as opportunity offered without waiting to form line of battle.

In the running fight which resulted, de la Clue made good use of the French practice of firing high, with the aim of damage to masts and spars rather than to hulls and men. Boscawen's flagship, the *Namur*, lost her mizen and both topsail yards, and fell astern. The admiral ordered a boat to be hoisted out, in which he made for the *Newark*, the nearest ship to him. On the way over the boat was holed by a French shot. Boscawen, pulling off his wig, stuffed it into the leak, reaching the *Newark* unscathed. No wonder the sailors loved him.

The rearmost French ship, the *Centaure*, Captain de Sabran Grammont, put up a stout defence, holding up several of the enemy until her captain and more than half of

88

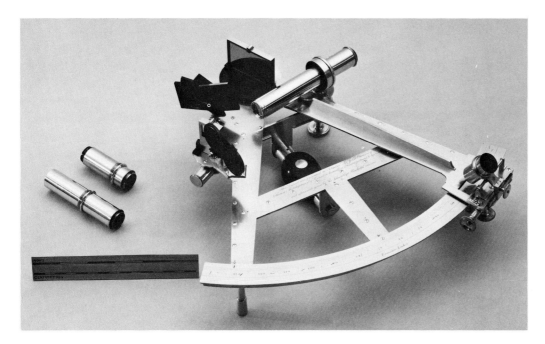

the company were killed or wounded. When she surrendered, towards nightfall on 17 August, time had been lost, but the pursuit was continued during the hours of darkness.

At dawn on 18 August, Boscawen was rewarded by the sight of four ships of the line standing towards the Portuguese coast. Two others had broken away, unknown to de la Clue, heading for Cadiz. The four which were within sight of the British entered the Bay of Lagos, where, to the astonishment of all beholders, de la Clue's flagship, the *Océan*, which had fought with distinction, ran ashore with all her sails set. As a result of the impact, the masts went by the board, falling across the bows. It was a tremendous sight, and the incident was explained (if not very fully), in a letter from Captain Buckle of the *Namur* to the Duke of Newcastle. In this he said: 'Mr de la Clue had one leg broke, and the other shot through. He was hastily put ashore to avoid being taken.' For conciseness and understatement, these few words would be hard to equal.

Boscawen, eager to get among the enemy, was not one to let delicate considerations of neutrality deter him. He followed the French into the bay, set fire to the *Océan* and the *Redoutable*, and towed away the *Téméraire* and *Modeste* as prizes. 'I flatter myself,' he wrote to Pitt, 'that my conduct in this affair will be approved by you. It is easier to satisfy that Court [Portugal] than for the French to build four men of war.' When he had the news, at his station off Brest, Hawke, with his usual generosity, wrote to Boscawen, 'No man in England can be more pleased with your good fortune.'

Hawke's day was soon to come.

After the annihilation of de la Clue's squadron the French had only the Brest fleet under Conflans with which to sustain an invasion. Wise counsel would have deferred the whole business, seeing that the summer was well advanced, and seeing that Hawke, in a phrase which he himself used later, was watching his opponent as a cat watches a mouse, and in much the same spirit.

Hawke was master of two utterly different ingredients of sail warfare: the chase

Isle of Man Action 1760
Richard Wright

This action was fought between three French frigates under the command of François Thurot, a famous privateer, and three British frigates under Captain Elliot. Thurot had landed troops in Carrickfergus Bay where, after a siege, they took the castle, but, hearing of reinforcements, re-embarked. Off the Isle of Man, Thurot's ships fell in with Elliot's squadron, *Æolus*, *Pallas* and *Brilliant*. At 9 a.m. fighting began, in effect three concurrent single-ship actions. After an hour and a half, during which Thurot was killed, all the French ships were taken.

action, and the patient, gruelling trial of close blockade of an enemy coast. As summer gave way to autumn, he was occasionally driven off station by westerly gales, but frigates, under Commodore Duff, remained at sea. It was they who, in November 1759, when the main fleet had been forced to shelter in Torbay, gave him news that Conflans, taking advantage of a favouring wind, had moved south, ready to embark the army of invasion at Morbihan, the soldiers encamped on the cliffs.

The weather on 16 November caused Conflans to heave to, but sped Hawke towards the French. 'I have carried a press of sail all night,' he reported in a dispatch to the Admiralty on the 17th, 'with a hard gale at south-south-east, in pursuit of the enemy, and make no doubt of coming up with them at sea or in Quiberon Bay.' Back in London, to which his words were directed, the admiral was being burnt in effigy by the mob for what they believed his failure to bring the enemy to account. From past experience, they should have known their man better.

Early in the morning of 20 November, one of Duff's ships made the signal for a fleet in sight. Hawke's response was to form line abreast, which gave the best spread of search. One hour later, it was confirmed that the admiral was approaching the main French fleet. Conflans had set course for Quiberon Bay, reasoning that, once inside, he could take up a strong defensive position in which to hold off an attack.

The most practicable approach to the roadstead at Quiberon lies between the Cardinal Rocks on the one hand and the Four Shoal, a dangerous rock-strewn cluster, on the other. Conflans was abreast of the Cardinals by 2.30 in the afternoon, but any

hopes he may have had of anchoring in a good position were dashed by the speed of Hawke's approach. With his blue flag at the main top-masthead of the *Royal George*, ordering every sail to be set which his ships could carry, oblivious of the gale, the rain squalls which from time to time blotted out the land, and the dangers of inshore rocks, his fleet swept on. Hawke was reaping the reward of gruelling months on watch, battered by gales and with never a glimpse of the enemy.

As the rear division of the French fleet rounded the Cardinals, the British van, eagerly obeying Hawke's signal to 'Form as you chase', which was the most electrifying order in nautical language, was in action. No 'shyness' or doubt appeared that day, and it was not Hawke alone who was savouring the hour of crisis. His second-in-command was Sir Charles Hardy, with his flag in the *Union* of 90 guns. Hardy had been denied his share in the taking of Quebec, but at least he was at Quiberon.

As the afternoon wore on, the wind, which had been high to start with, increased its velocity. It helped to throw the French line into disorder, and enabled the later British ships to come into action sooner than they would otherwise have done. Once the greater part of both fleets was within the confines of the bay the battle developed into a series of single-ship duels, each captain finding an opponent.

Hawke, in his splendid flagship, rounded the Cardinals a little before four o'clock, meeting the *Soleil Royal*, flying the flag of Conflans, trying to lead out of the bay back

Havana 1762
Dominic Serres

War having been declared with Spain in January 1762, a large expedition was despatched from Britain, which succeeded in taking all the allied French and Spanish islands in the West Indies. All that was left was Cuba, of which Havana, protected by Morro Castle, was the capital. Admiral Pocock and General Lord Albemarle were in joint command. After a long and unsuccessful bombardment, and an epidemic of sickness, Sir James Douglas arrived with reinforcements, instilling renewed vigour into the attack. Havana capitulated on 11 August, the garrison receiving the honours of war.

91

to sea. The vessels engaged broadside to broadside, and the Frenchman was driven so far to leeward that she could not weather the Four Shoal. Her captain, Bidé de Chésac, was forced to wear, and to try to retrace his course.

The short day closed in darkness, rain and storm. Hawke then anchored to await the morning light, when he would see for himself how his captains had done, and how best he could exploit what he knew to be victory.

Victory it was. The French *Formidable*, flagship of Rear-Admiral Saint-André du Verger, had been so battered by British gunfire that she struck her colours to Captain Speke of the *Resolution*. The *Thésée*, a brand-new 74-gun ship, encountered the *Torbay*, Captain Augustus Keppel, but heeled over and sank when her men opened the lower gun-ports to reply to Keppel's fire. The *Héros*, raked by Lord Howe's *Magnanime*, lost all her officers and four hundred of her crew before she surrendered. The *Superbe* foundered in the rough sea after receiving attention from the *Royal George*: seven ships, tacking to keep clear of rocks and shoals, got trapped in the estuary of the river Vilaine.

So far, no British ship had been lost, but during the night, wild with storm and with cries of men in distress, the *Resolution* ran ashore on the Four Shoal, and could not be got off, though most of her men were saved. The darkness enabled a few French ships to grope their way to sea and to make for the shelter of the Basque Roads. They were shepherded by the Chevalier de Bauffremont in the *Tonnant*, who came in for castigation later from his Commander-in-Chief. One ship, the *Juste*, ran ashore in the mouth of the Loire and broke her back.

The dawn scene which met Hawke's eyes was amazing. The *Soleil Royal*, uncertain of her exact whereabouts, had anchored in the midst of the British fleet. When her captain saw what he had done, he cut his cable and ran his ship ashore on the south side of the bay. The *Héros*, which had struck her colours but had not yet been taken in prize, since the sea had been too high for a boarding party, also cut her cable. The *Essex*, ordered to engage her, got wrecked on Four Shoal, and this was the only British loss in daylight. The *Soleil Royal* was later set on fire by her own crew, much to the disappointment of the British sailors, who had hoped for rich salvage from so illustrious a ship. They had to be content with souvenirs.

Hawke had achieved near annihilation, for even the seven ships in the Vilaine did not escape damage. By jettisoning all their guns they just managed to get across the bar into the river in a desperate effort to escape from Hawke. In the event, four of them broke their backs in the shallow waters.

Hawke's dispatch was worthy of the man. He wrote:

> When I consider the season of the year, the hard gales on the day of action, a flying enemy, the shortness of the day, and the coast they were on, I can boldly affirm that all that could possibly be done has been done. As to the loss we have sustained, let it be placed to the account of the necessity I was under of running all risks to break this strong force of the enemy. Had we had but two hours more daylight, the whole had been totally destroyed or taken; for we were almost up with their van when night overtook us.

Quiberon helped to dim the memory of Barfleur, and in its turn was to some degree effaced by the impact of later battles. But, by any standard, it was one of the great triumphs in warfare. As at Barfleur, the action was witnessed by French troops ashore.

For the rest of the Seven Years War the French relied, for such success as they achieved, on their privateer commanders. Some of them deserved a better fate than was accorded them. Among them was Thurot, who was deserted by the regular French captains under his command. This led to failure of the foray off the coast of Northern Ireland, and to Thurot's own death. There never was a greater fiasco than the proposed invasion of 1759, not even the attempt by Philip II.

IV

Away in the East, French and English were striving for a dominating position in the Indian sub-continent. The original contenders on the British side were Clive by land and Rear-Admiral Watson by sea. They recaptured Calcutta, drove the enemy out of Chandernagore, and brought the whole of Bengal under British control. After Watson's death, Commodore Steevens took over command of the slender British naval force in the area. Both he and his successor, Pocock, had the advantage of the brains of Captain Richard Kempenfelt, who was then in his forties, and, because he had lacked influence to obtain early promotion, was not of seniority in his rank.

Yet every officer with whom Kempenfelt served felt the benefit, and this was particularly so when Pocock faced the Comte d'Aché, who had arrived in India with a squadron partly made up of East Indiamen. D'Aché was on the worst of terms with the impetuous Lally, who had gone out in charge of all French forces in India. Pocock and d'Aché fought several duels which, though in themselves indecisive, resulted in control of the Indian theatre of war by the British. This was owing to d'Aché's retreat to Mauritius after his third and last battle with Pocock on 10 September 1759. He suffered heavy casualties, but damaged the British so much aloft that Pocock could not pursue him. Lally, defending Pondicherry, surrendered after a ten-month siege, in which he felt himself deserted by the Navy.

Lally went back to England as a prisoner of war. The son of an Irish Jacobite, he had served in the expedition to Scotland with Bonnie Prince Charlie. Hearing that his honour was impugned, he agreed to an exchange, only to find himself confined in the Bastille on his return to Paris. When his trial at last came on, after two whole years, d'Aché was one of the witnesses against him. Lally went to the guillotine. Voltaire, who had tried in vain to come to the help of the unfortunate Admiral Byng, was at least successful in aiding Lally's son to vindicate a reputation which had been shockingly traduced.

Pocock was sent from the East Indies to the West, after Spain joined France at the worst possible moment for herself. Within a few months she had lost Havana, as the result of a combined operation in which disease caused far more loss than the battle. She also lost Manila, to an expedition mounted jointly by the Navy and the East India Company. The naval commander, Rear-Admiral Samuel Cornish, had Kempenfelt as his flag captain, and Kempenfelt's was a major share in the admirable way in which the operation was carried out. It was one of the last in which Anson was concerned, for he died before it was put in train. As in the case of his own world voyage, it resulted in the capture of a galleon, and rich reward for those who took part. Never, perhaps, had so short a war cost a country so much as did the few months of hostilities in which Spain engaged.

By the time peace was made Britain had a new king in George III, very different in outlook from his predecessor, eager to make his countrymen respected for feats additional to those of arms, in which it was clear that they excelled.

At the Peace of Paris, which was signed in 1763, many conquests were handed back, for it was no part of the British design to aspire to supremacy everywhere. Although Britain gained an Empire, so little did this weigh with her that serious consideration was given to handing Canada back to France, and to take Guadeloupe instead. The idea came to nothing for the voice of the Americans was made clear, even though indirectly. They had been cheated once before of Louisbourg. They did not mean to be robbed now of protection to their northern frontier just for the sake of one more sugar island. The war, so Pitt had said, had been begun on their behalf. Let them benefit from the credit which had been gained by British arms.

V

One age-long battle reached a further stage during the Seven Years War, affecting the wooden ships of every nation. It was against *Teredo Navalis*, the ship-worm which had plagued mariners and shipwrights ever since antiquity, and the barnacle. Countless experiments had been tried to combat the boring creature which fed on ships' timbers, and marine growths which fouled their bottoms and slowed them up.

In Elizabethan times, Sir John Hawkins and his son Richard had done much with a layer of felt over which was a sheathing of elm. The Spaniards and Portuguese tried lead, but it was heavy and costly and, as Richard Hawkins noted, 'it is nothing durable, but subject to many casualties.' Nevertheless, the English made some use of lead, as was noted by Pepys who, in 1675, had some discussion with Charles II because, so the King remarked, sheathing appeared to affect the ship's ironwork when it was tried on the frigate *Phoenix*.

An effective answer proved to be copper. The frigate *Alarm* was sheathed with this metal in 1761. Beneath the metal was a layer of brown paper. The process was a qualified success, more so when the constructors had learnt to avoid fastening the copper with iron bolts, which corroded. The *Alarm* herself had a useful life of nearly sixty years, and was present at the capture of Havana. Another frigate, the *Dolphin*, was given the same treatment, and was the first coppered ship to go round the world. Her captain, Samuel Wallis, discovered Tahiti shortly before Cook began the first of his three great voyages of exploration. By 1783, coppering had been extended to the whole Navy, and officers were certain of its value. It was not a perfect process, but it was better than any other remedy then known.

EIGHT

THE WAR OF AMERICAN INDEPENDENCE

Canada attacked — Burgoyne's surrender — French intervention
The West Indies — Ushant and Keppel's trial — Paul Jones's adventure
Timber famine — Threat of invasion — Rodney at St Vincent
De Grasse at Chesapeake — The battle off Dominica
Howe relieves Gibraltar — Suffren and Hughes in India

ALTHOUGH THE SEVEN YEARS WAR had safeguarded the American colonists from danger from the French in the New World, Montcalm had foretold that if the British annexed Canada they would lose their other North American possessions. This proved to be so, after a prolonged struggle (1775–83), the outcome of which was made certain, ironically enough, by the sea power of France. The French navy had been revived, in a burst of nationwide enthusiasm, largely owing to Choiseul, one of Louis XV's ablest ministers. It was to be deployed in aid of the colonists. The combination, during a war in which, for the first time, Britain had no ally, gave the country a task to which it was unequal. Matters grew worse when Spain and Holland took an active part against her.

In the broadest context, the war was one of the most important events in the history of Western man, significant far beyond what could have been realized at the time. As regards warfare at sea, the events which marked its course as it spread across much of the world, were of importance both in themselves and in the way in which they affected tactics. They were also a testing time for many officers who came to the height of their powers in a later and still more protracted struggle.

At first, so far as the high seas were concerned, Britain maintained ascendancy, since the colonists had no navy. However, they were full of resource, and they soon followed the French practice of privateering. This caused heavy loss among ships sailing independently. Privateers usually left convoys alone, which meant that the British could supply forces ashore in North America when opposed only by the rebels. The Navy could even influence such land actions as the first considerable battle, fought at Bunker Hill near Boston by troops under the command of General Howe, brother of the distinguished sea officer. There, parties, such as that led by Cuthbert Collingwood, had their first taste of action, supplying the army with what was necessary from the ships.

The colonists not unreasonably supposed that the British would be vulnerable in Canada. Here they were disappointed. Thanks partly to a statesmanlike Act, passed in 1774, giving full freedom for the practice of the Catholic religion, the French in that country remained loyal to George III. Even so, General Carleton, the Governor of Quebec, who had been Wolfe's Quartermaster General in his campaign fifteen years earlier, found himself with a weak garrison, short of supplies, and with the likelihood of

Engagement at Lake Champlain 1776
Pub. Sayer & Bennett

The scene of two naval battles, the first on the waters of Lake Champlain took place during the War of the American Revolution. Sir Guy Carleton, needing a fleet to carry his troops south from Canada, hastily constructed boats on the lake, the largest of which was the *Inflexible*, 18. Benedict Arnold, with his equally hastily built fleet, was hiding behind Valcour Island and the British turned into a strong northerly and opened the attack on 11 October. Two days later came a resounding British victory, but the presence of the rebels on the lake delayed any further advance for another year.

having to sustain a siege. This was indeed mounted, the crisis being a vigorous assault made during a snowstorm on 31 December 1775 by Americans under Richard Montgomery and Benedict Arnold. In this affair, Montgomery was killed and Arnold wounded. The attack failed; the siege continued.

Captain Charles Douglas, commanding the 50-gun ship *Isis,* who had been thwarted by ice in 1775 in bringing supplies to Carleton, pressed up the St Lawrence at the earliest moment in 1776. He relieved Quebec in May in the same dramatic fashion as had occurred in 1760 when the *Lowestoft* was sighted from the ramparts. After Carleton had driven the besieging forces from the neighbourhood of the city, he advanced to the head of Lake Champlain.

Here, on fresh water, occurred the first action between British and American naval forces. Douglas was an officer of ingenuity and drive, a master of ballistics as then known, and able to inspire others. By ordering the construction of the *Inflexible* from local resources, and arming her with eighteen 12-pounder guns, a comparatively junior officer, Commander Thomas Pringle, was able to dominate the fighting which occurred on 11 and 13 October 1776. Arnold's smaller force, also improvised, was practically wiped out, but the Americans had imposed such delays on the British that no further advance could be made that year.

In the military line, Carleton's second-in-command had been General 'Johnny' Burgoyne, soldier, dramatist and wit. Burgoyne had not hesitated to criticize his super-

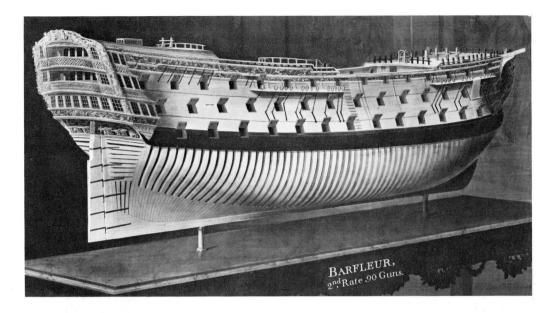

BARFLEUR,
2ⁿᵈRate 90 Guns.

Allegedly a model of the
second *Barfleur*, a ship
launched in 1768, she was of
1,947 tons and mounted 98
guns, her length, beam and
draught being 177 feet, 50
feet and 21 feet respectively,
and she carried 750 men. She
saw much action in the West
Indies and the North
American Station, and
received the surrender of the
Ville de Paris in Rodney's
victory over de Grasse. She
was the flagship of Admiral
Bowyer on 1 June 1794, when
commanded by the future
Lord Collingwood and she
also took part at Cape St
Vincent and Calder's action at
Ferrol. She was broken up in
1819.

ior for methods which, though they may have seemed dilatory, were based on experience. When campaigning was resumed in 1777, Burgoyne was given command of an
independent expedition. He got off to a good start, thanks to naval efforts on Lake
Champlain. There, a newly-built ship, the 26-gun *Royal George*, had been added to the
original flotilla. Even so, Burgoyne ran into increasing difficulties as he moved south.
Supplies ran low; communications broke down; no help came from British forces
deployed elsewhere and, in spite of his self-assurance, he was never Carleton's peer in
campaigning. By October, just a year after the success on the lake, he was forced to
surrender at Saratoga to much superior American forces under Horatio Gates.

The resilient Burgoyne in the end survived the humiliation, but Saratoga marked a
turning-point in the war. France, encouraged by British difficulties, hoping to avenge
her earlier losses, signed a treaty of commerce and friendship with the rebels in
February 1778. They were already being helped by volunteers such as the young
Lafayette, a favourite with George Washington, the American Commander-in-Chief.
France was hesitant to commit herself to outright war, partly because Louis XVI, on
principle, had no wish to ally himself with rebels. It was not until he had some
assurance from his uncle, Charles III of Spain, who wished to regain Gibraltar and
Minorca, that Louis allowed himself to become fully committed.

II

After a Pyrrhic victory at Bunker Hill, the position of the British under General Howe
became increasingly difficult. By the spring of 1776 town and harbour were under
bombardment, and Howe decided to move his forces north to Halifax, the nearest well-
equipped base available. Early in the summer, the decision was taken to proceed south
to assault New York.

General Howe arrived at New York harbour on 25 June with three ships, the
vanguard of his forces. Within five days he had his entire army assembled. On 2 July,

two days before the American Declaration of Independence, he landed unopposed on Staten Island. He was then joined by his brother, Admiral Lord Howe, with 150 ships of various kinds, and reinforcements from England. Within four weeks, the Howes had under command some 31,000 men of all ranks to execute the first amphibious assault in history to be led by brothers.

On the morning of 22 August 1776, after a night of thunder, lightning and 'prodigious' rain, the General advanced across the Narrows to Long Island, an action which eventually brought about the capture of New York City. Once in firm possession of New York and Rhode Island, Narragansett Bay became Lord Howe's focal area for the rest of his time in American waters.

The admiral had arrived with a document which allowed him and his brother 'to treat with the revolted Americans, and to take measures for the restoration of peace within the Colonies.' The dual rôle of war-makers and peace commissioners played an important part in their conduct. If neither admiral nor general appeared to press such successes as came their way, it was because other thoughts distracted them. Their elder brother, the third Viscount Howe, had been killed in action at Trout Brook, Lake George, in the previous war, and his gallantry had been held in particular respect by the Americans. This was one reason why it was believed that the Howes were suitable for the difficult rôle which had been assigned them, but once Lord Howe faced opposition at sea from the French, the whole aspect of affairs altered for the worse.

Admiral Howe's adversary proved to be the Comte d'Estaing, who, when younger, had transferred from the army to the navy, a practice sometimes allowed in the French service. D'Estaing arrived in American waters after a long but unchallenged passage. This was a reflection on the Admiralty in London, for the Board had had warning of his sortie from Toulon, but had not taken steps to intercept it.

D'Estaing made his landfall near the mouth of the Delaware. The result was that General Clinton, who commanded at Philadelphia, which the British had taken the previous year, withdrew from the town and marched overland to rejoin General Howe at New York. D'Estaing turned northward up the coast. He reached Sandy Hook, near the entrance to New York harbour, on 22 July 1778, with a force much superior to that of the British. Admiral Howe had with him only six ships of 64 guns, three of 50 guns, and seven frigates. They were intended for coastal work, to which they were well suited, not for battle against heavier ships. D'Estaing missed a great opportunity. Instead of attacking, he sailed away for Rhode Island to join the Americans against the beleaguered British garrison.

Despite his lack of numbers, Admiral Howe went to the rescue, intending to play with d'Estaing, whose measure he had, until the arrival of reinforcements from England under Vice-Admiral Byron, who was expected daily. 'Foul Weather Jack', as Byron was nicknamed, duly arrived, but not before the British and French fleets had been dispersed by a violent storm. Afterwards, in spite of American entreaties, d'Estaing insisted on proceeding to Boston to refit. He then departed for the Caribbean. It was perhaps as well for him because Byron, thanks to the weather, arrived at Sandy Hook too late to be of any use to Howe.

Having survived threats and storm, Admiral Howe had a final adventure before sailing home on 26 September. His flagship, the *Eagle*, was attacked in New York harbour by a submersible! This craft, named the *Turtle* from the shape of its 'pressure hull', was the ingenious invention of a former Yale student, David Bushnell, and embodied such

A First-rate Taking in Stores
J. M. W. Turner

One of Turner's most
famous paintings, it shows, in
his inimitable style, the
provisioning of a fleet before
leaving port on an expedition
or to seek battle. Until 1832
the Victualling Board oversaw
this side of things, entering
into contracts with merchants
for stores, clothes and other
provisions, and some of these
purchases are here seen being
taken inboard.

Nelson Receiving The French Colours after the Battle of the Nile
Guy Head

Guy Head painted this somewhat romantic portrait of Nelson, never before published in colour, soon after the *Vanguard* arrived at Naples after the Nile action. Said to have been painted from life, it was given to Emma by the sitter. Nelson, always a vain man, disdains the green eye-shade he always wore after Calvi; neither he nor the midshipman, who was far too junior an officer to be presenting his superior with the enemy's sword and *tricoleur*, looks as if he had just survived a fierce battle conducted throughout the night, and there is no sign of the bandage encircling Nelson's head after his wound in the battle, when he was convinced his time was come.

Trafalgar: End of Action
Engraved by J. Fittler after Nicholas Pocock

After an action, the epitome of the 'pell-mell' battle, both British and Combined Fleets were in sad case, with the weather rapidly worsening. The British suffered particularly in their hulls and rigging, several ships being partially or totally dismasted. The Franco-Spanish fleet lost eighteen ships captured or sunk, of which one, the *Achille*, blew up. This picture shows the confusion into which both fleets were thrown at the conclusion of the encounter.

Evening of Trafalgar
Water-colour by Harold Wyllie

Behind the darkened windows of *Victory*'s great cabin lies Nelson's body. Confirmation of his death came during the hours of darkness when it was seen that his Admiral's lantern above *Victory*'s poop was extinguished and the night signal was carried by the Commander-in-Chief, Collingwood, in the *Euryalus*. Repairs are afoot aboard the *Victory*, and a jury mizen has been set. With the ship cleared for action, wooden furniture and temporary bulkheads have been put overboard and are towing alongside. Vice-Admiral Collingwood, now in command of the fleet, having shifted his flag from the dismasted *Royal Sovereign*, is approaching in the frigate *Euryalus*.

This painting is here published for the first time.

Battle of Camperdown, 1797
P. J. de Loutherbourg

In spite of disaffection amongst his ships' crews Admiral Duncan had managed to keep a blockade on the Texel, but when news that the Dutch fleet was out arrived, he was refitting at Yarmouth. Setting sail with fourteen of the line, he met de Winter with eleven. No strict line was formed by the British, and a 'pell-mell' battle ensued, ending in complete defeat for the Dutch. Admiral de Winter, the only unwounded man on deck, surrendered his sword to Admiral Duncan on board his flagship, *Vrijheid*.

Battle between HMS Brunswick *and* Vengeur
Nicholas Pocock

HMS *Brunswick*, next in line to Howe's flagship *Queen Charlotte*, played a brilliant part in the action of 1 June 1794 – the 'Glorious First of June'. Commanded by Captain John Harvey, she ran on board *Vengeur*, 74, Captain Renaudin, and there then ensued the most tremendous battle between the two. Harvey, after several injuries, was compelled to go below, command devolving upon Lieutenant Cracroft. After three hours the ships separated, the *Vengeur* surrendering, but the *Brunswick* was in no state to take possession, having lost her mizen-mast, and having other masts and yards badly damaged, rigging and sails almost non-existent, 23 guns unserviceable and her bower anchor dragging.

The *Vengeur* sank quickly after the action with great loss of life, although Captain Renaudin and his twelve-year-old son survived, not meeting, however, until they reached Portsmouth.

advanced features as a breathing-tube for the operator, pre-dating the snorkel, ballast tanks, a depth gauge and a detachable charge. Propelled manually, it could be moved in any direction. Sergeant Ezra Lee, the pioneer submariner, actually reached Howe's ship, but was unable to attach the explosive device, and barely escaped with his life.

At the conclusion of hostilities, Bushnell practised medicine with some success.

With his powerful and as yet unblooded fleet of twelve ships of the line and attendant frigates, d'Estaing, cruising among the West Indian islands, could have looked for some conquests in an area where Dominica had already fallen to the French. In December 1778, he appeared off St Lucia, important as being only thirty miles to the south, that is, to windward, of the main French base of Fort Royal, Martinique, the centre of their West Indian activities.

D'Estaing found at St Lucia seven ships under the command of Rear-Admiral Samuel Barrington, with his flag in the *Prince of Wales* of 74 guns. Barrington repelled every effort to dislodge him from his anchorage across an inlet, driving off successive attacks with loss to the enemy. In spite of the fact that d'Estaing landed 9,000 troops on the beaches, whose task was to defeat a force under Major-General James Grant, which was established in strong positions, fierce assaults were hurled back and the island was retained in British hands. D'Estaing, learning that Byron was on his way to reinforce Barrington, withdrew to Martinique, to Barrington's astonishment.

The occupation of St Lucia was an important success in an area where, over the earlier course of the war, British losses were greater than their gains. 'Our islands must be defended,' wrote George III of his West Indian possessions, 'even at the risk of an invasion of *this* island'—meaning Britain. 'If we lose our sugar islands, it will be impossible to raise money to continue.'

III

The risk of which the King spoke came about in due course. When, in June 1779, Spain fulfilled her promise to France to join in the war, it was with two main purposes: one was the recovery of Gibraltar and Minorca; the other, which was strange in view of the past, was a serious attempt at invasion of the British Isles. But, before that could be attempted, there was likely to be a trial of strength between the main opposing fleets. One such had already occurred in the Atlantic in July 1778, when the elderly French admiral, the Comte d'Orvilliers, faced Augustus Keppel, a popular character of Dutch descent, who had refused command when Britain was at war with the Americans, but accepted to serve against France.

In itself, the encounter was one of those inconclusive affairs which could have been held to justify an astounding remark attributed to M. de Maurepas, sometime French Minister of Marine, that he 'did not think much of naval battles, which were "piff-poff" on either side, and afterwards the sea is just as salt!' No ships were lost at the battle of Ushant, but when the 'piff-poff' was over, and the gunsmoke dissolved, echoes reverberated in strange places.

Keppel's view was that he might have achieved a marked success had he been better supported by Sir Hugh Palliser, one of his subordinate flag officers and, incidentally, a member of the Board of Admiralty. Keppel did not say so publicly, but he refused Palliser's demand to deny rumours derogatory to Palliser's conduct in action. The

George Brydges Rodney
after Sir Joshua Reynolds

Rodney entered the Navy at the age of fourteen. In 1747, as a captain, he distinguished himself at Ushant. Commanding the Leeward Islands station, he captured Martinique, Santa Lucia, Grenada and St Vincent. After a spell of six years as Governor of Greenwich Hospital, he retired abroad owing to debt; but went back to sea, taking part in the relief of Gibraltar in 1780. Coming home in 1781, he was back in the West Indies the next year, when he defeated de Grasse at the Saintes.

The Comte de Grasse
(1722–88)
After A. Maurin

Entering upon his naval career at sixteen, he saw much action, once being taken prisoner. He was Commander-in-Chief of a force sent to the West Indies early in 1781, and was of material assistance to Washington in defeating Graves's fleet at Chesapeake Bay in September, thus preventing the relief of Yorktown, and hastening American independence. Early the following year he was himself defeated by Rodney at the Saintes and again taken prisoner. Returning to France, his efforts to vindicate himself only ensured his banishment from court.

result was that Palliser most misguidedly called for a court martial on his Commander-in-Chief. Keppel's acquittal was a matter for public rejoicing, the charges being dismissed as 'ill-founded and malicious'. But his trial, and that of Palliser which followed (resulting in an acquittal by a packed court), divided the Navy, and it was largely political in background.

The most serious immediate result was that no admiral of the first reputation would serve as Keppel's successor in chief command. Charge had to be given to Sir Charles Hardy. This man, so zealous in the Seven Years War, was by now an invalid, Governor of Greenwich Hospital. It was a dire reflection on the government of the day, and the state of feeling in the Service, that the safety of the realm was entrusted to such a decayed personality. Hardy was dead within a year of his appointment.

IV

Byron's clash with the French, after he had joined Barrington in the West Indies in January 1779, was as unsatisfactory as Keppel's later meeting with d'Orvilliers. The British at last had temporary local superiority in the Caribbean, but, possibly because his crews were reduced by sickness, and his ships in a poor state, Byron failed to run down d'Estaing who, in consequence, was able to seize the islands of St Vincent and Grenada. Not until July did the rivals meet, off the newly captured Grenada. There, d'Estaing, despite advantages, refused a close engagement, though he did serious damage to four British ships. After the battle the approach of the hurricane season precluded further operations. The French admiral, answering one of Washington's many appeals for help, sailed for Savannah at the end of August, with twenty-one ships of the line and 5,000 troops.

Savannah had been captured by the British the previous year, but the defences were still in a vulnerable state. D'Estaing, on his arrival, did not feel himself equal to a long-drawn-out and costly siege. Early in October, after an assault during which he himself was wounded, he withdrew, and took no further serious part in the war. He lived for fifteen more years, meeting his death on the guillotine during the French Revolution. His subordinate, the handsome Comte de Grasse, tall, meticulous, accomplished, although present at Savannah, was to make his mark at a later stage of the conflict.

In the meantime, attention focused on the exploits of a young man who ranks as one of the founding fathers of the navy of the United States. John Paul, who added the name Jones after he had settled in America, was the son of a gardener of Kirkbean, Kirkcudbrightshire. He first went to sea from Whitehaven and, with nautical experience behind him, offered himself to the rebels for a commission to serve at sea. He had some success, and caused great annoyance to the British in command of the *Ranger*, with which he took prizes in the Irish Sea.

More serious were his adventures with a small squadron of American and French vessels in the late summer of 1779. On 23 September, when Captain Richard Pearson of the 44-gun *Serapis* was escorting forty-one ships of a Baltic convoy towards the Yorkshire coast, he saw to the south of him, near Flamborough Head, a ship approaching, flying the British flag. It was Paul Jones, in the *Bonhomme Richard*, originally a French East Indiaman.

Owing to adverse winds, Jones could not close with Pearson for some hours, by which time the convoy had reached safety. When the two ships were near enough to engage, Jones struck the Union flag, hoisting one with red, white and blue stripes. Battle then began, and continued for three and a half bitter hours, the later stages being lit by moonlight. Pearson failed to use his superior armament to best advantage, and allowed Jones to grapple. Eventually, with the *Bonhomme Richard* sinking under him, and the

Serapis in a sorry state, Jones boarded Pearson's ship and forced the Englishman to strike his flag. Not long afterwards, the *Bonhomme Richard* sank, and Jones brought the *Serapis* to the Texel, where he was received as a hero.

The acclaim was justified, as was Jones's later fame in France. The glory was not altogether on one side however, for Pearson, although defeated, had done the job for which he had been appointed and had saved his convoy. He was court martialled, acquitted, and knighted by George III. On hearing the news, Jones remarked sardonically: 'Should I have the good fortune to fall in with him again, I'll make a lord of him!'

In considering the episode, historians have sometimes overlooked the importance of Pearson's convoy, for Britain at that time was desperate for naval stores, and in the midst of one of a succession of timber famines. The last consignment of masts from North America had arrived at the very beginning of the war, and both sides were feeling shortages in naval stores of all kinds. So much was this so that the French, when they could not make use of Dutch bottoms, had to bear the enormous expense of journeys overland to their dockyards. The merchants of London and other cities were in no doubt as to the merit of Pearson's action, for they too rewarded him as if he had won a victory.

Apart from shipwrights and ship designers, merchants and importers were in the best position to realize the extent of an eighteenth-century fleet on timber drawn from diverse sources. The sheer quantity needed was prodigious. A three-decked ship, the largest type afloat, required $5739\frac{1}{2}$ cartloads of oak, elm and fir, each cartload representing the amount of timber cut from a full-grown oak. Even a frigate required an entire wood of mature trees.

The best main-masts came from the forests of New England or Canada; the best top-masts from the Ukraine; the best spars from the mountain slopes of Norway. Part of the planking of the yellow sides of British ships of the line would have been imported from Danzig. The curved frame timbers—always in short supply—were made from tough hedgerow oaks, mainly from the Wealds of Kent and Sussex. It was no wonder that, with worldwide commitments, with an expanding fleet, and with resources liable to be cut off altogether, dockyard repairs were apt to be scamped, and unseasoned wood used in new construction.

Contractors in all countries at war tried every expedient in their search for alternative sources of supply. Holland, as a principal carrier, thrived on the needs of the belligerents. When she joined in the war alongside France and Spain, as she did in November 1780, there were those in Britain who argued that the country, as a recognized enemy, was less troublesome than she had been as a neutral.

Spain was another matter. Although her contribution to the war effort in North America was confined to the taking of Pensacola, unimportant and far to the south of the main areas of combat, from the outset she showed determination in attacks on Gibraltar. The rock fortress was now to sustain the longest and most arduous of its various sieges. Moreover, by adding thirty-six ships of the line under Admiral Cordoba to thirty under d'Orvilliers, Spain made possible one of the most serious threats of invasion of the British Isles which had ever been posed.

Some 40,000 French troops had been earmarked for service against England, and on 30 July 1779 the combined Franco-Spanish fleet sailed northward from its rendezvous off Corunna. Winds were unfavourable, and it was not until 14 August that it was sighted off the Lizard, nearly two hundred years after Elizabethan watchers had been warned by the sight of Medina Sidonia. At the time, Sir Charles Hardy, with a fleet of thirty-nine, little over half the strength of his opponents, was vainly searching the area south-west of the Isles of Scilly in weather which afforded poor visibility. When frigates gave him news of the enemy's advent, Hardy realized that he was cut off from his home base. The prospect of a beach-head on British soil—Gosport or the Isle of Wight figured in enemy plans—had never seemed so well founded; yet, with success apparently within their grasp, the two admirals, Cordoba a septuagenarian and d'Orvilliers only slightly younger, lacking in operational experience, bedevilled by sickness, hampered by shortage of victuals, and suffering the inevitable handicaps associated with allied command in which divergent systems of signalling and tactics were concerned, made no effort to pursue the object of grand strategy. It seemed as if it was all just a parade.

Had Hardy known the true situation, he would almost certainly have tried to force a battle. Infirm as he was, no one ever accused him of lack of courage, but he was keenly aware of his numerical inferiority, and of the condition of the poorer among his ships, about which Keppel had complained. As a result, he avoided action, slipping away to anchor at Spithead.

By mid-September, the threat was over. The French, accompanied by twenty-one Spanish ships, withdrew to winter at Brest. The remaining Spaniards went south to Gibraltar to strengthen the blockade. When members of the Board of Admiralty could breathe again, their first thought was to organize the passage of supplies and reinforcements to General Eliott, defender of the Rock. Such a task demanded strong nerves, skilful tactics, and a measure of luck. The man chosen was Sir George Rodney, a veteran whose extravagant habits had led him into debt. A loan from a French friend, the Marshal Biron, enabled him once more to serve his country at sea.

Rodney was not the easiest of men. He was autocratic, conservative in his methods, gouty, and well past his youth, but he was a thorough seaman with the habit of command. He sailed shortly after Christmas Day, 1779, his health being such that he was confined to his cabin. His orders were transmitted through his flag captain, Walter Young, a nominee of the First Lord, Sandwich, who was taking a risk in appointing Rodney after the veteran had been some years on the shelf.

Sandwich need not have worried. Rodney did him credit, for, on 16 January 1780, when in the neighbourhood of Cape St Vincent, he came upon a division of the Spanish fleet covering a convoy. Although he himself had the Gibraltar transports to protect Rodney, with twenty-two of the line, was in greatly superior strength. He captured the entire convoy, and in a chase action took four men-of-war under Admiral Langara, and destroyed a fifth.

This was the first naval victory of the war, and was the sort of tonic the country needed. Rodney was made much of at home, particularly as one of the King's sons, Prince William Henry, who was to make the Navy his career, was serving as a midshipman in the fleet. Gibraltar was provisioned and supported, and Rodney, who had orders to proceed to the West Indies once his first task was accomplished, felt a new man as a result of his success. As had been the case at Flamborough Head, much of the action had taken place by moonlight. Rodney acknowledged special benefit from the coppering of his ships. 'Without it,' he said, 'we should not have taken a single Spaniard.'

On 13 February, after a pause for celebration at Gibraltar, Rodney sailed for the

Rear-Admiral Sir Charles Douglas
Henry Singleton

Becoming a lieutenant in 1753, he took part in the operations in the St Lawrence leading to the capture of Quebec in 1759–60. A gunnery expert, Sir Charles Douglas was Captain of the Fleet to Rodney in the *Formidable* when the British fleet met de Grasse in the West Indies. Several actions took place in the next few days until the French surrendered to Rodney at 6 p.m. on 12 April 1782. Rodney, suffering from gout, had spent most of the action sitting in a chair on the quarter-deck while directing operations. Sir Charles, on going aboard the French flagship the *Ville de Paris*, 112, exclaimed that the *Formidable* was but a bumboat to her, her size was so enormous. He was appointed Commander-in-Chief of the North American Station from 1783 to 1786 and again in January 1789, but died suddenly the next month.

Caribbean. No attempt was made to stop him. It was the winter season. Many of the Spanish ships were laid up; and there was even a pause in the work of harrying the garrison on the Rock.

Owing to the fact that the well-tried policy of close blockade of the French Atlantic ports had been abandoned for lack of resources, a more enterprising man than d'Estaing, the Comte de Guichen, was able to sail from Brest with sixteen of the line for the same area as Rodney. Neither admiral was aware of the other's movements, or of the likelihood that, soon after their arrival, the West Indies would be the scene of activities far-reaching in their consequences.

The gift of creating understanding among his captains was not one with which Rodney was endowed. Although he told them that the painful business of thinking was his own prerogative, in taking on the burden he did not always make his intentions clear. This was all too apparent off Dominica in April 1780, before he had had time to rehearse his fleet in his tactical methods.

On 13 April, de Guichen, equally new to his responsibilities, had left Fort Royal Martinique, with twenty-three of the line, five frigates and a troop convoy, with the intention of attacking Barbados, by far the most valuable of the smaller British 'sugar islands'. He was sighted by Rodney, who had twenty of the line with him, beating to windward in the channel between Martinique and Dominica. By the early hours of 17 April, the fleets were on a parallel course heading north. Rodney intended to turn and

attack de Guichen's rear and centre with his whole force, as soon as a chance arose. Sensing the danger, de Guichen wore his fleet around and steered south. Rodney did likewise and, at 11.50. a.m., made the signal: 'Every ship to bear down and steer for her opposite in the enemy's line.' This was followed five minutes later by one to engage.

His captains failed to understand. Most of them had been brought up in the tradition that the engagement of ship to ship all down the line must be rigidly followed. Concentration on one particular section of the opposing fleet, though sometimes tried, was not within the experience of many. The entire van, led by Captain Robert Carkett, in the *Stirling Castle*, the warrior, who, as a young lieutenant, had captured the great *Foudroyant*, carried all sail so as to reach his advanced station in the regular Order of Sailing.

It was a repetition of what had occurred in Byng's fleet off Minorca, and Rodney's plan was ruined. The action became totally disjointed and the flagship, the *Sandwich* of 90 guns, was heavily attacked and received much damage, though she gave better than she got. Rodney was furious, not only at what he considered to be his captains' stupidity, but because he thought that the flagship herself had not been properly supported. Carkett was the main sufferer from his spleen, but all the senior officers were treated like delinquents. Hyde Parker, an abrasive character nicknamed 'Vinegar'

Action Between HMS Quebec *and* Surveillante
Marquis de Rossel de Cercy

This, another of the famous single-ship actions, took place early in October 1779. In company with the *Rambler* cutter, Lieutenant George, *Quebec* sighted *Surveillante*, a larger frigate, with her attendant cutter, and was fired on before being able to range her own guns. Captain Farmer withheld his fire until within pistol-shot; the encounter was so fiercely fought that both ships were dismasted, and the *Quebec*, finally catching fire, blew up, killing most of her crew including her captain.

(which would equally have served for Rodney), was thought by his Commander-in-Chief to be almost treasonable.

De Guichen knew just how the case stood and, in a graceful way, he conveyed his sympathy to Rodney, as one tactician to another. Yet, whatever his disappointment, Rodney had saved Barbados.

After a visit to North America, during which the idea was discussed of an attempt to recapture Rhode Island, which had been pointlessly surrendered, Rodney returned to the West Indies. There, he learnt that a freak hurricane had devastated sugar plantations, and wrecked six ships of the line, three French and three English. Soon afterwards, he was notified that the Dutch were among his country's enemies. This led him, in February 1781, to capture the island of St Eustatius, a Dutch possession. It had served as a thriving centre for contraband trade, in which, to his extreme fury and disgust, Rodney found that English merchants had been participating.

Rodney's attitude towards St Eustatius, where he hoped to reap a golden harvest of prize money, is considered as being a notable instance of how such an irrelevant factor could affect an admiral's dispositions. Sir Samuel Hood had joined the command in January 1781, once again giving the British preponderance in the Caribbean. It was known that the French would make every effort to restore the position by sending a fleet to the West Indies under de Grasse, and it was of the first importance to prevent further enemy successes in the area.

Faced with the difficult choice of stationing a strong force to watch Brest and to prevent de Grasse from sailing but, by so doing, lacking strength to succour Gibraltar, which was once more in dire need of provisioning, the Admiralty chose Gibraltar. The Rock was relieved a second time by a fleet of twenty-eight ships of the line under Vice-Admiral George Darby, who had succeeded Geary in command of the Home Fleet. No confrontation resulted. Cordoba's Spanish ships, despite superiority in numbers, remained quiescent; but, as there was nothing to prevent him, de Grasse reached Martinique in April, after a fast passage from Europe.

Rodney had been warned that the French were coming. Had he concentrated his whole fleet well to windward of Martinique he might have won a second victory or, at least, have inflicted severe losses on the store-ships which accompanied de Grasse. Instead, he divided his forces. One squadron, with himself in charge, guarded St Eustatius; another was ordered to watch the French base at Fort Royal. 'Never was a squadron so unmeaningly stationed,' wrote Hood later, perceiving as he did that sound strategy would have been to ensure interception of de Grasse at all costs, with every available ship. As it was, the French admiral was able to shepherd his flock into Fort Royal without loss. Hood made an effort to prevent him, suffering casualties in the process, but he fought at long range, since he was outnumbered. In the circumstances, he might well have been more aggressive despite his numerical inferiority. Afterwards he withdrew to join Rodney, and the Commander-in-Chief then proceeded to Barbados. Rodney's obsession had cost him a chance of further glory. As if to underline his error, de Grasse, refreshed after his voyage, captured Tobago.

V

The year 1781 was marked by three naval actions, one in America, one in the North Sea, and one off the French Atlantic Coast, which were of particular interest in that they typified the character of the admirals involved. The first, which occurred in August near the Dogger Bank, was the only engagement between Dutch and British of any consequence. It was a slogging-match in the traditional style of the Anglo-Dutch wars of the previous century. As the British admiral was 'Vinegar' Parker who, to Rodney's fury, had been given a new command by Lord Sandwich, nothing else could have been looked for in the way of tactics. The Dutch lost one ship, and the British ensured the safety of a Baltic convoy, so that they may be said to have had the better of the encounter.

During the following month there occurred an action off the Capes of the Chesapeake which was decisive for the future of the war. And in December, Richard Kempenfelt, although in much inferior force, gave an illustration of a perfectly executed operation.

Such difficulties as Rodney had had with his captains, which were largely his own fault, were not to be compared with those surmounted by Kempenfelt in the Channel Fleet. Known throughout the Navy as one of the most thoughtful of men—Keppel called him 'a favourite with the Admiralty, and he deserved to be so'—Kempenfelt served throughout highly critical times as First Captain or chief of staff to successive Commanders-in-Chief, continuing in the post after his own promotion to rear-admiral in 1780.

The men who were wet-nursed were a sad succession: first, the infirm Hardy; then Sir Francis Geary, another decayed pupil of Lord Hawke, whose tenure of command lasted a few months only; finally, George Darby, perhaps the most colourless of all. Kempenfelt was in continuous correspondence with Sir Charles Middleton, the Comptroller of the Navy, who consulted him on every matter of principle or importance. He had adopted a much extended system of signals, as first used by Lord Howe in America. A keen student of French methods, he had studied the work of Pierre Bouguer, the Chevalier du Pavillon, the Vicomte de Morogues; the Chevalier de la Bourdonnais, and, above all, Bourdé de Villehuet, all distinguished writers on signals and tactics who had their following in other countries. Kempenfelt's introduction of a system of numbered flags led to difficulties with crusted admirals and captains. This was amusingly illustrated in the case of Geary.

One day, when in pursuit of what they mistook at first for a French fleet, but which was, in fact, a convoy, Admirals Geary and Kempenfelt consulted together on the quarter-deck of the flagship. An account in the *Naval Chronicle* said:

> Kempenfelt had contracted the habit of using more signals than men less practised in that particular branch of service thought necessary. As soon as the enemy were discovered, and the signal made for a general chase, Kempenfelt, burning with as much impatience as his Commander-in-Chief to get up with the enemy, brought up the signal book, which he opened, and laid on the binnacle with the greatest form and precision. Admiral Geary, eagerly supposing the chase to be the Brest fleet, went up to him with the greatest good humour, and squeezing him by the hand in a manner better to be conceived than expressed, said quaintly, 'Now my

dear, dear friend, do pray let the signals alone today, and tomorrow you shall order as many as ever you please!'

In Darby's relief of Gibraltar, Kempenfelt was the only flag officer present of any distinction, although there were a number of redoubtable captains in a fleet containing twenty-nine of the line. Kempenfelt's sole opportunity to exercise independent command came after an action off the Chesapeake had had a cataclysmic effect on the course of the war so that a description must await its chronological place. Meanwhile, it could be said without dispute that affairs in home waters would have been much worse but for the presence of this very junior rear-admiral. Lord Sandwich justly said to him: 'No one has given more satisfaction to the nation than yourself. They have a confidence in you which could not easily be transferred.'

Certainly there was no one across the Atlantic who, after Rodney's failure to damage de Grasse, inspired those at home with complete trust.

Early in July 1781, de Grasse sailed for San Domingo, where he found urgent messages from Washington asking for immediate co-operation. His own view, which carried the day, was that if American troops, in company with a French contingent already helping Washington under the Comte de Rochambeau, were prepared to march

At the Treaty of Utrecht in 1713 Gibraltar had been ceded to Britain by Spain, but it was an embarrassment to them, and over the years they continually tried to retake it. By 1782, when Lord Howe relieved the British garrison, under Lieutenant-General Eliott, later Lord Heathfield, the place was under its fourth year of siege. A convoy was required at least once a year to revictual the defenders, and in September 1782, Howe sailed with thirty-four of the line and attendant ships, including several convoys, totalling 134 merchant ships. French and Spanish ships were anchored off Algeciras, but had already failed in their attempt to retake Gibraltar. The merchantmen, not entirely clear as to their instructions, made their way to the Rock in various ways, with Howe directing them to their destination, much in the manner of a sheepdog rounding up his recalcitrant flock. It was not until 18 October that all arrived safely and the siege was raised, probably Howe's greatest achievement.

into Virginia, where the British were operating under General Cornwallis, a combined effort might be the means of eliminating the British threat.

De Grasse sailed from San Domingo on 5 August, with twenty-seven ships of the line and 3,000 troops, every sailor and soldier at his disposal. A few days earlier, Rodney had left for England with a convoy, intending to restore his health, which was much in need of it. He left his command in charge of Hood.

As New York was believed to be under threat, Hood left for North American waters on 10 August with fourteen ships of the line. He found on arrival that the French Rhode Island squadron had left Narragansett Bay for an unknown destination. He also found at New York an officer senior to himself. This was Thomas Graves, who had only six of the line and one 50-gun ship ready for service. At the end of the month Graves and Hood sailed southward, hoping to gain news of de Grasse's movements.

On 5 September the British appeared off Cape Henry, to learn that Cornwallis was established at Yorktown in need of supplies, and that de Grasse was in Chesapeake Bay. The odds against the British, nineteen against twenty-four ships of the line, were serious, but de Grasse was in a difficult position, for he could not beat out of his anchorage in regular order. His ships were bound to stand out to sea on different tacks before they could find mutual support in line ahead.

Graves was no Hawke. He was of the orthodox breed, and preferred to delay his attack until he could assess the French strength, and then to fight them in regular fashion. The result could have been anticipated: there was an inconclusive fight at fairly long range, resulting in damage to British masts and spars. One ship, the *Terrible*, was so much injured that she became a total loss.

De Grasse, reinforced by the squadron from Rhode Island, re-entered the anchorage on 11 September, and the British were forced to retire to New York to refit. The fate of Cornwallis ashore was sealed. Sea power had failed the army and—although the fact was not immediately apparent—the Americans and French had won the war.

If Graves's engagement disheartened his country, the last memorable action of the year brought a little comfort to those in England. It was also to have its effect on the concluding stages of the war at sea.

In December, Kempenfelt, with his blue flag in the *Victory*, was given command of twelve of the line, a 50-gun ship, four frigates and a fire-ship, his orders being to intercept a force under de Guichen bound for the West Indies to reinforce de Grasse. He sighted the enemy on the 12th, but, to his chagrin, found the French in such superior strength—nineteen of the line, including first and second rates—that he could not hazard a general action.

With the advantage of the wind, he sailed parallel with the enemy in line abreast, watching for the chance to bear down upon de Guichen's rear and to isolate the convoy. During the course of some hours, the van and centre of the French fleet got well ahead of the rear, and the convoy thus stood far to leeward.

Observing this, and choosing the right moment, Kempenfelt changed formation into line ahead, engaging the French rear with his van. The rest of his ships, running free, cut off and captured seventeen of the convoy, including troop-carriers, driving off or destroying the frigates which attempted to defend them. Kempenfelt had proved himself in action as distinguished as he was in thought. This time there was no occasion for a courteous note from de Guichen to his opponent. Kempenfelt had done what he wanted.

Gibraltar: Beginning of the
Siege 1780
A. Paton, engraved by Fittler

The later events of the war at sea lacked nothing in interest and variety, even although the main issue had been decided, and the Government of Lord North, which had conducted the war on behalf of George III, did not see it concluded. The French, who had participated as much in the hope of extending their possessions in the West Indies as of helping Washington, were now in a position to plan a full-scale invasion of Jamaica, by far the largest of the British West Indian islands. It was to that end that de Grasse made his dispositions, but instead of having to deal with Graves or Hood, his opponent was to be a Rodney restored and invigorated. The veteran had made an exceptionally good return passage from England, in spite of bad weather. On arrival at his command he had had an amicable interview with Hood, which had not been common in the past. With him in his flagship were two exceptional men: Sir Charles Douglas, baronet, Captain of the Fleet, hero of the operations of 1776 at Quebec, and Gilbert Blane, Rodney's personal physician. Blane, a pupil of James Lind, was to keep the fleet in remarkably good health, compared with what was usual in the Caribbean. The *Formidable* of 98 guns was a notable ship, bigger and better equipped than the *Sandwich* in which Rodney had won at the moonlight battle off Cape St Vincent.

The ship also carried, on her upper deck, a new weapon, one of the most important to come into service during the age of sail. This was the carronade. It was made by the Carron Ironworks of Falkirk, Scotland, and was the invention of Lieutenant-General Robert Melville (1723–1809). It was a stubby, short-range gun of large bore, firing heavy shot. It was light, relative to its fire-power, mobile, and easier to handle than older types of naval ordnance. It had not yet become standard equipment in the fleet, but Douglas's advocacy ensured that it was well represented in the command to which he had been appointed.

Melville's original 'Smasher', as it was nicknamed, was a short-barrelled eight-inch gun weighing only 31 cwt, yet firing a 68 lb ball, with a charge of only $5\frac{1}{2}$ lb of gunpowder. The 'Smasher' proved its value in defensively armed merchant ships, for which it had been designed. The Navy Board, representing the Admiralty, at first favoured smaller carronades of varying calibre, although the Ordnance Board did its best to block progress. The breakthrough came as the result of an action by the *Rainbow*, an old 44-gun ship which, as an experiment, was armed entirely with carronades. She fell in with the French frigate *Hébé*, which was armed with 18-pounder long guns. Closing, the *Rainbow* poured the weight of her broadside into the Frenchman. The result was instant surrender, and a prize of exceptional value as a model for frigate design.

Good equipment certainly helped to give Rodney a mellower outlook than he had displayed hitherto, and when Hood gave him the news, sent with speed across the Atlantic, that such reinforcements as de Grasse might receive were unlikely to be up to his expectations, he could view future prospects with measured optimism.

Meanwhile, de Grasse had made the most of his success against Graves. Moving to the West Indies, he retook St Eustatius, and two or three smaller islands. Then he attacked St Kitts, the scene of the first English settlement. Hood, with twenty-two of the line, hastened to the rescue, but owing to a minor collision which delayed him, he lost the element of surprise. Alerted, de Grasse put to sea with his twenty-six ships. Hood, slipping in behind him, seized his anchorage. De Grasse made two attempts to

Its name a corruption of Jebel el Tarik (Tarik's Mount) after Tariq ibn Zaid, who took it from the Spanish in 711, Gibraltar has always been a bone of contention. First coming under British rule after its investment by Rooke in 1704, its importance as the entrance to the Mediterranean was never overlooked by the home government. Rodney relieved it in 1780, having fallen in with and captured a Spanish convoy. Sir George Elliot defended the Rock with great skill, and Howe's relief of Gibraltar should be regarded as his greatest achievement.

Grundlicher Abriß von GIBRALTAR
Explication der Buchstaben
A. das Schloß. B. die Stadt. C. der neue Molo.
D. St. Maria von Europa. E. der alte Mola.
F. Das Spanische Lager. G. Runde Thurn H. Alag

A. Castillo. B. la Ciudad. C. Muelle nuevo
D. Sevestia Señoia de Europa. E. Muelle Viejo
E. Campamento. G. Fuerza dela Redondeta.
H. Ataque.

dislodge the British ships, but failed to do so. Unfortunately, the small infantry garrison on the heights above lacked the strength to contain a series of assaults and the soldiers were forced to surrender. Hood was lucky to escape in darkness by cutting his cables. He joined Rodney, fresh from England, in the last days of February 1782.

De Grasse, reinforced to bring his strength up to thirty ships of the line, was able to leave Martinique, with troops and stores destined for the invasion of Jamaica, on 8 April. Rodney's fleet, totalling thirty-six of the line, caught up with him next day, and some sporadic firing occurred. Then, at last, on 12 April, a decisive meeting took place between the great West Indian fleets which, for so long, had been striving for predominance. They met on opposite courses, near the group of islets called The Saints, which lie between Dominica and Guadeloupe. While passing each other in line formation, closely engaged, the wind suddenly shifted towards the south-east, almost in the teeth of de Grasse. His ships were taken aback, getting into confusion.

This crucial event enabled Rodney to steer through a gap which appeared towards the rear of the French centre. Contemporaries referred to this as an 'incision'. The word was apt, and the action was not premeditated. The *Formidable* was followed by ships astern, and the French were attacked from both sides.

111

As de Grasse's van drifted to leeward, Hood's division severed it into unco-ordinated groups. After about two hours' fighting, in which British gunnery showed to advantage, the bulk of the French fleet made off to the west, leaving five badly damaged ships, including de Grasse's own *Ville de Paris*, at Rodney's mercy.

Such was the famed occasion of 'breaking the line', but as Lord St Vincent remarked later, 'Rodney passed through the enemy's line by accident, not design, although historians have given him credit for the latter.' There was no tactical originality, and the results were due partly to luck.

One of Rodney's midshipmen, Joseph Yorke, a boy of fourteen, wrote home the day after the battle saying, 'Sir Charles Douglas went on board the *Ville de Paris* and said that the *Formidable* was a Bomb Boat to her.' Rodney was so overwhelmed by his success, by the capture of de Grasse, by the removal of all danger to Jamaica, that, to Hood's fury, he omitted to follow up his victory. Hood himself, now given further occasion to criticize his chief, was able to take in prize two more ships. Sad to say, the *Ville de Paris* foundered during a storm on her way back to England, severe weather and indifferent masts accounting for this and other losses, including the *Ramillies*, in which Graves flew his flag.

Nine days after the Saints, Captain John Jervis, later to become Lord St Vincent, who was then commanding the *Foudroyant*, which he turned into the smartest ship in the Navy, fell in with the French *Pégase*, 77 guns, near Brest. After one of the comparatively rare single-ship actions between large vessels, the British boarded and captured the Frenchman. Jervis was wounded in the head by a splinter during the fight, which was severe. He was knighted shortly afterwards, and was marked down for important commands, being near to achieving his flag by seniority. His immediate assignment was to a fleet to be commanded by Lord Howe, for whom he had the utmost respect.

The change in ministry which saw the resignation of Lord North and the displacement of Sandwich enabled Howe once more to offer his services at sea. Keppel at the Admiralty was acceptable where Sandwich was not.

It was the Spaniards who claimed Howe's immediate attention. Owing to British weakness in the Mediterranean, a Spanish expedition had been able to capture Minorca in February 1782. This inspired the nation to crown their efforts against Gibraltar. General Eliott was by now in urgent need of supplies, and although he was able to beat off the most sustained of all assaults, made in September, further provisioning was essential if starvation was not to succeed where attack had failed.

Lord Howe, with his flag in *Victory*, was now given what he considered to be the most difficult task in his career. This was to conduct a fleet of thirty-four ships of the line, with a large convoy of merchantmen, over a long stretch of uncommanded sea, with a hostile fleet under Cordoba, forty-nine in number, ready to intercept him.

The assembly of the British force at Spithead was the scene of a tragedy which affected the nation. Kempenfelt, who had transferred to the *Royal George*, was drowned on 29 August, together with hundreds belonging to the ship's company, when Hawke's historic flagship sank at anchor while undergoing a minor repair. The ship's structure gave way when her lower tier of guns was shifted, the reason being that her timbers were rotten. This was affirmed by expert witnesses, including Sir John Jervis, who gave evidence at the formal court martial of the captain, Martin Waghorn, who survived. The ship, and those who drowned in her, were victims of the timber famine which prevailed throughout the war.

112

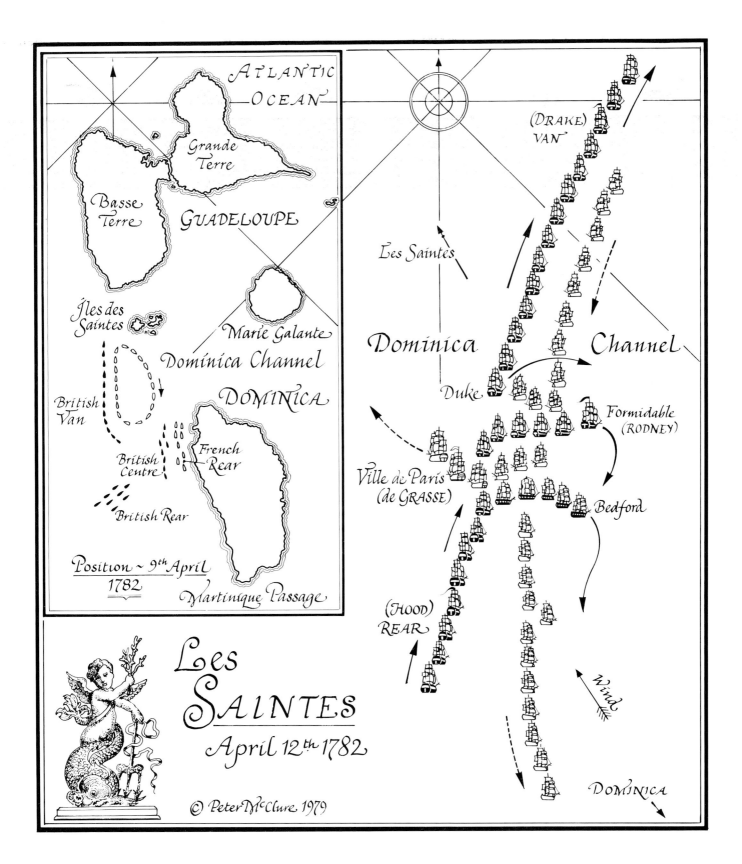

ATLANTIC OCEAN

Grande Terre

GUADELOUPE

Basse Terre

Îles des Saintes

Marie Galante

Dominica Channel

DOMINICA

British Van

British Centre

French Rear

British Rear

Position ~ 9ᵗʰ April 1782

Martinique Passage

(DRAKE) VAN

Les Saintes

Dominica

Channel

Duke

Formidable (RODNEY)

Ville de Paris (de GRASSE)

Bedford

(HOOD) REAR

Wind

DOMINICA

Les SAINTES
April 12ᵗʰ 1782

© Peter McClure 1979

Shortly after the loss of the *Royal George*, Howe sailed. He anchored off Gibraltar on 16 October, reprovisioned Eliott, and—his mission achieved—prepared to face Cordoba. By this time, the Spaniards knew that all attacks on the fortress were doomed to failure, and Cordoba contented himself with a distant cannonade, which Howe knew to be little more than a gesture. In the way of casualties, the cost of the foray had been light, and Howe returned home without further molestation.

VII

Only in the Far East did serious fighting extend into 1783. There, two opponents, stout in every sense of the word, conducted a duel which extended from February 1782 until June 1783, and included five regular battles, fought by both sides with great fury. The French admiral, Suffren, and Sir Edward Hughes were indeed well matched, for Suffren was the only Frenchman of stature whose idea coincided with that of the British that outright defeat of an enemy fleet was the first object of warfare by sea.

Unfortunately, Suffren could never depend on the obedience and understanding from his captains which Hughes took for granted. He had important strategic successes, such as seizure of the Cape of Good Hope on his way out to India, and the capture of Trincomalee in Ceylon after he got there, but in the upshot he was unable to shift the balance of power in the sub-continent which had swung in favour of the British.

The Suffren–Hughes engagements, although sanguinary, were conducted with mutual respect. William Hickey, a British civilian, was at one time or another a guest of both admirals. He admired Suffren's gallantry as much as his cuisine, but he could not help observing that whereas the French *Héros* was in a filthy state, and the admiral himself none too clean, Hughes's *Superb*, with the same armament of 74 guns, was as spick and span as her commander.

News of the peace reached these distant warriors belatedly. Both admirals received honour on their return to Europe, and what pleased Suffren as much as anything in his life was a delegation of British captains who attended him at the Cape of Good Hope on his way home. It was to congratulate him on the magnificent way he had fought. It was one of those gestures which were to become ever rarer in the final phases of sail warfare.

NINE

INTERLUDE
IN THE NORTH

The Armed Neutrality — Russo-Swedish war — Northern shipbuilding
Greig and the battle of Hogland — Swedish attempt on St Petersburg
Victory at Svenskund — The Treaty of Värälä

THE CHIEF, perhaps the only clearcut, gainers from the War of American independence had been the former colonists, whose separate nationality was recognized. The belated resurgence of British sea power, exemplified by Rodney and Howe, enabled George III's government to make a better peace than might otherwise have been looked for. France restored Grenada, St Vincent, Dominica, St Kitts, Nevis and Montserrat. Britain returned St Lucia, increased French fishery concessions in Newfoundland, and surrendered her treaty right to prevent the fortification of Dunkirk. Spain kept Minorca. As for Holland, conquests of either side were restored, except in the case of Negapatam on the Coromandel Coast, which was ceded to Britain.

Holland had been a special case, for it was Britain who had declared war on her, not the reverse. The reason had been the formation, in 1780, of what became known as the Armed Neutrality. This was an association agreed to by Russia, Denmark, Prussia, Holland, Portugal, Austria and the Two Sicilies. The object was to assert the right of trading with opposing sides in war. In simplified terms, the principles involved were that neutrals might sail without fear of arrest or search even along belligerent coasts; that the flag covered the goods except for contraband, a definition of which was agreed; and that, to be respected, a blockade must be efficient. It could not be maintained or even observed merely as the result of an official declaration.

Britain was against Holland because the country was the most important member of the association, so far as volume of shipping was concerned. Her navy was in no great shape; little need be feared from that source. Portugal, Austria and the Two Sicilies were of minor account at sea, but the Northern Powers, Russia, Sweden and Denmark, which had enjoyed a spell of relative peace in the Baltic lasting thirty years, had navies able to protect convoys when necessary. It would therefore have added pointlessly to her own difficulties if Britain had antagonized the Scandinavians. This was all the more so as their produce, in the way of naval stores, had become not merely useful but essential. As the war dragged on enormous quantities were involved and the dockyards, their reserves exhausted, lived from hand to mouth.

Apart from the severe action in 1781 off the Dogger Bank between British and Dutch, when a formal state of war existed between the two countries, the Armed Neutrality led to no fighting, and to fewer incidents than might have been expected. There were, however, clear indications of sympathy. For instance, Sweden, which had a

long tradition of friendship with France, was among the first to recognize American independence. A number of her naval officers saw active service in the French fleet, and others got their early training in French ships. Sweden, Russia and Denmark all maintained squadrons at sea almost until the end of hostilities, the Russians making use of Copenhagen as an advanced base.

Four years after the Peace of Versailles settled matters between the various belligerents, Turkey declared war on Russia. This gave Gustavus III of Sweden, with some encouragement from Britain and Prussia, though with no support from either country other than pressure on Denmark to stay neutral, a chance he had long hoped for. This was to recover territory in Finland lost by his predecessors, and in particular a stretch of seaboard which included Viborg. The Empress Catherine II occupied the throne of Peter the Great but, for all her varied endowments, she was unlikely to wish to lead her fleet in person. On the other hand, the war gave Gustavus the chance to exert his personal influence on naval affairs. He was the last king to lead a fleet in battle.

Gustavus, a man of diverse talents, was one of the most lavish patrons of his age. The Swedish monarchy had been in eclipse since the later years of Charles XII, and Gustavus was determined to revive its strength. So far as his fleet was concerned, he had the good fortune to employ the services of one of the ablest ship designers in Europe. This was Fredrik Henrik af Chapman (1721–1808), a man of Yorkshire descent who worked at Karlskrona. Chapman's *Architectura Navalis Mercatoria* (1768) was influential in its day among naval constructors, and has been valued ever since.

Chapman was responsible for building a number of unusual types of ship and smaller craft for use in an area of sea where the old mixed fleet, containing both oar-propelled and sailing ships, such as had vanished elsewhere, was a regular feature, so peculiar were the conditions of the northern littoral. The frigate *Amphion*, which Chapman built for the King, was a prototype of the 'Command Ship' essential to modern naval operations on any scale.

116

Captain William Locker
Gilbert Stuart

William Locker was the commander of the first ship Nelson served in after passing his lieutenant's examination, the frigate *Lowestoffe*. When Nelson moved on into the *Bristol*, Collingwood took his friend's place. Locker remained an intimate of both for the rest of his life. He was an ardent follower of Hawke, even naming his son Edward Hawke Locker, and through him Nelson imbibed many of the tactical skills he later put to good use.

Other classes evolved on Chapman's drawing-board and produced in his yard were sometimes original, sometimes based on historical models. With the need to design vessels for fighting in shallow waters, Chapman produced the square-rigged turuma, and the hemmema, where a variation of the lateen was employed. These, together with the pojama and the udema, combined oar and sail. They were not altogether successful. Their shallow draught made them poor sailers, and on account of their weight they were hard to row.

More approved were the gun sloops and gun launches which Chapman began to build in 1776. They were prized by Gustavus, and were satisfactory in action. Compared with older Swedish types, the sloops were well armed; they offered a relatively small target and were easily manoeuvred. The crews did not sleep on board but pitched tents ashore with the fall of darkness. Later versions appeared, mounting 18- or 24-pounder guns. Both sloops and launches carried lugsails, and Swedish bomb vessels, similar to types developed by both the British and the French, carried their ordnance almost amidships.

Such were some of the smaller units supplementing orthodox ships of the line and frigates which were at the service of Gustavus and his brother commander, Charles, the Duke of Södermanland, members of the illustrious house of Vasa, very different from the Howes in the American war. They had the advice of a British officer, William Sidney Smith, a pupil of Rodney, who, although young, had tremendous self-assurance and much natural ability. Gustavus thought well of him, and gave him one of the Swedish Orders of Chivalry. On his return home, Smith held forth so often on his northern adventures that his contemporaries referred to him sardonically as the 'Swedish Knight'.

Sweden and Russia both relied on imported talent for naval expertise. The King and the Duke of Södermanland were opposed by a navy in which the most important constructor was an Englishman, Sir Samuel Bentham, and the leading strategist a Scot,

Sir Samuel Greig. Greig had persuaded a number of his fellow-countrymen to enter Swedish service, following a tradition which went back to the time of Gustavus Adolphus.

Gustavus III's qualities did not extend to realism in foreign affairs, and his brother was more drawn to the occult than to tactics. In underestimating Russian resources, which were massive enough to sustain the effort of separate wars, one in the Baltic and the other against Turkey, Gustavus was repeating errors made by Charles XII earlier in the century. Even in the Baltic Russia could command numbers and, as Denmark did not long remain neutral (an unnatural condition for her where Sweden was involved), Catherine's fleet was able to make use of Copenhagen as a base, as in the time of the Armed Neutrality.

The first considerable encounter of the war at sea took place off Hogland, an island high up the Gulf of Finland, in July 1788. This was the last action in which Sir Samuel Greig took part, for he died shortly afterwards. He had first made his name in the service of the Empress against the Turks in an earlier war, in the Aegean. At Hogland his duty was to defeat the Duke of Södermanland, the Swedes being present in support of a land advance towards Viborg. The action itself was severe but indecisive, each side losing one ship of the line. The ultimate advantage was with Greig, for the advance was checked.

During the following summer, off Öland, the Swedes, again led by Duke Charles, missed their greatest opportunity. The Russians had three separate squadrons available for operational service, based on Reval, Copenhagen, and Kronstadt. The Reval force, consisting of twenty ships of the line under Admiral Tchitchagov, sailed for the Swedish base at Karlskrona, the Copenhagen squadron being ordered to rendezvous with him. The Duke and Tchitchagov met before the Russian squadrons had joined forces, but although he was in superior strength, having twenty-nine of the line, Charles had not skill enough to defeat his opponent during the course of an action lasting six hours. Such a moment would not recur.

In 1790, as a result of great exertions, with his country enthusiastically behind him (as was not so during the early stages of the war), Gustavus had at his disposal forty-two first-line ships, mainly sailing vessels. Duke Charles took command, the King himself having charge of the oared flotillas, numbering over 250 vessels of all sorts, and the troop transports, of which they formed the close escort. As Denmark had by now withdrawn from the war, Gustavus could bring all his strength to bear upon his main antagonist.

The Swedish armada sailed from Karlskrona on 30 April, which was earlier than usual, the breaking-up of the winter ice making such a move possible. Two weeks later, the first opposition was encountered—a Russian fleet under the Prince of Nassau-Siegen, a man described by his subordinates as precipitate as a madman.

In the fighting which followed, one Swedish ship of the line was captured and another sank after storm damage, but Gustavus and his brother succeeded in their aim. This was to force their way into the port of Fredrikshavn. A number of Russian coasters were seized, and the arsenal was destroyed, but the place was not occupied. Gustavus put troops ashore nearer Viborg, which he hoped might serve as his forward base in an ambitious movement towards Petersburg.

Duke Charles should have joined the King at Viborg, but on 7 June he was attacked by a squadron from Kronstadt under Admiral Kruse. As so often the battle itself was indecisive, but shortly afterward Kruse was reinforced by twenty-four of the line under Admiral Tchitchagov, which gave the Russians considerable superiority in numbers. In the circumstances, the Duke was fortunate in being able to reach Viborg and to anchor there. He found that his brother had been forced to withdraw from his shore positions.

The Swedish fleet was disposed in a line across Viborg Bay, somewhat in the manner of Barrington and Hood in the West Indies. The Russians did not attack. Instead, they anchored well beyond gun-range. Their idea was blockade, and this was sense, for the Swedes had no means of replenishing food and water. Before long Charles would be forced to make an effort to break out—somehow to make his way to the open sea.

The move was made on 22 June. At first, through boldness and surprise, he inflicted more damage than he received. One of the Russian ships of the line, commanded by a British officer, Richard Trevenen, suffered badly, Trevenen himself receiving a mortal wound. Unhappily for the Swedes, when almost half their fleet had passed through the Russian lines, a fire-ship ran aboard a ship of the line, which in turn collided with a frigate. All three ships blew up, a dramatic illustration of the hazards of fire-ship warfare, even to the attacking side. The explosion, added to the all-pervasive smoke accompanying a naval action, resulted in confusion. Four other large Swedish ships, two frigates and some smaller vessels went aground or were captured. The rest escaped momentarily, but two more ships were lost before they could reach the comparative safety of Sveaborg, the principal Swedish coastal fortress on Finnish soil.

Gustavus, with the flotillas, also escaped destruction, though not without some intricate fighting in which he himself had a narrow escape from capture, the ship pursuing him being recalled at the last minute through the misinterpretation of a signal. As it was, Gustavus was able to reach Svenskund, south of Fredrikshavn, to join an inshore force already occupying the fjord.

It was Nassau-Siegen, by an undisciplined attack, which was made in unfavourable weather on 28 June, who met with disaster. In order to celebrate the birthday of the Empress he deferred his movement until that date. This gave Gustavus time in which to take up good defensive positions. He drew up his force in supporting formations behind the low rocks of the fjord, which gave them strong natural protection. When the Russians advanced with complete recklessness and sublime over-confidence, but in no regular order, they were met by such deadly fire that 9,500 were killed, wounded or taken prisoner. Swedish losses were fewer than three hundred. Nassau-Siegen himself narrowly evaded capture, a fate which befell his flag captain. As the Prince had prepared quarters for Gustavus, in the expectation that his opponent would be forced to surrender, this circumstance added an ironic note to victory.

The belated triumph for the Swedes marked the end of the fighting. The Russian main fleet was intact, but the flotillas had been decimated. The capture of Petersburg, which throughout the war had been the Swedish goal, was far beyond Gustavus's power: indeed, Sweden was never again in any position to challenge Russia. Peter the Great's foundation of a navy had been justified. In his own time, it had been the means of extending his territory. It had safeguarded his successors.

The Russo-Swedish war ended at the Treaty of Värälä. The Empress Catherine, who had other preoccupations, was content that the *status quo* in the Baltic should not be disturbed, but she made no concessions of territory. Gustavus had only two more years to live. He was mortally wounded by one of his own subjects at a masked ball, an episode recalled in a famous opera by Verdi, *Ballo in Maschera*.

TEN

WAR WITH REVOLUTIONARY FRANCE

Impressment — Howe and Hood — Toulon — The Glorious First of June
Descent on Ireland — Jervis at St Vincent — Mutiny at Spithead and the Nore
Duncan at Camperdown — Nelson at the Nile — Bruix at large
The Northern Confederacy — Attempt on Boulogne — Keith in Egypt
The Peace of Amiens

THE LAST MAJOR WAR in which sail played a predominant part extended, with one formal interval, over twenty-two years, from 1793 to 1815. If his birth had coincided with the outbreak of hostilities, a man with the all-important 'influence'—friends in the right places—added to some degree of merit, could have commanded a ship of war when the time came for demobilization.

Such wars as this, and the one which had preceded it, involved not only immense labour in the dockyards and on the building slips, but mounting difficulties in finding men to serve—hence the hardship of forcible impressment. This was an unavoidable expedient until regular conditions of naval employment were belatedly established in the nineteenth century.

The French, though they had their difficulties, managed things reasonably well, thanks to their long-established rota system, and to patriotic fervour. The Spaniards were forced to draft soldiers to the fleet, with results which could have been expected. Their time at sea was short. There was insufficient opportunity to train them in active service conditions, yet when they sailed, it was almost always due to some emergency.

Complaint in Britain about impressment was of very long standing—older by far than the time of Pepys. Even in the Middle Ages a sovereign with the prestige of Edward III had difficulty in raising men for his ships. A later illustration of the reputation of the fleet, as applied to the common seaman, is afforded by an incident in the life of Dr Johnson. After a visit to a man-of-war as a guest of one of the officers, he remarked: 'A man in jail has more room, better food, and commonly better company.'

That Johnson meant what he said was proved by the case of his Negro servant, Francis Barber. As a youth, in the heyday of the Seven Years War, in a fit of enthusiasm Barber actually enrolled as a volunteer. Johnson was so disturbed, not selfishly, at the loss of his services, but at the prospect before Barber, that he moved heaven and earth (including Tobias Smollett) to get him released. He was successful, and Barber did not try again. He may have heard of a detail in a ship's books which still causes surprise to researchers, as does the diversity of sources from which seamen were drawn. The books contained regular columns headed 'R' and 'D'. 'R' stood for 'Run',

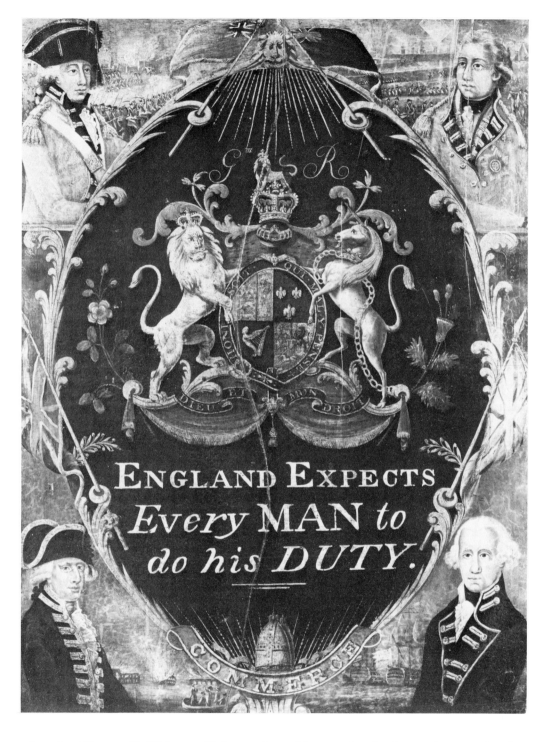

This panel is surrounded by four naval commanders, including Sir John Jervis and Sir Roger Curtis. The British Lion at the top of the oval emanates rays of light, while at the bottom there reposes a bishop's mitre. Inside the oval is displayed the Royal coat of arms, which then included the White Horse of Hanover, below which are the words 'England Expects Every Man to do his Duty'— later to become famous in the Trafalgar signal. Behind the oval are scenes of battle, and below it the word 'Commerce', by which Britain lived.

otherwise 'Deserted'. This act, if detected, could carry the death penalty or a flogging round the fleet, from ship to ship, involving hundreds of lashes, yet attempts were common. 'D' stood for 'Discharged' or 'Deceased', which would have been merciful release from servitude, suffering and sickness.

The efforts involved in the war to come far exceeded those of 1776–83, which were

HM Ships Boyne *and*
Caledonia *off Toulon*
Thomas Luny

The *Boyne* and the
Caledonia, the latter wearing
the flag of Vice-Admiral Sir
Edward Pellew, were part of a
force watching the French
port of Toulon. This picture
shows the running action of 5
November 1813, when the
French fleet ventured forth
into the Mediterranean while
the blockading fleet were
blown to leeward.

themselves remarkable. When the American war had opened, the British Navy numbered 340 ships of all kinds in commission, and could muster 15,062 men. By 1783,
under pressure of what had developed into a world conflict, such as was now to be
repeated, the figures had swollen to 617 ships and 107,446 seamen. The inevitable run-
down had its tragedies. Not all seamen could find employment in merchant ships or
ashore. Many had to beg their bread. In ten years, all the old problems recurred.

II

The immediate cause of war was revolution in France. The execution of Louis XVI in
January 1793 brought matters to the point of no return, and on 1 February France
declared war on Britain and Holland. William Pitt the Younger, George III's First

The Cutting out of HMS
Hermione
Thomas Whitcombe

HMS *Hermione*, built in
1782, was under the com-
mand of the tyrannical
Captain Hugh Pigot in 1797
when the crew mutinied after
two of their number had been
killed in falling from the
yards. All but three of the
officers were murdered and,
to compound the felony, the
crew handed the ship over to
the Spaniards, in whose
service she remained for the
next two years. On the night
of 24 October 1799, the boats
of the *Surprise*, Captain
Hamilton, six in number, cut
out the *Hermione* from the
strongly defended harbour of
Puerto Cabello in Venezuela.
Nearly all the mutineers were
caught and hanged. *Hermione*
was rechristened first
Retaliation and then
Retribution, and it was some
time before her original name
returned to the Navy.

Minister, stated that French provocation included occupation of the Netherlands, with
the aim of establishing a subservient regime. This was a continuation of the policy of
Louis XVI. Pitt added that his country went to war to maintain the rule of law in
Europe, and for the security of her possessions overseas.

Britain became a member of the first of several coalitions, for a feature of the struggle
was the way in which nations were forced to withdraw or to change sides. The original
combination included Sardinia, Portugal, Spain, Austria and Prussia. In the nature of
things, only Spain might afford some help at sea. On that element, the main burden
would be Britain's. It was one of the constant factors.

The Royal Navy was better prepared than on some similar occasions in the past. In
1790 there had been a dispute with Spain over the right to trade and settle on the
Pacific coast of North America. The matter had ended peacefully, but not before a fleet
had been mobilized. Many officers who had been on half-pay since 1783 had the chance
of going to sea in ships brought out of reserve.

There were two flag officers with outstanding claims to high command, Howe and
Hood. Both were elderly, but whereas Howe was conscious of the fact, Hood never
would be. Howe would have agreed with the perplexed creature who once remarked
that a man's mind and hand were apt to tremble at sixty, and that he himself was always
the last to perceive it. Nevertheless, Howe was very much the country's leading
admiral, with a fine record in three separate wars. He had held every rank and post,
including that of First Lord of the Admiralty. At the desire of the King, he was to fly
the Union flag at his mainmast and to command the Channel Fleet.

Hood was different. He had come to responsibility later in life than Howe, and met
more setbacks. He was arrogant, and conservative in outlook. Although Nelson, in a
moment of partiality, wrote words in his favour which have been remembered, his

letters show him to have had little generosity, which is putting it kindly. He was given charge of the Mediterranean fleet, together with some of the best ships.

Hood had the first opportunity, in August 1793, when Royalists at Toulon opened the port to him. The affair started well but ended in disaster. A Spanish squadron, sent to co-operate, proved useless. There were not enough troops to hold the enclave, and a rising officer of genius, Napoleon Bonaparte, helped to drive the Allies from their shore positions into the sea. Sir Sidney Smith, returned from Sweden to British service, did less well than he might have done when ordered to destroy the French ships in the harbour before Hood left, for the French soon had a southern fleet in being. Hood was constrained to use Corsica as his base, entailing the task of reducing the French garrisons. Nelson was prominent in the land actions, where he lost the sight of his right eye.

The following year opened promisingly for Britain, with success in the West Indies. There, Sir John Jervis and General Grey, a veteran trained under Wolfe, took Martinique and other French islands, not all of which were held.

To crown the year, Howe defeated Admiral Villaret-Joyeuse in a battle fought four hundred miles out into the Atlantic, on 1 June. This was an important moral and tactical success, though Howe failed to prevent a vital grain convoy reaching France from America.

Both admirals were engaged in covering merchantmen, and both were successful, though the inward-bound traffic to Brest was of more consequence than that leaving Britain. Villaret-Joyeuse being at sea at all with a strong fleet was the result of extra-ordinary efforts on the part of the Revolutionaries, for they had destroyed the old naval hierarchy completely. The Comte de Bougainville, Cook's rival as a circumnavigator, had been among the last to try to maintain order in a community which was in process of dissolution. By the time of the Terror he was himself in prison, and was only saved by the death of Robespierre. Nearly all his contemporaries had been eliminated or were in exile.

Villaret-Joyeuse had been trained by Suffren, but had no experience of high command. To keep an eye on him, the authorities sent a Revolutionary Commissar to sea with the fleet. This man, Jean Bon St André, was satirized as:

> . . . in battles much delighting,
> He fled full soon at the First of June
> But he bade the rest keep fighting.

This was unjust, for he was an example of the dedicated zealot with appropriate drive. He infused new life into the dockyard at Brest, and in a remarkably short time made it possible for Villaret-Joyeuse to be equipped. It was an early instance of a political appointment to an operational force, and the tradition continues in doctrinaire communities.

Howe's foray began early in May. After he had ordered Rear-Admiral George Montagu to escort the British merchantmen on their way south, and then to keep a look-out for those of the French, he sent two frigates to reconnoitre Brest. The captains reported that the French fleet was still there, but Howe knew it would not remain so. He then sailed west, practising the tactics he had long studied. Thanks to his efforts, continuing and expanding those of Kempenfelt, his signal system was in advance of anything then extant, even in France. The official Signal Book of 1793 grouped signals

124

alphabetically, under appropriate headings. Of special importance was to be No. 75, which provided for 'Breaking the Enemy's Line at All Points.'

On 28 May, Villaret-Joyeuse was seen to windward. Howe ordered his leading ships to try to get into action as fast as possible. Rear-Admiral Thomas Pasley, with his flag in the *Bellerophon* of 74 guns, showed skill in so doing, and a French three-decked ship was soon damaged and in danger of capture. Night saved her, as it did one of her attackers, the *Audacious*.

Next day, the 29th, Howe was able to bring on a general action. It was less satisfactory than he had hoped, partly due to the failure of his leading ship, the *Caesar*, to steer close enough to the enemy to break through their line as Howe had intended. This was disappointing because the *Caesar* was a new 80-gun ship and her captain, Molloy, had done well under Rodney during the American War. The intervening years had affected his nerve. However, thanks to others, two Frenchmen were cut off. In steering down to their rescue, Villaret-Joyeuse sacrificed the weather-gauge. Howe was careful to retain this during the days which followed.

It was clear that the French would stand in defence of the distant convoy, which was by then nearing its destination, but it was not until the early morning of 1 June that the prevailing mists cleared sufficiently for Howe to ensure perfect visibility for his attack. This would be a tactical innovation, although it was one which he and others had long considered practicable. According to Sir John Jervis, who, though not present himself, had such a reverence for Howe that he treasured every scrap of information about him, the Commander-in-Chief ran down on the enemy:

> in a line abreast, nearly at right angles with the enemy's line, until he brought every ship of his fleet on a diagonal point of bearing to its opponent, then steering on an angle to preserve that bearing until he arrived on the weather quarter, and close to the centre ship of the enemy, when the *Queen Charlotte* altered her course, and steered at right angles through the enemy's line, raking their ships on both sides as she crossed, and then luffing up and engaging to leeward.

The flagship executed the intricate manoeuvre perfectly. As the fleets were in size well-matched—twenty-five British opposed by twenty-six French, with an unusual number of frigates and ancillaries, including a hospital ship, the ill-named *Charon*—Howe prophesied that for every ship which was able to follow his example, he would take one prize. Six ships did so, and six prizes were brought into Spithead. A seventh Frenchman, the *Vengeur*, was sunk by gunfire. There were no losses in British ships, but casualties and damage were heavy.

Although Admiral Montagu failed to intercept the French convoy, so that Villaret-Joyeuse and St André could return elated, their main task achieved, the occasion was a tonic to the British Navy, the best it had had since Rodney's victory of 1782. It was not followed up to the fullest extent, Howe being so weary at the close that he had to be supported by his officers. 'Why,' he said gently, 'you hold me as if I were a child!' What touched him greatly was a delegation of sailors, headed by James Bowen, the Master of the Fleet, to express their respect, congratulations and thanks. Howe answered in a faltering voice. 'No, no, I thank *you*—it is you, my brave lads, it is *you*, not I, that have conquered.'

The 'Glorious First of June', as George III referred to the occasion, was celebrated by both sides. The French created a myth about the *Vengeur* sinking to the last man

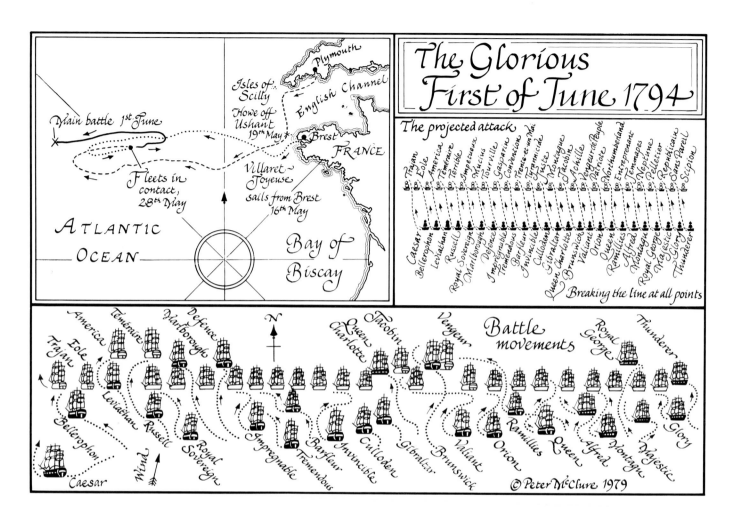

The Glorious First of June 1794

The projected attack — *Breaking the line at all points*

Battle movements

© Peter McClure 1979

(who was said to have drowned shouting patriotic slogans), after a terrific duel with the *Brunswick*. This was hard on the British, who, at great risk, picked up many of the crew in their boats. In England, artists produced popular scenes. A favourite, by Mather Brown, shows a group on the deck of the *Queen Charlotte* (the planks running the wrong way). Every uniform is meticulous. Howe, in admiral's full dress splendour, had his sword drawn, for what purpose it is hard to imagine. Lieutenant Neville of the Queen's Regiment, which had detachments with the fleet, collapses nearby with a mortal wound, but very gracefully.

Such pictures, of which every generation and country had multitudes, should be seen not as strict realism but glorification. According to a note set down by an ancestress of the present writer, who took passage in a West Indiaman shortly after the battle, she heard a sailor who had served on board Howe's flagship say that:

he was below before the action began, and saw many of his comrades killed before Lord Howe would allow them to fire a gun, as he wished them to wait for the French admiral's ship to engage. But the men said: 'My lord, an Englishman can't bear to receive blows without returning them and we must fire!' Lord Howe replied: 'Then fire, lads, and be damned!' His Lordship then went on to encourage the soldiers, and he was dressed during the action like a sailor, in a blue jacket and fur cap. When the battle was over he was in appearance like a chimney sweep with gunpowder.

Such were the realities, like the comment of the badly wounded lad who, when visited in hospital and congratulated on his share in the glory, could only murmur that it wouldn't give him back his leg.

III

Neither Howe nor Hood endured the strain of operational service for more than a limited time. Hood went to Greenwich Hospital. Howe, who in the King's mind was always *his* admiral, retired to Bath, although he remained nominal Commander-in-Chief of the Channel Fleet. In practice, his place was taken by Alexander Hood, Samuel Hood's younger brother, who had been created Lord Bridport for his part in the June battle.

Howe and Bridport were distant. Howe remembered Bridport's partiality for Palliser in the controversy over Keppel in 1778, when Bridport had been suspected of cooking entries in his log. Indeed, Bridport, brave in battle, was less good in the conduct of the fleet. This was illustrated on 23 June 1795, when Villaret-Joyeuse was intercepted in a foray. Although the French, inferior in numbers, were chased back to Brest after losing three ships off Groix Island, the result was considered less than satisfactory. There was a widespread feeling that an admiral who, when younger, had served as flag captain to Saunders, and had been with Hawke at Quiberon, had not inherited the attributes of either. A modest success might well have been turned into a resounding one.

Only six days earlier, a very different spirit had been shown by William Cornwallis, brother of the general who had met with misfortune at Yorktown. 'Billy Blue', as he was called because it was said he kept the Blue Peter flying all the time he was in port, when he was cruising with a mere five ships came across thirty Frenchmen, including ships of the largest size. With such a vast disparity in numbers, he might well have experienced disaster. Instead, his defence was so skilful that he was able to save the brand-new *Mars*, of 74 guns, after she had received severe damage to hull and rigging. Cornwallis made use of the ruse of signalling, via his frigates, to a force supposedly over the horizon, which in fact did not exist, and his bold front caused the enemy to ease their pressure. His feat was so impressive that in the official list of Battle Honours promulgated by the Admiralty, 'Cornwallis's Retreat' is the only example of its kind.

Recognition of merit was, on the whole, marked during the long war. In due course Cornwallis rose to the chief naval command—that of the Western Command, which, in the later stages of the struggle, became the hinge of strategy, as Vernon had stressed that it should be. Howe and Bridport did not believe in close blockade, as did so many of their predecessors. The tradition was to be revived after Howe's death in 1799, and its most famous exponents were Jervis and Cornwallis.

Further afield, there was more of importance occurring by land than sea. The French overran Holland. Spain changed sides. Coastal operations by the British, one to Quiberon Bay, ended in failure through lack of support, when disaffected groups were worsted by the Revolutionaries under General Hoche. France recaptured St Lucia and added the island of St Vincent to her temporary West Indian annexations. Successors to Hood in the Mediterranean proved indifferent. A new Coalition was tried—this time, Britain, Austria and Russia. Ireland was in constant ferment. The brightest news for Britain came from far away. A force under Admiral Elphinstone, later Lord Keith, took the Cape of Good Hope in the name of the dispossessed Prince of Orange, gaining the most valuable staging-post for India.

The year 1796 was marked by French thrusts on land, including Bonaparte's brilliant campaign in Italy, which secured his fame, and that of his army. More captures were made of Dutch overseas possessions, including Demerara and the Moluccas. St Lucia and St Vincent changed hands once more, this time falling to Rear-Admiral Sir Hugh Christian, a man who had too few opportunities in his career, and General Sir Ralph Abercromby, who was later to serve in Egypt.

The year ended with a French fleet, led by Admiral Morat de Galles, making a descent on Ireland. Villaret-Joyeuse had been against the idea, and was replaced by a contemporary, also trained under Suffren. Hoche was in command of the troops, but the winter season was entirely wrong for such a venture. A few ships reached Bantry Bay without interference from Bridport, but no troops were landed, the weather precluding any other course but a return to France.

The return led to a brilliant individual exploit. Sir Edward Pellew who, the previous April, had captured the frigate *Virginie* of 44 guns after a fifteen-hour chase in the *Indefatigable*, 44, was in company with the frigate *Amazon*, Captain Reynolds, when they sighted and engaged the *Droits de l'Homme*, a 74-gun ship of the line, returning from Bantry Bay. Action began on 13 January 1797, late in the afternoon. It continued throughout the hours of darkness, in dreadful weather, and off the perilous coast of northern France. In the end, the *Indefatigable* alone escaped wreck on the Penmarch Rocks. Great loss of life by storm was added to that of the battle.

The action did nothing to lighten the gloom in Britain. Many described the hour as 'the darkest in English history'. Such statements had been made before, often with apparent truth, but the year was in fact to be one of mixed fortune. Even so, nothing could disguise the fact that French success in Europe, including the re-occupation of Corsica, compelled the British to abandon the Mediterranean.

Ironically, having found in Sir John Jervis the best possible Commander-in-Chief, it fell to him to withdraw from the area. Jervis's discipline, seamanlike ability, and a reputation which extended back to the Seven Years War, inspired the best of his captains, and galvanized or shamed the rest. Among the best was Nelson, who was one of the last to leave a scene of activity he had come to know better than any of his contemporaries.

After a foray which included withdrawing forces from Elba, and a sharp action in which he defeated the Spanish frigate *Sabina* off Cartagena, Nelson sailed to join Jervis. The fleet was based on Lisbon, which offered better facilities than Gibraltar. On his way, Nelson, flying a commodore's broad pendant, passed through an enemy group in mist and darkness, undetected. He was thus able to give Jervis first-hand news of the size and course of at least some of the ships of war he was likely to meet. The Spaniards had been destined for a part in one of those grandiose schemes for the invasion of the British Isles which so often tempted strategists who planned in offices far from the sea. The French and Dutch fleets were also to figure. It fell to Jervis to deal with the Spaniards, and he came upon them about thirty miles from Cape St Vincent, on 14 February 1797, St Valentine's Day.

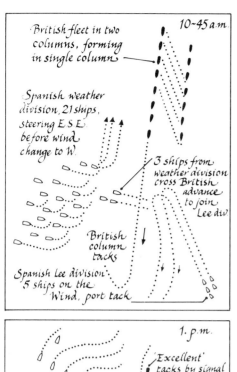

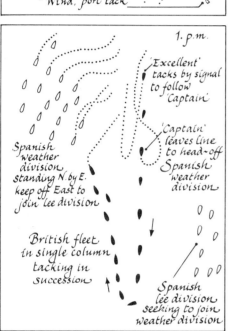

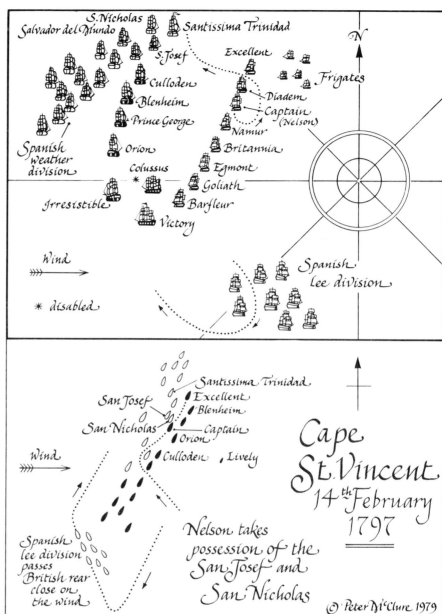

To all appearances, they were a formidable crowd, except that crowd was the word. Don Josef de Cordova, the Spanish Commander-in-Chief, had his ships in no sort of order, but they were in two distinct groups. One was to windward of Jervis, the other to leeward. Among the twenty-seven or twenty-eight ships, the *Santissima Trinidad*, with four rows of gun-ports and 130 guns, was the largest man-of-war afloat, and there were at least six three-decked ships, the rest being 80s or 74s. What Jervis did not know was that the group to leeward contained three or four urcas, laden with mercury from the mines at Almaden and destined, after putting in to Cadiz with the rest of the fleet, for

129

the silver mines of Central America, the mercury being used in the process of extracting silver from its ore. Any one of them would have been valued as a prize.

As a follower of Howe, Jervis was accustomed to manoeuvre his fifteen ships in highly disciplined formations. But against such a mass as that now facing him all he could be fairly sure of achieving was that the separated bodies of Spaniards should not unite. His line ahead, first in two columns and then in one, divided the foe as with a ruler. His attack was concentrated on the larger group, which was to windward.

De Cordova's moves were those of evasion—flight would not have been too strong a word. Numbers in themselves were nothing, an attitude in which he coincided entirely with his adversary. His fleet was short-handed; it was ill-trained; and it included many soldiers. Even to Jervis's opening broadsides, replies were ragged, and the standard grew worse, not better. Nice judgement was required on Jervis's part as to when he should order his ships to alter course in succession, to prevent the leading Spaniards escaping his fire altogether, and to make their progress back to port as hard as possible.

Jervis may have left his signal a shade late. The *Victory*, his flagship, was not leading the fleet, and the Commander-in-Chief's view may not have been too clear, particularly with smoke blowing down on him from Spanish guns. Whether this was so or not, Nelson decided on an act of initiative as bold as it was successful. He wore his ship, the *Captain*, 74, out of the line, steering for the foremost Spaniards. For the next few hours he, and the rest of the fleet except the *Colossus*, which had been damaged in collision, were furiously engaged. The burden fell on five ships. These were the *Captain*, the *Blenheim*, a three-decker commanded by Captain Frederick, the *Excellent*, commanded by Nelson's old friend, Cuthbert Collingwood, the *Prince George*, flagship of Rear-Admiral William Parker, and the *Culloden*, Captain Troubridge, Jervis's favourite captain and another close friend of Nelson. These ships had the only heavy casualties of the day, sixty-five killed between them against a total of eight elsewhere.

Nelson's exploit in boarding two large Spanish ships, and the splendid gunnery of the *Excellent*, were the most remarked features of the battle. Four Spaniards were made prize; no British ships were lost, and the only serious disappointment was that the towering *Santissima Trinidad*, which actually lowered her colours to Sir James Saumarez in the *Orion*, was saved by the appearance of a number of undamaged ships before a boarding-party could secure her.

Valentine's Day brought Jervis the earldom of St Vincent, and Nelson the Knighthood of the Bath. The transcendent merit of the victory, which would have been even fuller but for the restricted hours of winter daylight, deserved the words which Collingwood wrote about his chief: 'Should we not be grateful to him, who had such confidence in his fleet, that he thought no force too great for them?'

No one grudged Jervis his laurels, but there were those who resented the way in which Nelson trumpeted his own exploits, which were, indeed, exceptional. Only those who, like Collingwood, knew Nelson well, felt that he scarcely needed forgiveness. He had shown ability under lesser leaders. Under a great one, he excelled.

When dispatches from Lisbon first reached England, the country was in a state of inspissated gloom. The Bank of England had suspended cash payments, and the little party of naval officers, bursting with good news, even had difficulty in raising a few pounds for the expenses of posting to London.

There, the authorities were considering reports of one of the oddest invasion fiascos which ever occurred. Four French ships had embarked 1,500 men of a so-called Black

Legion, with orders to burn Bristol. The idea had originated with General Hoche, who had learnt from his Bantry Bay experience how easily Bridport's watch could be evaded.

The captains did not reach Bristol, or attempt the Bristol Channel. Instead, the Legion was put ashore at Fishguard, at the southern extremity of Cardigan Bay. The men, half of whom were convicts, were under the command of an American adventurer who called himself General Tate. Once the Legionaries were disembarked the ships promptly sailed back to France. So far from proving a threat, the invading force surrendered to a hastily assembled body of local Fencibles, headed by Lord Cawdor, without having fired a shot. There were many stories current about the affair. One of them was that Tate saw a number of Welsh women in tall hats and scarlet cloaks, and concluded that this was the uniform of a regiment of Guards!

There had been suitable illuminations in honour of the battle of St Vincent, but the fireworks had scarcely burnt out before very different news came from the Navy. The Channel Fleet was in mutiny. It was the direst threat that had ever been used by a major fighting force in a crisis of war. The reason was the outrageous conditions under which sailors were expected to work, fight and die. They were enduring what has been called the longest pay pause in history. Seamen's wages had not been increased since the time of the Commonwealth, and they had a score of other grievances. Not all of them were set down in the very moderate Petition, sent by Delegates from every ship at Spithead, to those in authority. The date of the first missive, which was addressed from the *Queen Charlotte*, was 18 April 1797.

The seamen were thoroughly patriotic, and knew their power as Britain's bulwark in defence, and her spearhead in attack. 'We should suffer double the hardships we have hitherto experienced,' said their Petition, 'before we would suffer the Crown of England to be in the least imposed upon by that of any other Power in the world.' But they wanted an increase in their derisory pay; better and fresher food, particularly when in port; and a remedy for the way in which they were habitually cheated of their dues by pursers and others. To these were added later a plea for regular leave, which was impracticable, such was the rate of desertion, and sick pay for those in hospital.

The requests were so reasonable that most of them were granted, at least in principle, an able seaman's pay being increased from 24s to 29s. 6d. a month. Even so, it generally remained in arrears. It is just possible that had Lord Howe continued in active command the mutiny would not have occurred in the form it did—direct refusal of duty. He had, however, not acted promptly on petitions which had reached him at Bath. Moreover, even had he been able to stay at his post, it is doubtful, to say the least, if he would have persuaded the Admiralty to act in the seamen's interest. What is certain is that, when grievances had been met, he paid a visit to every ship, at the cost of much personal suffering. His presence ensured a peaceful ending at Spithead and Portsmouth, with a procession and a glass of wine taken with the Delegates.

Unfortunately, no sooner were the Spithead ships back on duty and the Petition attended to than much more serious trouble broke out at the Nore. This was partly a matter of poor communication, partly because the disaffected found an eloquent spokesman in Richard Parker, a man of strong personality. The trouble was suppressed in due course, but not without great alarm in London. Parker, with other ringleaders, was hanged.

St Vincent allowed no such threats in his more distant fleet. His remedy was the

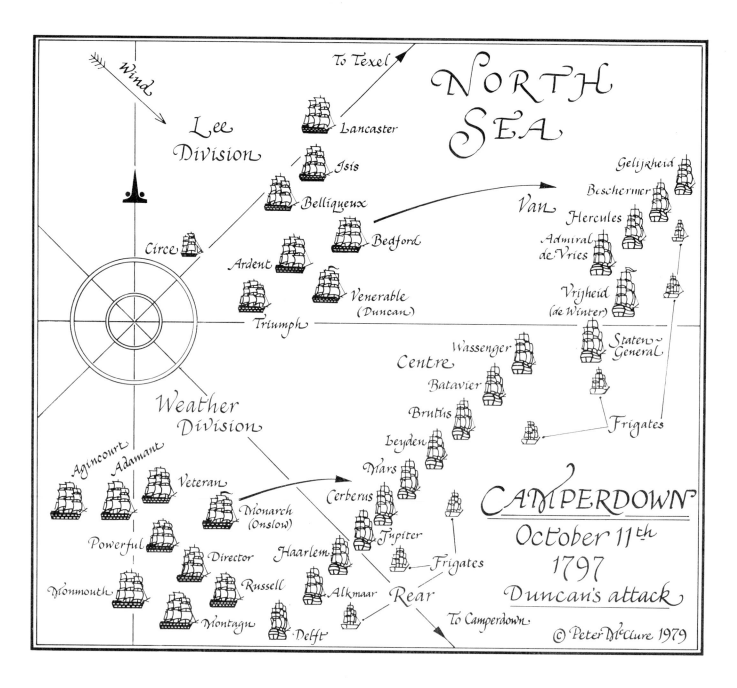

NORTH SEA

Wind

Lee Division

To Texel

Lancaster

Isis

Belliqueux

Bedford

Ardent

Venerable (Duncan)

Triumph

Circe

Weather Division

Agincourt

Adamant

Veteran

Powerful

Monarch (Onslow)

Director

Haarlem

Monmouth

Russell

Alkmaar

Montagu

Delft

Van

Gelijkheid

Beschermer

Hercules

Admiral de Vries

Vrijheid (de Winter)

Staten-General

Wassenger

Centre

Batavier

Frigates

Brutus

Leyden

Mars

Cerberus

Jupiter

Frigates

Rear

CAMPERDOWN
October 11th
1797
Duncan's attack

To Camperdown

© Peter McClure 1979

yard-arm. As for the men of the Nore, many of them made noble amends on 11 October, only a few months after the disturbances. A scratch fleet, led by Admiral Duncan, won a victory at Camperdown over the Dutch, defeating a force under de Winter which was destined for the invasion of Ireland. Duncan was a Scot, a big man in every sense of the word. He stood 6ft. 4in. in an age when great height was far less common than now. His age was sixty-six.

Lord St Vincent, who loved Duncan, as did all who knew him, once commented that he had no idea of tactics, 'trusting that the brave example he set would achieve its object, which it did completely.' This was less than just. Although it was Duncan's resolution in keeping the North Sea in all weathers, watching the Dutch, which gained the admiration of all who realized what it entailed, particularly when, at the time of the mutiny, he was reduced to two effective ships and Cornwallis's ruse of signalling to non-existent forces in the offing, he conducted his battle with decision which equalled that of St Vincent.

His first dispatch after Camperdown was one of the briefest on record.

> *Venerable, off the coast of Holland*
> *Camperdown ESE eight miles*
> *Wind N by E.*

Sir

I have the pleasure to acquaint you, for the information of the Lords Commissioners of the Admiralty, that at nine o'clock this morning I got sight of the Dutch fleet; at half past twelve I passed through their line, and the action commenced, which has been very severe. The Admiral's ship is dismasted, and has struck, as have several others, and one on fire. I shall send Captain Fairfax with particulars the moment I can spare him.

I am &.,

ADAM DUNCAN

The phrase 'I passed through their line' must have been forgotten by Lord St Vincent, for what Duncan had done, according to his signal log, was to give an order with similar effect to that of Howe's No. 75 at the Glorious First of June. It was No. 34—to 'pass through the enemy's line and engage them to leeward.' This was to prevent the Dutch from making for the safety of their notorious shoal waters, where no fleet could pursue them with impunity. Duncan captured eleven ships without loss to his own force, but their state was such that all needed reconditioning before they were fit for further service. Duncan was made a viscount, and no one deserved the honour more.

IV

The British re-entry into the Mediterranean resulted in one of the many remarkable sea battles of this ramified war. It was fought in Egypt between Nelson and the French on 1 August 1798, and was the first Anglo-French of major importance since Howe's Atlantic fight four years earlier.

Since his exploits off Cape St Vincent Nelson had fared sadly. He and Troubridge, able as they were, had failed in an attack on Santa Cruz, Teneriffe. This had been attempted in July 1797 in the hope of emulating Blake's feat in destroying or capturing Spanish treasure. For once, an expedition had underrated Spanish skill, and Nelson lost his right arm during the affair. He made a good recovery at home, then sailed for Lisbon as a Rear-Admiral, with his flag in the *Vanguard*, 74. When he rejoined St Vincent, the Commander-in-Chief said that his mere presence gave him new life.

In April 1798 St Vincent, to the chagrin of at least one senior officer, gave Nelson an independent command. His orders were to make a reconnaissance in force, to discover the purpose of a vast armament the French were preparing in every southern port under their control. Bonaparte was to be in overall command, Brueys its admiral.

Everyone in Europe realized that something had been planned on a vast scale. Only the French command knew more. Napoleon was in fact intent on an Empire in the East.

Owing to lack of frigates, Nelson made one false cast to Alexandria, to find the harbour empty. Actually, his track had crossed that of Brueys, but ahead. After a successful summons to Malta to surrender, Bonaparte went on to land his 'Army of Egypt' without opposition shortly after Nelson's ships had disappeared over the horizon on their way back to Sicily. By the time the British squadron had returned (the senior captains agreeing with their Admiral that Alexandria must, after all, have been the French destination), Nelson had been able to transform his officers into a 'band of brothers'. They knew how he would meet any tactical situation.

When the French fleet was at last found, it had been deliberately embayed. The scene was Aboukir, near the Rosetta mouth of the Nile. Brueys remembered how formidable Barrington and Hood had made such a position in the West Indian fighting during the American war. If the French were discovered, so it was thought, the British would attack. If they did so, they would be driven off with heavy loss. Brueys even had a small battery on Aboukir Island, near which the unlucky Troubridge ran his ship ashore, but it proved of no help in the action which followed.

Nelson and his captains had had a tedious chase to find their quarry. When they had done so, they did not even wait to form a regular line before sailing straight into the bay. Fighting began with little daylight left, and continued throughout the soft Egyptian night. The climax came with the shattering explosion of the French flagship, *L'Orient*, which was far bigger than any ship of Nelson's. The noise and confusion were so awe-inspiring that firing ceased on both sides until the *L'Orient* had settled on the sea-bed, carrying with her treasure looted from the Knights of Malta.

Dawn on 2 August showed a scene of which Nelson said that victory was 'not a name strong enough'. It was annihilation. Of ships of the line, each side had thirteen. The French had four frigates in addition, and many more guns. Only two French ships of the line and two frigates escaped the holocaust. In one of them was Pierre Villeneuve, flying from horrors which would haunt him for the rest of his days.

Part of the secret of Nelson's success was that he allowed full initiative to his captains. One of them, Foley of the *Goliath*, reasoned that where there was room for large ships to swing, there would also be room for an attacker to approach from inshore. He did so, and he was followed by others, notably Sir James Saumarez in the *Orion*. Some of the French ships were in consequence 'doubled'—fired at from both sides. They fought with desperation, but the impetuosity of the approach was beyond anything in their experience.

A few months later Nelson received a letter from Lord Howe expressing his admiration and surprise that every captain had acted with such intelligence and valour. Such had not always been his own experience in a long career. Pressed as he was with a crowd of urgent business, Nelson answered with one of the best short accounts of his masterpiece.

> My Lord
>
> It was only this moment that I had the invaluable approbation of the great, the immortal Earl Howe—an honour the most flattering a Sea Officer could receive, as it comes from the first and greatest Sea Officer the world has ever produced. I had the happiness to command a Band of Brothers, therefore, night was to my advan-

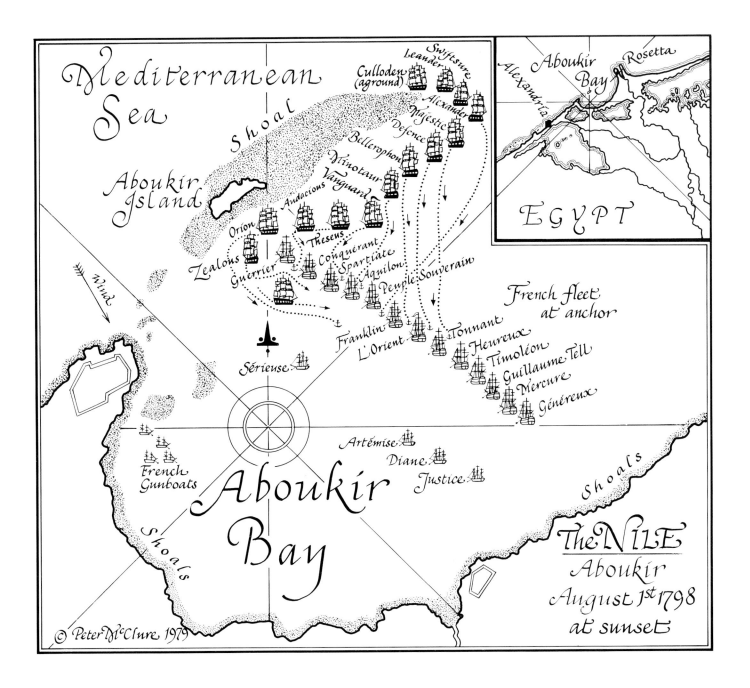

The map shows:

Mediterranean Sea

Aboukir Island

Shoal

Culloden (aground) · Leander · Swiftsure · Alexander · Majestic · Defence · Bellerophon · Minotaur · Vanguard · Audacious · Orion · Theseus · Zealous · Guerrier · Conquerant · Spartiate · Aquilon · Peuple Souverain · Franklin · L'Orient · Sérieuse

Tonnant · Heureux · Timoléon · Guillaume Tell · Mercure · Généreux

French fleet at anchor

Wind

French Gunboats

Artémise · Diane · Justice

Aboukir Bay

Shoals

The NILE
Aboukir
August 1st 1798
at sunset

© Peter McClure 1979

EGYPT

Alexandria · Aboukir Bay · Rosetta

tage. Each knew his duty, and I was sure each would feel for a French ship. By attacking the Enemy's Van and Centre, the wind blowing directly along their Line, I was enabled to throw what force I pleased on a few ships. This plan my friends readily conceived from the Signals (for which we are principally, if not entirely indebted to your Lordship) and we always kept a superior force to the Enemy.

At twenty eight minutes past six, the sun in the horizon, the firing commenced. At five minutes past ten, when *L'Orient* blew up, having burnt seven minutes, the six Van ships had surrendered. I then pressed further towards the Rear; and had it pleased God that I had not been wounded and stone blind, there cannot be a

Adam Duncan, Viscount Camperdown (1731–1804)
After Raeburn

Entering the Navy at the age of fifteen, he took part in many actions, and was captain of HMS *Blenheim* at Gibraltar in 1782. Flying his flag in HMS *Venerable*, he suppressed a mutiny aboard in 1797, and, although some ships deserted, he kept a blockade on the Texel with two ships, using the ruse of signalling to non-existent ships over the horizon. Reinforced, he brought the Dutch fleet to action off Camperdown in October that year, gaining a notable victory. He died suddenly in 1804.

doubt that every Ship would have been in our possession. But here let it not be supposed that any Officer is to blame. No; on my honour, I am satisfied each did his very best.

I have never before, my Lord, detailed the Action to anyone; but I should have thought it wrong to have kept it from one who is our great Master in Naval tactics and bravery . . .

The letter is valuable in showing that Nelson, who was by then a peer, concurred with his own Commander-in-Chief, Lord St Vincent, in recognizing Howe as supreme in his own profession, an eminence which Nelson himself came in time to occupy. Howe died shortly after he received the account. He was the only man ever to have received the Order of the Garter for services purely naval in character, and he was as great a man in his own day as Hawke had been in his: moreover, he combined some of the administrative skill of Anson with other qualities. One gift he lacked, the magic and trust which inspires others to exceed their own best. St Vincent once remarked that Troubridge and Nelson were supreme in this characteristic, but Troubridge, unfortunate both at Teneriffe and Aboukir, never had the opportunity to justify his reputation on an adequate scale.

At first, the war seemed transformed by Nelson's feat. Earl Spencer, the First Lord, fell flat on the floor outside his room at the Admiralty, so great had been his suppressed anxiety, so intense his relief. Other good news followed: the defeat of a French squadron engaged in yet another attempt on Ireland, four prizes falling to Sir John Borlase Warren. This occurred on 12 October: less than a month later a modest force under Commodore John Duckworth, with his pendant in the *Leviathan*, 74, took Minorca from the Spaniards without resistance, showing how little their heart was in the business. By regaining the use of Port Mahon, which had been so valuable in the past, Britain now only needed Malta to have adequate bases from which to protect her considerable trade with the Levant. Malta proved a tough nut. Napoleon left a commander at Valetta, Claude-Henri Vaubois, who was to cause much trouble.

Nelson's fame soon began to dim. The wound to which he had alluded in his letter to Lord Howe had appeared slight, but was in fact troublesome—a deep scar on his forehead was an outward sign. He was flattered by the adulation he received at Naples, to which he proceeded from Egypt. There he involved himself in land strategy which led to nothing but disaster. The French swept all before them when the Neapolitans, at the admiral's urging, attempted to drive them from Papal territory. Nelson was obliged to convey King Ferdinand to Sicily with his court and treasure in the face of the enemy's advance. To all intents and purposes he was lost to his country's service for over two years: 'Sicilifying his conscience', he described his condition. He was also ruining his marriage by his attachment to Emma Hamilton, wife of the British Minister. This was a liaison which proved lasting.

All-conquering as he seemed by land if not by sea, Napoleon was marooned. When he attempted to enlarge his successes by an attack on Acre, he met with repulse from the Turks, whose suzerainty extended over most of the Middle East. The soul of the defence, the animator of the Turks, was Sir Sidney Smith, and it was his finest hour.

After his withdrawal from Syria in May 1799, Napoleon determined to return to France, to re-animate the war effort, which appeared to be slackening. The authorities in Paris were well aware of the effects of the battle of the Nile, both in general and on affairs in the Mediterranean. Vice-Admiral Bruix, the Minister of Marine, went in person to Brest to stimulate efforts in the dockyard and to take command of the main fleet.

Before he put to sea Bruix sent a cutter, the *Rebecca*, with the intention that she should be captured, which she duly was. She carried a dispatch to the rebels in Ireland saying that help was on the way. Bridport swallowed the bait, and made the necessary division of his fleet to cope with such a threat. Shortly afterwards Bruix emerged from Brest with twenty-five of the line and six frigates, his flag in the *Océan* of 120 guns. Collingwood, now a Rear-Admiral, described the escape as 'horrible bungling work', which was true. Here was a newly-equipped French fleet, considerable in size, with orders to join up with the Spaniards, wherever they might find them. The task was to relieve Malta, which was blockaded, and then to succour the Army of Egypt.

Bruix sailed at a moment when the British forces were so scattered that, with vigorous action, they might have been defeated in detail, and the aims of the foray realized. Unfortunately for his country, he did not prove the man for the job. He succeeded in putting better seamen than himself into a flutter, including Bridport, Keith, St Vincent, Nelson and Duckworth, but he achieved nothing, and the Spaniards would not play. His was one of the most dangerous cruises ever undertaken. Its failure was all the more disappointing.

Shortly after Bruix's return to Brest, which occurred in June, Napoleon left his army. On the night of 22–23 August 1799, with a south-east wind blowing, the general embarked in the frigate *Muiron*, a product of the famous Arsenal at Venice. It was not quite two years since the ship had been seized, at the time when the French extinguished the Venetian Republic by the terms of the Treaty of Campo Formio. The *Muiron* served her new master well. Pursuit was avoided, and Napoleon landed at Fréjus without mishap. He was welcomed vociferously, and was soon master of France, with the title of First Consul.

IV

It was the new century—September 1800—before Valetta fell, after a two-year siege by the Maltese and blockade by the British. The Tsar, Paul I, who had been an inactive ally against France, had become Protector of the Knights of Malta in their exile, and had designs on their island. Napoleon was able to play on his vanity and ambition, and as Paul had already begun to consider reviving the former Armed Neutrality of the North, in which he found Denmark an eager accomplice, Sweden and Prussia acquiescent, it was soon clear that the Baltic would once again become a major concern to Britain, who now more than ever depended on supplies from its shores.

When Vaubois capitulated, Nelson was returning home from Sicily overland. He had not long reached England when he was appointed to a fleet being assembled under the command of Sir Hyde Parker, whose destination was the North. The Armed Neutrality had become a major consideration with the Government. In December, Denmark placed an embargo on British vessels in her ports, and closed the Elbe. Russia seized British shipping and imprisoned the crews. This was no great matter at the moment, except for the men, for the harbours were ice-bound, but during the coming months they would be free, and their cargoes of timber were urgently required.

The choice of the rich, elderly, newly-married and lethargic Parker to lead an expedition requiring the greatest skill and resolution was one of the few failures of the British naval administration. In February 1801 Pitt resigned as First Minister, Addington replacing him, and Lord St Vincent took over the Admiralty from Lord Spencer. But if Parker was a bad choice, that of Nelson as his second was inspired. From the moment Parker admitted Nelson into his confidence, the pace quickened. Nelson understood total war, and had waged it. Parker did not.

The shape of things to come was foreshadowed when the fleet, eighteen ships of the line and thirty-five smaller vessels, reached Elsinore. The guns of Kronborg Castle thundered, but wasted shot. What they did make clear were Danish intentions. The country would not submit to threats. Sweden was different. The batteries on the eastern shore of the Sound stayed silent. Gustavus IV Adolphus, the last of the Vasa dynasty to rule the country, had privately decided that Napoleon was the Beast of the Apocalypse. His officers preferred not to risk hostilities. Parker would have an unimpeded run to Copenhagen.

Nature and human artifice combined to make a seaward assault on the Danish capital a matter of great hazard. Besides removing all navigational aids the Danes had drawn up a line of eighteen ships, which had been turned into floating batteries, along the eastern side of the harbour approach, which in any case was rendered difficult by shoals and a sandbank called the Middle Ground. Beyond the range of ships was the Trekroner, a fortress bristling with big guns.

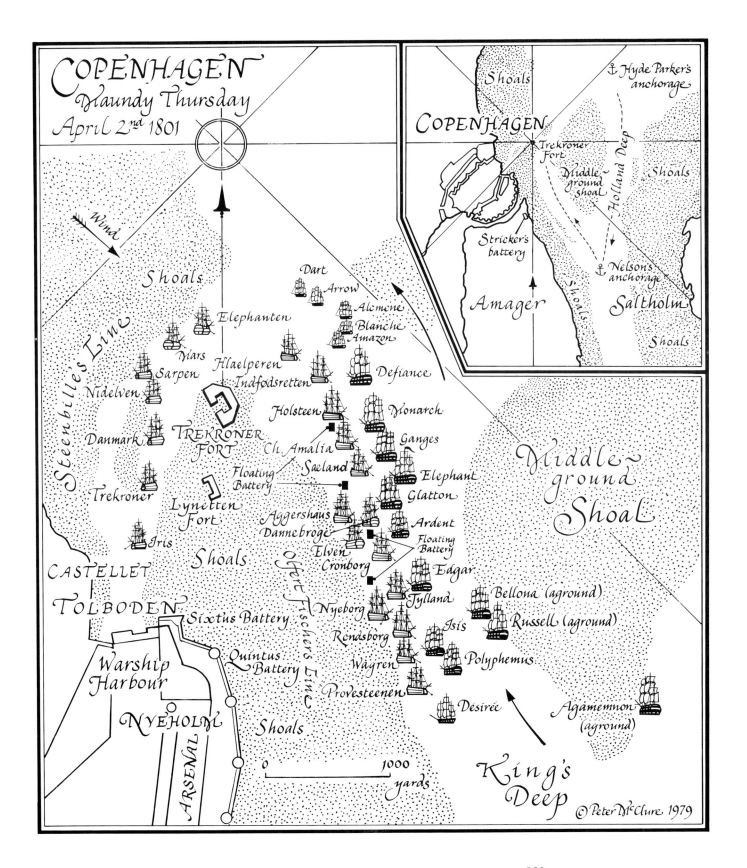

COPENHAGEN
Maundy Thursday
April 2nd 1801

Wind

Shoals

Steenbille's Line

Elephanten
Mars
Sarpen
Nidelven
Danmark
TREKRONER FORT
Trekroner
Lynetten Fort
Iris

Dart
Arrow
Alcmene
Blanche
Amazon
Defiance

Holsteen
Indfodsretten
Ch. Amalia
Floating Battery
Saeland
Aggershaus
Dannebroge
Elven
Cronborg
Nyeborg
Renosborg
Wagren
Provesteenen

Monarch
Ganges
Elephant
Glatton
Ardent
Floating Battery
Edgar
Tylland
Isis
Polyphemus
Desirée

Bellona (aground)
Russell (aground)
Agamemnon (aground)

Middle-ground Shoal

CASTELLET
TOLBODEN
Warship Harbour
NYEHOLM
ARSENAL
Sixtus Battery
Quintus Battery
Shoals

Ofert Fischer's Line

Shoals

King's Deep

0   1000
                     yards

© Peter McClure 1979

COPENHAGEN

Shoals

Hyde Parker's anchorage

Trekroner Fort
Middle-ground shoal
Holland Deep
Shoals

Stricker's battery

Amager

Nelson's anchorage

Saltholm

Shoals

139

Parker allotted twelve ships of the line to Nelson to silence the batteries, together with five frigates, two sloops, five bomb vessels and two fire-ships. Nelson transferred his flag from the large *St George* to the *Elephant* of 74 guns, for only the smaller ships of the line were likely to be able to negotiate the shallows, and even then with difficulty. Parker sailed the larger ones, including the *London*, his own flagship, to seaward of the harbour, to ensure that no force within it could put to sea without a battle.

When Nelson took his ships into action on the morning of 2 April the masters were so ignorant of local conditions, and pilots borrowed from merchantmen so scared, that several captains conned their ships themselves. Three ships of the line, a quarter of the main force, grounded, and of them only two could take even a distant part in the action. They were the *Bellona*, 74 guns, commanded by Thomas Thompson, one of the Nile captains, the *Russell*, 74 guns, and the *Agamemnon*, 64 guns, Nelson's own first command in the long war. Anchoring his remaining ships in succession opposite the batteries, with the frigates nearest to the Trekroner, Nelson began a furious close-range cannonade against an enemy who had had all the time in the world to prepare, who had the resources of a dockyard at his back, and a steady supply of reinforcements when casualties occurred. The Danes were uniquely placed and against anyone but Nelson they would probably have made a successful defence.

By noon, however, the flagship, *Dannebrog*, had been so damaged that Admiral Fischer shifted his flag to the *Holstein*. An hour later, when British fire was at last beginning to tell, Hyde Parker, from his distant station, signalled Nelson to discontinue action. This was the most extraordinary signal ever made at the height of a battle. It could not be obeyed without disaster; Hyde Parker was too far away to see exactly what was happening, and when Nelson, putting his telescope to his blind eye, said he had a right to be blind sometimes, he was only acting as any commander of calibre would have done. Even as it was, the order cost the life of the best of the frigate captains, Riou of the *Amazon*, who was killed by a shot from the Trekroner as he turned his ship.

By the early afternoon resistance had almost ceased, and Nelson sent ashore to propose a cease-fire. This was agreed, and the British then withdrew, but with great difficulty, two more ships grounding on their way out. Nelson called it the hardest battle of his life, with reason. The countries were not officially at war, the action being 'preventative'. The casualties were heavy, the Danes having 1,035 killed and wounded, and the British 944. Saddest of all, the whole business proved to have been unnecessary. A few days before it took place Paul I had been murdered by members of his entourage, and in the hands of his successor, Alexander, Russian policy was reversed. The news was not known, at the time, to the combatants.

Despite Nelson's endeavours and inevitable exhaustion, the supine Parker allowed him to conduct negotiations ashore, resulting in an armistice. Nelson prophesied that there would be more trouble with Denmark, in which he was right. Not unnaturally, the Danes remembered bitterly what they considered an unjustified attack. It added to sympathy with the cause of France.

When Lord St Vincent received accounts of the action, he recalled Parker, giving Nelson chief command, which he should have had in the first place. Although gratifying to Nelson—who also became a viscount—the admiral was longing to return home, hating as he did the chill of the Baltic. St Vincent was pleased to grant even this request, so much did he approve of his conduct. He sent Sir Morice Pole to ensure that the terms of the agreement were kept. Baltic trade was resumed, and the immediate purpose of the sortie achieved. On a longer view, the whole affair had been unfortunate, but a country fighting for its life, as Britain was by this time, would have been unwise to risk the consequences of a Northern Confederation through scruples about how to break it.

While Nelson was engaged in the north, Lord Keith and Sir Ralph Abercromby were completing the work begun in Egypt three years earlier. Keith, commanding the naval side of a large expedition, whose purpose was to defeat the French army, landed a force in which, next to Abercromby himself, John Moore was the most brilliant, though not the senior, officer. He, and Sir Arthur Wellesley, the future Duke of Wellington, who was winning battles in India against Tippoo Sultan of Mysore and other potentates acting in the French interest, were the most outstanding army officers of their generation. Abercromby was killed in Egypt, but his successor, John Hely-Hutchinson, defeated the French in a campaign which stretched over several months. The army was sustained by the complete ascendancy of the British fleet and, at one time, some of Keith's ships actually dropped anchor on the wrecks of vessels which had been sunk at Aboukir.

In the summer Sir James Saumarez, who had recently been promoted to flag rank, turned a repulse into triumph. On 5 July he made an attack on a squadron under the French admiral, Linois, which was anchored in the Bay of Algeçiras. Linois ran his ships, three of the line and a frigate, under the batteries inshore. Unfortunately, during the course of the action, the *Hannibal*, 74, went aground too near the forts and was captured.

After lightning repairs at Gibraltar, Saumarez had his revenge six days later, during the course of a bizarre night action. A Franco-Spanish squadron was sighted from the Rock, the intention being to cover the withdrawal of the captured *Hannibal* to a safer refuge. The sighting was made towards nightfall, and Saumarez instantly weighed and gave chase. At around midnight, Captain Richard Keats in the *Superb*, 74, came up with two Spanish first-rates, the *Real Carlos* and the *San Hermenegildo*, and fired a broadside into them before pressing on to chase a ship more the *Superb*'s own size. Apparently what happened was that the British shot flew over the *Real Carlos* and into the *San Hermenegildo*, which mistook the *Carlos* for an enemy. The result was that these powerful ships engaged one another furiously until both caught fire and blew up.

The senior officers of the allied force, Linois and the Spaniard, Moreno, escaped from the scene in a frigate, the *Sabina*. Saumarez completed his success, and redeemed the reputation of his flagship, the *Caesar*, which, under Molloy, had done less than well at the Glorious First of June, by the capture of the French *St Antoine*. The action, besides illustrating Spanish ineptitude, stressed the peculiar difficulties of night fighting without the most careful preparation and training.

At the time of Saumarez's success, Nelson was employed in anti-invasion measures. These were necessary, for Napoleon never relinquished the hope of a massive cross-Channel invasion, for which flotillas had been assembled in the harbours of the Low Countries and in northern France. Britain took the threat more seriously than many have supposed, as evidence along the south coast still proves. To reassure public opinion, Nelson was appointed to the command of forces inshore, with his flag in a frigate. He injected an aggressive spirit into his officers and men, but an elaborate attack which he mounted on Boulogne met with repulse, possibly because he did not lead it himself.

Commemoration of Copenhagen 1801

An unusual wine coaster in that it is in the form of HMS *Elephant*'s jolly boat, and can carry two decanters. Made of *papier mâché*, it has a silver mounting, around which are the names of the ships which took part in Nelson's victory at Copenhagen in 1801, when his flagship was the *Elephant*.

A Pair of Decanters

These two decanters must once have belonged to the Collingwood family, as their coat of arms is emblazoned on the back of each. On the front of one is engraved, around the appropriate ship: 'The *Excellent*—Capt. Collingwood, Feb 14 1797' and around the other 'The *Vanguard*—Adml. Lord Nelson, Aug 1 1798'. They were discovered by chance in an antique shop in Cambridge about fifteen years ago by the great-great-nephew of Admiral Lord Collingwood, and are now back in the family.

In May 1802 came the one formal pause in the war, brought about by the so-called Peace of Amiens. Stalemate had been reached. Both sides needed time for reflection and reorganization. Although few percipient people believed peace to be permanent, so little had been settled, it did not prevent thousands of English from flocking to France, deprived as they had been for so long of Continental travel. Some returned home safely, but not others. Against the accepted rules of international behaviour Napoleon detained all Englishmen between eighteen and sixty years of age when, in May 1803, he decided he was ready for the next round. He knew well enough that no crowds of eager Frenchmen were holidaying in 'nook-shotten Albion'.

ELEVEN

THE NAPOLEONIC WAR

The Trafalgar Campaign — Strachan's action
Collingwood in the Mediterranean — Saumarez in the Baltic
Battle of Lissa — War of 1812 — Peace

BY THE TIME the war reopened, St Vincent had put British naval affairs into disarray. In trying to purge the dockyards of corruption he had stirred up every kind of trouble from vested interest. The result was that the chief operational commanders, Cornwallis in the Western Squadron and Nelson in the Mediterranean, endured shortages of every kind, including ships in adequate numbers. This was an instance of good intentions bringing sad results.

It was fortunate that Cornwallis and Nelson understood their business so well; that they knew enemy weakness by sea; and that they were friends of long standing. Both men were utterly professional and without jealousy towards each other. Nelson regarded himself as in some sense Cornwallis's pupil. He had had the good fortune to have taken part in more spectacular events than his senior, and Cornwallis never questioned Nelson's claim to celebrity. The understanding between them was of great value to the security of the country, for it was plain that the massing of troops across the Channel by the 'Emperor of the French', as Napoleon became in May 1804, was no bluff. He really believed that one day he could get command of the narrow seas, ferry his men across, sweep all before him, and dictate terms in London. He even approved the striking of a medal to that effect, and the date on it was 1804! His orders to his admirals specified precise dates, courses, rendezvous. What a lubber they must have thought him, if ever they dared to consider him objectively. It seemed as if he had learnt nothing from his voyages to and from Egypt, not even that the wind took no account of imperial commands, and that the British might have ideas of their own.

No considerable sea battle took place for some time after the renewal of war, the chief events being those incidental to blockade. This was work so arduous that Collingwood could write: 'I have hardly known what a night of rest is these two months; this incessant cruising seems to me beyond the powers of human nature.' He, and thousands like him, would have welcomed battle as a tonic after the ceaseless perils of storm, rock and shoal. On one occasion, when he had his flag in the *Venerable*, 74, which had been Duncan's flagship at Camperdown, he reported that when at last she docked it was found that they had been 'sailing for the last six months with only a sheet of copper between us and eternity.' Such were the realities of keeping the sea with ill-conditioned ships. It was wonderful that the tragedy of the *Royal George* was not repeated.

Of actual encounters there were so few, such was British ascendancy, that the official Admiralty list of battle honours shows a long gap. This was between 1801, and the

Battle of Trafalgar
J. M. W. Turner

A detail of Turner's *Battle of Trafalgar* which shows Nelson's fall, shot through the backbone by one of the marksmen in the fighting tops of the French *Redoutable*, Captain Lucas. The fire was immediately returned from the poop of *Victory*, and it was at first claimed that a Midshipman Collingwood—no relation to the Admiral—had avenged Nelson's death, but it was finally established that the avenger was an officer named John Pollard.

Keith–Abercromby campaign in Egypt, and February 1805, when the defence of a Mediterranean convoy by the *Arrow*, sloop of war, and the *Acheron*, bomb vessel, against two large French frigates, saved the merchantmen, although at the cost of the small and gallant pair, who were hopelessly outgunned. The action occurred off Cape Tenez, and was a classic example of rewarded self-sacrifice on the part of a naval escort. The British captains survived, and won immediate promotion.

In the very month that Napoleon made himself Emperor, Pitt resumed office as First Minister to George III. He had all his old determination to prosecute the war. His aim, which was achieved the following year, was a new coalition, the members being Britain, Russia, Austria and Sweden. Meanwhile, off Brest and Toulon, where Nelson made his stately home in the *Victory*, the ships kept close or distant watch. They inspired that famous sentence of Alfred Mahan, true of this time and for all the remaining years of the conflict—'those far-distant, storm-beaten ships, upon which the Grand Army never looked, stood between it and the dominion of the world.'

Before the year 1804 was out, Spain declared war on Britain. The event had been anticipated by the Royal Navy, which seized some treasure ships in the high-handed way which was sometimes its style, but it was in any case inevitable, so subservient had

One of the chivalrous episodes at Trafalgar: a young lady from the burning French *Achille* is seen being rescued from a watery grave by men from the schooner *Pickle*. She was later transferred to the *Revenge*, where she learned that her husband had also survived the battle. Some women were carried by ships, which gave rise to the expression 'Show a leg'. If the leg duly shown on the bosun's call was proved to be female, the incumbent of the hammock was allowed an extra lie-in!

the Spanish Court become to the interests of France. The circumstance added to Britain's problems, but not to her alarm, least of all to that of her seamen, who anticipated rich pickings. On the other hand, it encouraged Napoleon's schemes for invasion, for the Spanish fleet was the second largest in Europe.

Spanish participation made 1805 the year of destiny for the main fleets of Britain and France. Napoleon now had a vision of combining the forces from Brest, Rochefort, Cadiz, Cartagena and Toulon in a grand-scale operation. The respective naval commanders were to elude or brush aside the watch on their ports, sail for the West Indies and then, in the shape of a second 'Invincible Armada' such as Philip II had once assembled, sweep back to European waters, defeating Cornwallis on the way, and secure the Channel for the crossing of his army.

In theory it seemed splendid, and some of the plan was successful. Villeneuve, in charge of the Toulon fleet, twice got away, in January and at the end of March. The first time he was driven back by weather, which gave him a poor idea of the seamanship of some of his captains. On the second attempt he got clear, and when Nelson had the news he feared, not unnaturally, for Egypt. He was not privy to the Emperor's plans, in this like every other British commander.

Once he knew that the enemy scheme was entirely different, and that Villeneuve's course was for the Atlantic, he was held back by adverse winds—'dead foul', as he dolefully described them. Having ensured the safe passage of a military convoy into the area of his proper command, he decided on a chase to the West Indies, with whose waters he had been familiar since boyhood.

Villeneuve's escape was at first the extent of his luck. As he approached the Spanish coast, he was informed by his allies that no ships from Cartagena or Barcelona were ready to sail. At Cadiz it was better. The Spaniards joined him, and when he reached

Stormy Night After Trafalgar
J. W. Carmichael

This is a descriptive if somewhat fanciful painting by the Newcastle artist, J. W. Carmichael, showing the condition of weather after the battle and the rocky lee shore on to which some ships were driven. The storm depicted illustrates how impossible it would be to anchor in such conditions, and how it thus aided the escape of some of the French prizes.

his Caribbean rendezvous at Martinique, he had a combined fleet of twenty sail of the line. There he waited for the Brest contingent, but in vain, for it had been punched back by Cornwallis's Western Squadron. He did a certain amount of damage to the rich trade of the West Indian islands, but, as soon as he realized that Nelson was in pursuit of him, he hurried back to Europe.

The original force with Nelson consisted of only ten ships of the line, some of them, the *Superb* in particular, with such foul bottoms that they affected his speed. He was never unwise enough to suppose that with the strength at his command he could defeat Villeneuve outright, but he intended to attack him whenever he found him, in the well-found expectation that he could inflict enough damage to render the combined fleet useless as a coherent force. All his life he had accepted a high degree of risk, in view of the possible rewards. The policy had been justified, even at Copenhagen, where every advantage except experience was with the Danes.

Owing to erroneous information, which he found it hard to believe yet could not disregard, Nelson made for Trinidad, which had been taken from the Spaniards in 1797 and retained at the peace. He himself had anticipated meeting Villeneuve further north, in much the same waters where Rodney had encountered de Grasse. As it was, Villeneuve was well on his way back to Europe before Nelson had true knowledge of his

movements. He then sent a fast-sailing brig, the *Curieux*, to warn Cornwallis and the
Admiralty of what he knew. The captain concerned, Bettesworth, did better than his
orders. He caught sight of the combined fleet, counted its numbers, and made a report
of the utmost value to the Admiralty. There, Lord Barham had taken charge. He was
nearly eighty, but had unrivalled experience in naval administration, and was the man
for a crisis. On the strength of what he knew, Barham felt that Villeneuve could be dealt
with by a detachment from Cornwallis's fleet. Sir Robert Calder was sent, with fifteen
of the line, to intercept.

When he heard of this disposition, Napoleon stigmatized it as crazy, once more
misunderstanding naval reality. Calder met Villeneuve off Finisterre on 23 July, and,
although in inferior numbers, gave better than he got, taking two Spanish prizes. It was
these prizes, as well as damage to one or two of his ships, which may have helped to
decide him not to press Villeneuve as relentlessly as Barham would have wished, and as
Nelson would certainly have done. There was an outcry that more had not been
achieved, and Calder, who had an exalted view of his own capabilities, felt aggrieved.

Nelson put in at Gibraltar on his return to European waters. Then, with permission
from the Admiralty to do so, he sailed for home. He was there for twenty-five days,
during which time he had news that the combined fleet were at Cadiz. There,
Collingwood was watching the port with a small force, which would shortly be reinforced by Calder. As it was thought by some captains, though not all, that Villeneuve
would attempt a sortie before the winter (in spite of the fact that Napoleon had by now
given up his idea of invasion), Nelson's place was obviously back at his post. Barham

*Greenwich Pensioners
Celebrating Trafalgar on
Observatory Hill*
S. P. Denning

A convivial scene—the
pensioners, wives, children
and grandchildren seem bent
on celebrating the great victory of Trafalgar rather than
mourning the death of
Nelson. No doubt having a
rare day out, naval cadets
from the academy at
Greenwich are also present.
In the background, the
Queen's House and
Greenwich, fronting the river,
can be seen.

got together as many ships as possible, so as to ensure that if Villeneuve did emerge,
he met with something stronger than the mild reverse he had suffered at Calder's
hands.

Nelson arrived in the *Victory* off Cadiz on 28 September. He ordered that no gun
salutes should herald his approach, his intention being that Villeneuve should remain in
ignorance of his strength and dispositions. His practice was for the bulk of his fleet to
keep well out to sea, and he was fortunate that Collingwood, from whom he took over,
was not only a devoted friend, but sympathetic to the ideas of his chief, which differed
in many ways from his own.

By no means all the captains of the twenty-seven ships of the line which eventually
joined his flag had served with him before, or were familiar with his methods, but
within a few days, by visits and conferences in the flagship, he had won their enthusiastic confidence. The spirit was that of the 'band of brothers' at the Nile.

He had at one time expected to have a total of as many as forty ships of the line, and
had prepared a memorandum explaining what his tactics would be in such circumstances. In the event, matters were simplified. He would attack the enemy in two
columns, one under his own direction, the other under that of Collingwood. He had the
advantage of a Telegraphic Signal Code developed by Sir Home Popham, through
which he was able to convey his orders precisely. He did so with such frequency that
Collingwood, who was of a more reserved disposition, was once heard to say that he
wished Nelson would stop signalling, since they all knew exactly what they had to do.

148

This was a tribute to the Popham Code, as well as an affectionate dig at Nelson's love of effect.

Napoleon, marching his army against the Austrians to break up Pitt's coalition, destroyed his own fleet by ordering Villeneuve into the Mediterranean. He reinforced the instruction by sending another admiral, Rosily, to replace a man in whom he had lost faith. Rather than bow to such humiliation, Villeneuve took his ships to sea before Rosily could arrive at Cadiz by way of the atrocious Spanish roads. In any case, supplies in the port were running low.

The combined fleet had cleared the harbour by 19 October, watched by Nelson's frigates, and heading for the Straits of Gibraltar. Once in the Atlantic, realizing that Nelson was in greater strength than he had expected, Villeneuve reversed the course of his thirty-three ships, hoping to regain Cadiz. Light airs, and a waiting enemy, were against him. Commodore Churraca, in the Spanish *San Juan de Nepomuceno*, exclaimed to his second-in-command when he saw the signal: 'The fleet is doomed. The French admiral does not understand his business. He has compromised us all.' Truer words were never spoken.

II

As a result of Villeneuve's manoeuvre, Churraca's ship became the rearmost in a long ragged line stretching for almost five miles, and in some confusion. After approximately two hours it had sorted itself out into what Collingwood described as 'a crescent, convexing to leeward.' Owing to the light airs there was considerable delay in closing the ten miles between the fleets, and Nelson took the opportunity to write up his diary, settle his worldly affairs, which included a 'legacy' to his King and Country—Emma Hamilton—and inspect every part of the ship, encouraging the men at their posts.

Collingwood's *Royal Sovereign*, heading the lee column, was the first ship into action. The *Royal Sovereign* had been an abominable sailer; she was sent home in July for repairs, and had rejoined the fleet early in October equipped with a new copper bottom which enabled her to sail faster than any other ship under Nelson's command. This resulted in Collingwood, having cut the weather line of the combined fleet and engaged the *Santa Aña*, being without support for several minutes. His flagship was at one point during this period engaged with five ships, the *Fougueux, San Leandro, San Justo, Indomptable* and *Santa Aña*. Said Collingwood: 'I thought it a long time after I got through their Line before I found my friends about me.' Nelson, watching, remarked in admiration to Blackwood of the *Euryalus*, 'See how that noble fellow Collingwood carries his ship into action!'

Belleisle, Captain Hargood, was very soon on her way to Collingwood's succour, drawing off the fire of the *Indomptable*, who was driven away, and the *Fougueux*. The *Belleisle*, being a two-decker, was somewhat at a disadvantage compared with the *Royal Sovereign*, but was no less forward for all that: her losses, however, were not as high as some, although her damage was severe: she lost all her masts, had her bowsprit and figurehead shot away, and numerous shot-holes in her hull. Despite this, she was able to take possession of the Spanish *Argonauta*, of 80 guns.

Victory came into the action less than an hour later. Nelson, at that point, did not know in which ship Villeneuve was flying his flag; he therefore steered for the

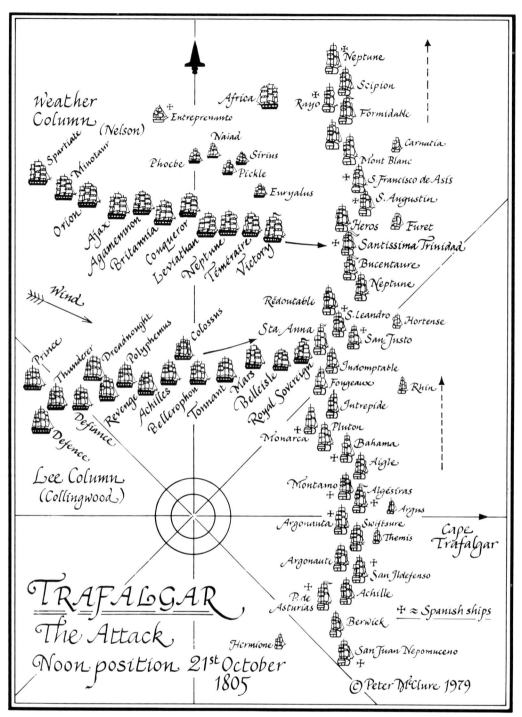

Weather Column (Nelson)

Wind

Lee Column (Collingwood)

TRAFALGAR
The Attack
Noon position 21ˢᵗ October
1805

© Peter McClure 1979

✠ ≈ Spanish ships

Cape Trafalgar

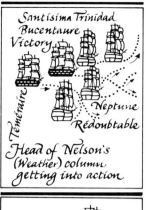

Santisima Trinidad
Bucentaure
Victory

Téméraire

Neptune

Rédoubtable

Head of Nelson's (Weather) column getting into action

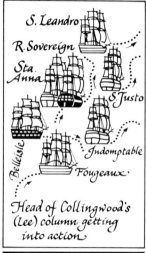

S. Leandro
R. Sovereign
Sta. Anna

S. Justo

Belleisle

Indomptable

Fougeaux

Head of Collingwood's (Lee) column getting into action

Santissima Trinidad, the largest ship afloat, but changed course for the *Bucentaure* when the commander-in-chief's flag was seen at her halyards. *Victory's* carronades hurtled into the stern windows of the *Bucentaure*, to be followed by a broadside, causing great damage. *Victory* was then raked by the *Neptune*, following close behind the *Bucentaure*, and replied with a starboard broadside into *Redoutable*, her larboard guns hitting the *Santissima Trinidad* in her stern. Then came *Victory's* fight with

Redoutable, Captain Lucas, probably the best French officer in the service. Knowing that his men could not compete with the British crews at gunnery, he had concentrated their training on musketry from the foretops. And, at about 1.15, he had his reward.

Nelson and his captain, Hardy, were pacing the quarterdeck, when, about to turn, the admiral fell to the ground, shot through the shoulder. He was taken below, his face covered with a handkerchief so that his men would not be disheartened at seeing their commander wounded. He himself knew that his wound was mortal—'Ah, Mr Beatty! [the surgeon] you can do nothing for me now. I have but a short time to live; my back is shot through.' He lingered, however, for about three hours, dying in the knowledge that at least fourteen ships had surrendered or been destroyed. The *Victory*'s log records his death as follows:

> Partial firing continued until 4.30., when a victory having been reported to the Right Honourable Lord Viscount Nelson, KB and Commander-in-Chief, he then died of his wound.

The fighting had been very severe; many ships were dismasted, owing to the French habit of firing into the rigging, and some were hardly able to move. For instance, the *Redoutable*, who had fought so well, found herself almost on board the *Téméraire*, with the *Victory* on her other side. The *Fougueux* now appeared to add to the confusion, and ran aboard the *Téméraire*, whose first lieutenant, Thomas Kennedy, took the Frenchman with a small detachment.

Dumanoir, commanding six French and four Spanish ships, was ordered to bring these ships into action, and, had he done so, things might have gone ill for those ships in the centre, *Victory*, *Téméraire* and *Royal Sovereign*. This threat was, however, beaten off, and Dumanoir has been criticized severely as to his conduct in holding off.

The battle was, in effect, brought to an end with the blowing up of the French *Achille*. She had fought bravely, but when the blazing mast and rigging fell onto her deck, the fire spread very quickly indeed. British boats saved many of those jumping into the sea, but when she finally exploded, at about 5.30, nearly five hundred of her crew were still aboard.

If Trafalgar was not annihilation as at the Nile, the result confirmed the superiority of British sea power, a state not called into question for over a century, although suffering a painful lesson in the unnecessary War of 1812 against the fledgeling United States of America.

III

The evening of Trafalgar was the time for counting the cost. The Combined Fleet, from its total of thirty-three ships, had lost eight French and nine Spanish vessels captured, not including the blown-up *Achille*. From the fifteen remaining, four, under the command of Dumanoir, had escaped, and eleven managed to return to their home port of Cadiz in varying states of damage. Not one British ship was lost, although casualties were heavy in some. Against the gains had to be put the death of the Commander-in-Chief, Nelson. He was, in reality, a national figure, and although many of the men in his command had never even set eyes upon him, there was an almost universal feeling of loss. In the Combined Fleet, the losses of personnel amounted to

Sir Thomas Masterman Hardy
(1769–1839)
Richard Evans

Hardy was the only one of
Nelson's 'Band of Brothers'
to have been present at all
his patron's major actions.
Nelson, at this time in
Agamemnon, sent him, with a
boarding party, to take a
Spanish frigate. Although this
was accomplished the ship
was recaptured and Hardy
taken prisoner. He was exchanged, but would have
been captured again when he
went to the rescue of a
seaman with the enemy in
sight. 'By God,' said Nelson,
'I'll not lose Hardy,' and
turned back to stand by.

Hardy commanded the
Mutine brig at the Nile, was
with Nelson as a volunteer in
the *Elephant* at Copenhagen,
and *Victory*'s flag-captain at
Trafalgar. First Sea Lord in
1830, he later became
Governor of Greenwich
Hospital.

152

Vice-Admiral Cuthbert, Lord Collingwood
From a miniature on a bracelet by an unknown artist

Ten years older than Nelson, his closest friend, Collingwood followed him in many of his appointments. After Trafalgar, although he had a family, he did not set foot on English soil again, dying on his way home in March 1810. A reserved man, his friendship was given to few; duty was his watchword. His ships were noted for their gunnery—the Royal Navy's Gunnery School at Whale Island is named after HMS *Excellent*, his ship at 1 June 1794. Floggings in the fleet were the fewest in the log-books of the era. Other punishments were imposed instead. As an ambassador, when he became Commander-in-Chief, Mediterranean, in the troubled times in which he lived he was unexampled, and the Admiralty never found fault with his decisions. The glory of a full-scale sea-battle was only denied him when, through false information, Ganteaume put to sea in 1808. His name lives on in the great shore establishment at Fareham, HMS *Collingwood*, the electricians' training base.

Charles Middleton, Lord Barham (1726–1813)
Unknown

Probably the most efficient administrator the Navy has ever known, Charles Middleton served his country well afloat, though without particular distinction. Like so many of his contemporaries, including Nelson, a great deal of that service was spent on half-pay. Appointed Comptroller of the Navy in 1778, he held that position for twelve years. Also a Member of Parliament for a short time, he became First Lord of the Admiralty in April 1805. He was raised to the peerage as Lord Barham the next month and was largely responsible for the successful planning of the campaign of that year, culminating in the great victory of Trafalgar, no mean achievement for an old gentleman of eighty!

nearly 7,000, with probably the same number captured. In the British camp, rather fewer than 2,000 were killed or wounded, though the dead included Captain Duff of the *Mars* and Captain Cooke of the *Bellerophon*.

Now the weather took a hand. Nelson had made a signal before the action started requiring the fleet to anchor at the end of the day. However, when Collingwood repeated the order, it was impossible for some; they had had their anchors and cables shot away in the action. That night, and the following day, the wind freshened to gale force. Difficult as it was for the British ships to keep the sea, it was almost impossible when attending to prizes as well. Many of those captured ran onto the rocks, and finally, only four of the prizes made the haven of Gibraltar. Commodore Cosmao-Kerjulien came out of Cadiz on 23 October with a small force, intent on recapturing some of their ships: they retook the *Santa Aña* and *Neptuno*, but the *Indomptable*, carrying *Bucentaure*'s survivors, ran ashore. *San Francisco de Asis* was wrecked, as was the *Rayo*, two days after, having had the misfortune to fall in with the *Donegal*, fresh from Gibraltar. Those prizes reaching the Rock were the French *Swiftsure*, and the Spanish *Bahama*, *San Ildefonso* and *San Juan Nepomuceno*, Churraca's flagship.

After the battle, Collingwood had transferred into the *Euryalus*, Captain Blackwood, the *Royal Sovereign* being badly damaged. In this ship he wrote his famous dispatch and the equally famous General Order:

> The ever to be lamented death of Lord Viscount Nelson, Duke of Brontë, the Commander-in-Chief, who fell in the action of the 21st, in the arms of Victory, covered with glory—whose name will ever be dear to the British Navy and the British Nation, whose zeal for the honour of his King, and for the interest of his

154

Sir John Thomas Duckworth
(1748–1817)
After William Beechey

Duckworth served at 1 June 1794, and was a Vice-Admiral with a fleet blockading Cadiz when he heard of a French squadron at sea. Losing it, but carrying on to the West Indies, he fought an action with another French squadron under Leissègues off San Domingo in February 1806. The French were completely annihilated in the manner of Aboukir. The next year Duckworth forced the Dardanelles to replace the British ambassador in Constantinople, from which he had fled. Later he became second-in-command, Channel Fleet, and Commander-in-Chief of the Newfoundland Station. Created a baronet in 1813, his last appointment was at Plymouth Dockyard.

The Battle of Lissa, 1811
C. Webster, engraved by Merke

Captain William Hoste, like Nelson a Norfolk clergyman's son, and a protégé of his immortal countryman, in command of a detached squadron in the Adriatic, came upon a combined French and Venetian fleet on their way to attack the British base of Lissa. Hoste, in the *Amphion*, 32, raised the signal 'Remember Nelson!' and achieved a notable British victory with his four ships against a much superior force.

The Battle of Navarino, 20 October 1827
Thomas Luny

The Battle of Navarino took place in 1827, ostensibly to help Greece overthrow the Turkish yoke. Unique for two reasons, it was the last battle fought wholly under sail, and it was fought between five nations, none of which was officially at war with any other. While her allies' commanders (French and Russian) were congratulated by their governments on their success over the Turco-Egyptian fleet, the British Commander-in-Chief of the whole expedition, Admiral Sir Edward Codrington, was recalled and censured by Whitehall for winning a politically inexpedient battle. He was, however, promoted Admiral of the Red in 1837. Navarino, while marking the beginning of the end of the sailing ship era, was also notable for the fact that it was the first occasion on which French and English had fought on the same side since Solebay in 1652.

Mural Depicting the Life of Admiral Lord Collingwood
Ralph Gillies Cole

Painted in oil on wood, this mural, which measures 8 × 34 feet, represents the life-story of Admiral Lord Collingwood. Its home is at the naval base at Fareham in Hampshire which bears his name, now the school for naval electricians.

Neptune and Britannia fore-shadow events; the clerical gentleman is the headmaster at Newcastle Royal Grammar School; watched by his parents, Collingwood is introduced into the Navy by his maternal uncle, Admiral Brathwaite. Naval instruments, including guns, on which he was to become an expert, are depicted, as is the battle of Bunkers Hill in 1775, on which day he was gazetted lieutenant. The group of four represents Lieutenant Haswell, Captain Peter Parker, Nelson and Collingwood. Below are the court martial scene and that of his wedding. The centre-piece is the battle of 1 June 1794 and Collingwood's ship, *Barfleur*. Howe and St Vincent are shown, while Collingwood can be seen scattering acorns for further 'wooden walls' to be built. He is then depicted as 'ambassador' in the Mediterranean before coming to rest at St Paul's.

Bombardment of Sveaborg seen from the French battery established on Abraham Island, 10–11 August 1855
Lithograph by M. Beeger

Near the end of the Crimean War, a Franco-British fleet in the Baltic, after making a show of force off Kronstadt, bombarded the strong fortress, Sveaborg, which protected Helsinki harbour. A great deal of shot was expended, but to no avail. The outstanding aspect of the naval war in the Baltic was its abysmal mismanagement and the senility of its commander.

Country, will be ever held up as a shining example for a British seaman—leaves me a duty to return my thanks to the Right Honourable the Rear-Admiral [Northesk], the Captains, Officers, Seamen and Detachments of Royal Marines, serving on board His Majesty's squadron, now under my command, for their conduct on that day.

But where can I find the language to express my sentiments of the valour and skill which were displayed by the Officers, Seamen and Marines, in the battle with the enemy, where every individual appeared a hero on whom the glory of Country depended? The attack was irresistible, and the issue of it adds to the page of naval annals a brilliant instance of what Britons can do, when their King and Country need their service . . .

The new Commander-in-Chief sent home Lieutenant Lapenotière with the dispatches, in the schooner *Pickle*. He arrived at the Admiralty early in the morning of 6 November, and Lord Barham was immediately called from his bed to hear the news of triumph and disaster. Two days later a commission was made out for Collingwood to take over officially the mantle of supreme command in the Mediterranean. He was also created a peer—Baron Collingwood of Coldborne and Hethpool, both places in which his wife's family had an interest—but, as he had two daughters only, the honour was not hereditary. Nelson's family, however, did better in this respect. His elder brother, William, was created an Earl, given a pension and allocated a large sum of money to buy an estate subscribed for by the grateful people of Britain.

IV

Not many days after Trafalgar, Sir Richard Strachan, with four ships of the line, his own *Caesar*, *Courageux*, *Hero* and *Namur*, all of them 74s with the exception of the 80-gun flagship, *Caesar*, came up with a French squadron which they believed to have come from Rochefort. After a battle of three and a half hours, during which 'the enemy fought to admiration', the French surrendered, and it was much to Strachan's surprise that he discovered that he had taken Dumanoir's ships from Cadiz.

Collingwood's most testing time now began. Not only was he Commander-in-Chief, Mediterranean, but he was also, whether he wished it or not, a diplomat. Crisis after crisis arose, and time after time Collingwood settled arguments and disputes long before the orders as to the course he should take reached him from home. Not once was he rebuked for his actions.

Sicily and the East were his most pressing problems, and the intrigues of Maria Carolina, Queen of the Two Sicilies, sister of the unfortunate Marie Antoinette, and nominal ally of the British, did nothing to smooth his path in dealing with the affairs of the former country. Sicily was the most desirable base for the Mediterranean fleet. Other island bases, like Sardinia and Minorca, were useful for specific purposes, such as watching Toulon, but the cost of defending squadrons and troops was too much. For the defence of Sicily it was essential that the mouth of the Mediterranean should be closed, and this led to the renewal of the blockade of Cadiz. British troops under General Craig occupied the island early in 1806, reinforced by ships from Collingwood's squadron, putting Sicily out of immediate danger. Craig, who was ill, was relieved by General Stuart, and Captain Sotheron, with his four ships of the line, was based at Palermo, ready for any enemy movement by sea.

155

HMS Arrow *and HMS* Acheron *Defending a Convoy* F. Sartorious

The sloop *Arrow*, 28, and the bomb *Acheron*, 8, while escorting a convoy of thirty-four merchantmen, encountered the French *Hortense*, 48, and *Incorruptible*, 42, and, after an action of two days, during which thirty-one of their charges were saved, the British ships struck. The *Arrow* sank almost immediately and *Acheron* was so badly damaged that she was burnt by her captors. Both British captains were promoted for their gallant defence.

The offensive in Sicily was taken when Rear-Admiral Sir Sidney Smith arrived in the theatre of war. Flying his flag in the *Pompée*, he was to put himself under Collingwood's command—Sir Sidney, however, had an exalted view of his own capabilities, and was determined that he would not act solely as an agent for carrying out Collingwood's orders. Collingwood, with misgivings, for Smith's boastful and volatile nature was well known, gave him command in the central Mediterranean and, supported by General Stuart and his troops, naval activity on the coast of the mainland increased. French batteries were attacked, partisans landed, enemy supplies cut off, and soon the Italian littoral was under the admiral's control. At the beginning of July 1806, Sir Sidney's ships put ashore 5,000 troops under Stuart, and they came up with and defeated a larger French force under General Reynier at Maida on 4 July. The weakness of the British force, however, forced its return to Sicily without following up the success. Stuart was rewarded with the K.B. and a pension; and the first medal commemorating a battle on land was struck. Sir Sidney, with his usual lack of discretion, had achieved something, but at a cost; the Queen, always dangerous, was encouraged in her thoughts of regaining Naples, this with no authority from the Foreign Office; Calabrians had been promised the support of the British, a pledge which could not be carried out; and at Court he had set factions against each other. Both Stuart and Sir Sidney were censured, but they had halted Joseph Bonaparte's advance on Sicily for the year, tying down his brother's forces in the area of Naples.

156

V

The other persistent problem which dogged Collingwood during his time in the Mediterranean was that of the East. Napoleon wished to separate Russian and British interests, held together by an uneasy alliance. To this end, Sebastiani, the French ambassador at Constantinople, was to use all his considerable talents. Turkey came increasingly within the orbit of Napoleonic France, partly owing to the conflict of interests between herself and the Russians in Greece. Endeavouring to halt this drift, the Commander-in-Chief sent Rear-Admiral Sir Thomas Louis with three ships to the danger area, an act in advance of Cabinet orders. Admiral Duckworth, who had won a victory over the French at Santo Domingo earlier in the year, was detailed to take his ships, reinforcing Louis, through the Dardanelles; but, by the time he arrived, the Turks had taken a firm stand on the side of the French. Arbuthnot, the British Ambassador to the Porte, was to be returned to his post—he had fled to the safety of the British fleet on 29 January 1807—and the only way was by forcible means. Duckworth was somewhat pessimistic about the prospects, but saw that the forcing of the Dardanelles was the solution. It was a disaster. In spite of Collingwood lending Sir Sidney Smith to Duckworth—he fought nobly in a spirited action—the expedition was badly mauled, and Duckworth had to retire, receiving further damage as he did so. The Russian admiral, Siniavin, who had been appealed to earlier by the British, now appeared, and suggested to Duckworth a second attempt on Constantinople. Duckworth refused; but the Russians achieved enough on their own: twice they beat Turkish flotillas, the second time capturing a ship of the line.

Copenhagen 2–5 September 1807
Pub. J. Rylands

The British Government, alarmed at French interference in the Baltic, despatched a fleet of sixty-five vessels under Admiral Gambier in the *Prince of Wales*. Joined by the army under Lord Cathcart, siege was laid to Copenhagen. The Danes, having only a few days to prepare their defences, capitulated after a three-day bombardment. Their entire fleet was surrendered to the British (though few of their seventy vessels were used by the Royal Navy). This infuriated the Danes who immediately built a fleet of gunboats which caused the British enormous trouble in the later Baltic campaigns.

Battle of San Domingo 1806
Pub. I. Hinton

Not long after Trafalgar
some of the French fleet
under Leissègues escaped
from Brest and made for the
West Indies, pursued by Sir
John Duckworth's squadron.
He came up with them off
San Domingo, anchored
in Occa Bay. Duckworth, in
the *Superb*, started action at
10 a.m. and all was over in
less than two hours, the
French *Impérial* and *Diomède*
being burnt and only their
frigates escaping.

VI

The area around the Baltic was also giving trouble to the British. It had been to dissolve the threat of the Armed Neutrality that a force had been sent to Copenhagen in 1801, and Nelson, in spite of his superior officer, Hyde Parker, had been successful. Now, after the Treaty of Tilsit in 1807, signed by Napoleon and the Tsar, it was very probable that Denmark would again join an alliance against Britain. To prevent this, an expedition under the command of Admiral Gambier and General Cathcart was dispatched against the Danes who, as yet, had no idea of the force's intentions. They did, however, strengthen the defences of Copenhagen. On 1 September, Gambier and Cathcart sent a demand for surrender, which was refused, and bombardment began. A document of capitulation was signed on 7 September, ceding the Danish fleet to England. The British and their prizes sailed for England in October, but only four of the captured ships were deemed fit for sea. Denmark was not subdued, and, as soon as the British departed, made an alliance with France, also building an enormous number of gunboats, which proved a great nuisance to the British.

Admiral Saumarez, who played a part in both the battles of Valentine's Day and the Nile in his ship, *Orion*, was appointed to the Baltic command. Like Collingwood in the Mediterranean, his post was as much diplomatic as naval and, as a Channel Islander,

158

his fluency in French was one of his assets. The duties of the British Navy in support of her ally, Sweden, were many, and included keeping the Sound open for trade, ensuring that communications between Denmark and Norway were disrupted, keeping a presence in the Belts so that passage was denied to French troops, bolstering up the Swedish fleet and blockading French-held ports on the German coast. In pursuit of these aims, a by no means large fleet was sent, Saumarez, with his flag in the *Victory*, having as his subordinates Rear-Admiral Samuel Hood in the *Centaur*, 74, and Rear-Admiral Richard Keats in the *Superb*, 74. There were ten other ships of the line, five frigates and a number of smaller craft. Numerous engagements with the Danes in their new gunboats took place, but against Russia the tendency was more towards fleet actions than skirmishes with detached ships. The Swedish navy had almost ceased to exist when the commander of the great fortress of Sveaborg, in a position of great strategic importance, surrendered to the Russians after a less than token resistance and, by so doing, allowed ninety-one ships to fall into the hands of the enemy. Seventy-one of these vessels, of varying kinds, were at once taken into Russian service. After some defeats, what was left of the Swedish fleet had to retreat to a position off the Åland

HMS Guerrière *Versus USS* Constitution
Engraving by Betrémieux

HMS *Guerrière*, a British frigate, was captured by the USS *Constitution*, Captain Isaac Hull, after half an hour's brisk action, the first naval encounter of the War of 1812. The *Guerrière* was an ex-French ship, captured by HMS *Blanche* in 1806, and had been added to the Royal Navy under her own name.

HMS Implacable *Joining in the Destruction of the* Vsevolod
W. L. Wyllie

Commanded by Captain Thomas Byam Martin, the *Implacable* was part of a small British force under Vice-Admiral Sir James Saumarez in *Victory* co-operating with the Swedes against the French, Danes and Russians in the Baltic. In August 1808 a Russian squadron was chased off Hangö; the *Implacable* and *Centaur*, being faster sailers than the Swedish ships, engaged the *Vsevolod*, 74, and poured a broadside into her with tremendous effect, and the Russian colours were hauled down in surrender. On *Implacable* being recalled, the *Vsevolod* rehoisted her flag and made off in tow of a Russian frigate, but grounded. Repairs to *Implacable*'s mast being quickly made, she and *Centaur* went off in pursuit, and the *Vsevolod* surrendered again. In the face of the advancing Russian fleet, the *Vsevolod* was set on fire and finally blew up.

Islands. In the middle of August 1808 Saumarez detached Hood in the *Centaur*, with the *Implacable*, Captain Byam Martin, to sustain the Swedes. In a general chase after the Russian fleet, the two English ships being far better sailers than the Swedish vessels, the *Centaur* and *Implacable* took the Russian *Vsevolod* in sight of her compatriots. The next year, the Treaty of Fredrikshavn was signed between Sweden and Russia, and in January 1810 the Swedes also made peace with France, a condition being that British ships were to be banned from Swedish ports. Duke Charles of Södermanland had succeeded to the throne, his nephew, Gustaf IV Adolf, having been declared insane. There were problems of succession as the new king was ageing and childless, and his designated heir, the Danish Prince Christian, had died. The Swedes therefore offered the throne to Bernadotte, a Gascon soldier, one of Napoleon's great generals. Although the arrival of Bernadotte in October 1810 led to a formal declaration of war by Sweden against her former British allies, there was little or no action taken against the Swedes. The Crown Prince, as Bernadotte was designated for the next eight years, made an alliance with Russia, which provided for the acquisition of Norway in exchange for Finland, which was formally ceded to the Russians. In March 1812 war broke out between France and Russia, and yet another of those shifting alliances was entered into when Britain made peace with Russia and Sweden. Saumarez hauled down his flag in November 1812, having adroitly sustained the balance of power in the Baltic in spite of the complexity of changing alliances. Denmark finally made peace with the Allies on 14 January 1814, the price of this being the confirmation of the cession of Norway to Sweden. The Norwegians were unable to sanction this and force had to be used against them. The Convention of Moss in August of that year finally brought the war to an end and bound Norway to Sweden, a state of affairs which continued until 1905, when the two countries again separated.

160

VII

Collingwood had died at sea on 7 March 1810, on his way home to a well-earned retirement after a life spent in the service of his country. His successor as Commander-in-Chief, Mediterranean, was Admiral Sir Charles Cotton, and it was under his control that the only sea encounter of any note took place in March 1811. Commodore William Hoste, a Norfolk *protegé* of Nelson's, flying his pendant in the *Amphion*, 32, was making use of Lissa as a base for his patrolling force consisting of the *Active*, 38, *Volage*, 22, and *Cerberus*, 32, in addition to himself. The French and Venetians, the latter having been under the French yoke since 1797, were sighted by the *Active* early on the morning of 13 March, and in greater force, five frigates, a corvette, a brig, two schooners, a gunboat and a xebec. Dubordieu, their commander, deployed his miscellaneous forces in two columns and bore down at speed to attack Hoste's little fleet, which was in the closest order. Having failed to break the line, the French commodore endeavoured to round the ship in the van and so place Hoste between two fires, but the shooting from the British ships was so fierce that he was unable to achieve his aim. Two hours after the action commenced the *Flora* struck, and shortly after the *Bellona* did likewise. The rest of the French force tried to make off, but were followed as closely as the damaged state of the British ships would allow. The *Active* and *Cerberus* forced the sternmost of the fleeing ships, the *Corona*, to submit, hearing in the distance the explosion of Dubordieu's *Favorite*—she had been ablaze for some time. Hoste, who had

A Bomb Ketch in the Sound
Dominic Serres

Ketch-built vessels used as tenders to the fleet were particularly suited for the purposes of bombardment as the space forward was ideal for the positioning of mortars. When attacking, the bomb ketches were moored by springs—rope hawsers—and the mortars trained on the target ashore. Until 1804, they were manned by the Royal Artillery; thereafter by the Royal Marine Artillery. With the development of naval gunnery the vessels became obsolete.

*Battle of Lake Erie 1813 —
Whale Tooth*

Scrimshaw work depicting
the battle of Lake Erie, which
was a notable victory for the
Americans. At the outset of
the War of 1812, Britain had
several ships on the Great
Lakes. America had none, but
by speedy building soon had
more, under Commodore
Perry, than the British who
were commanded by Robert
Barclay, a veteran of
Trafalgar. Meeting on 10
September, Perry's flagship,
Lawrence, named for the
captain of the *Chesapeake*,
was so badly damaged that he
transferred to the *Niagara*.
Barclay finally surrendered,
and the American victory was
the turning-point of the war
in the north-west.

flown the signal 'Remember Nelson!' on going into battle, was much mortified at the
fact that, while he had been taking possession of the *Bellona*, the *Flora* sped away,
although she had struck. Several acrimonious letters passed between the two forces, the
French maintaining that the *Flora*'s colours had been shot away: she was not given up,
in spite of unremitting efforts by the British commander.

The action now switched to the New World. Relations with the United States had
been deteriorating for some time, two of the chief reasons being trade and the boarding
of American ships by the Royal Navy. America's commercial life was slowly coming to
a standstill under the effect of British blockade of Continental ports, and real hardship
was being suffered in some of the New England coastal towns. The Royal Navy's high-
handedness in boarding American ships, ostensibly looking for 'deserters' but in reality
for the purposes of impressment, was very much resented. It has been estimated that,
by the establishment of the independence of the United States, the British Navy 'lost'
something like 18,000 seamen. This figure may be exaggerated, but Britain was so
starved of hands to man her fleet that she was not particular as to whom she 'pressed'.
If the men in ships boarded spoke English, that was good enough for the lieutenant in
charge of impressment. Over 6,000 Americans found themselves serving in the Royal
Navy by this method. Apart from these annoyances, the United States still had her eyes
on Canada and, as a result of this, a great deal of the fighting in the War of 1812 took
place on the Great Lakes, with both sides building small flotillas under regular naval
control. The war at sea resolved itself into a number of brilliant single-ship actions,
probably the most famous of which is the duel between Captain Sir Philip Broke in the
Shannon and Captain James Lawrence in the untried USS *Chesapeake*, who soon
succumbed. The *Chesapeake* remained in the British Navy List for many years.

On land, the British had some success and had captured Detroit, the defending force

162

of some 2,500 men under the command of General Hull surrendering without a shot fired to a Canadian contingent of 700 with 600 Indians, commanded by General Sir Isaac Brock and Tecumseh respectively. Ironically, the news of Hull's capitulation was received at the same time as his nephew, Captain Isaac Hull, arrived back at Boston having, in his frigate, *Constitution*—known affectionately as 'Old Ironsides'—destroyed the British *Guerrière* in a half-hour action off Nova Scotia. In contrast to the poor showing of the army, the United States navy was distinguishing itself in many skirmishes on the Great Lakes. Both sides had constructed miniature fleets, and by the time of the battle of Lake Erie on 10 September 1813, the Americans, under the command of Commodore Oliver Perry, had two brigs, six schooners and a sloop in commission. The British captain was Robert Barclay, a veteran of Trafalgar, where he had lost an arm. His flotilla consisted of two ships, the *Detroit* and *Queen Charlotte*, two brigs, a schooner and a sloop. Perry's flagship, named after Lawrence, flew his commodore's broad pendant embroidered with the dying words of the commander of the *Chesapeake*, 'Don't give up the ship!' Action commenced at 11.45. Perry, in the *Lawrence*, taking on the *Detroit* ahead of the rest of his ships, soon found himself without support. The *Niagara* having failed to come up to the attack on the *Queen Charlotte*, the latter joined in the pounding of the *Lawrence*, which was soon in parlous state. Two hours after the fighting began Perry, in the *Lawrence*'s only remaining boat, rowed over to the *Niagara*, carrying his pendant. In this fresh ship he broke the British line and, in trying to wear, the *Detroit* fell on board the *Queen Charlotte*, making an easy target for the *Niagara*, and she destroyed them both. At three o'clock, after fighting to the utmost, Barclay, who had again been wounded, surrendered, and, shortly after, the whole of the British force had followed suit. This battle was the turning-point of the war in the north-west, and it was not long before the Americans recaptured Detroit.

Battle of Lake Champlain 1814—Whale Tooth

Like the Battle of Lake Erie, a fine piece of scrimshaw work depicting the battle of Lake Champlain. This was the fiercely contested naval part of the British campaign against Plattsburg, and was the command of Captain George Downie. The small British fleet was opposed by that of Lieutenant Macdonough, whose tactics finally won the day for the Americans after a short but stiff action. This battle, in which Downie was killed, ended all threat of British invasion from Canada.

163

The following year, almost to the day, the battle of Plattsburg on Lake Champlain, in which a British squadron under Captain George Downie (who was killed in the action) was defeated, was the decisive action of the war, ending any danger of the British invading from Canada. The Treaty of Ghent at the end of December 1814 signalled the conclusion of the conflict, although news of its signing did not reach New York until the beginning of February, when it was immediately ratified. It was too late, however, to prevent the battle of New Orleans in January 1815, when a force of Peninsular veterans under General Edward Pakenham was defeated by Andrew Jackson, later to become President. The war had achieved nothing, and even the basic causes of its outbreak were ignored in the peace treaty. Until New Orleans, the British had probably had the best of it: her blockade of the coast had brought the American Treasury to the verge of bankruptcy, and her landing-parties had caused great hardship to coastal districts as they laid waste the countryside, burning and destroying as they went. The destruction spread as far as the White House, which was burnt, allegedly in retaliation for the burning by the Americans of York—now Toronto. Two important facts came out of the war, however: the British never again boarded American ships for the purpose of the 'press', and the Americans no longer entertained the idea of the invasion of Canada.

VIII

Meanwhile, the long war in Europe was at last coming to its climax. Napoleon, faced with a rebellion of his marshals, headed by Ney, was forced to abdicate in April 1814. At the end of the month, he sailed in HMS *Undaunted* for exile in Elba, ceded to him by the Allies, along with a guard of six hundred men and an allowance. Elba, however, was not the place to contain such a man as Napoleon and, having been kept in touch with events in Bourbon France, where the reinstated reigning family had soon proved unpopular, he made the decision to return, landing at Cannes on 1 March 1815. The country rallied around him, and he soon had a large enough force to put in the field against the Allies, who had avowed their intention of invading France. The campaign culminated in the Allied victory of Waterloo on 18 June, and a few days later Napoleon was forced to abdicate once more. His intention of escaping to the United States was foiled by the Royal Navy, who were blockading the coast, and he surrendered himself aboard HMS *Bellerophon*, later being conveyed to St Helena and final exile.

Thus the Napoleonic War came to an end, leaving Britain undisputed mistress of the seas and the Allies arbiters of Europe. But technology was advancing, and the following years would be those of change.

NAVARINO AND AFTER

New Inventions — Bombardment of Algiers — Battle of Navarino
Admiralty experiments — The end of an era

THE LATE EIGHTEENTH and early nineteenth centuries heralded the beginning of the end of the sailing navy. As early as 1698 one Thomas Savery had patented a steam engine, an improved form of which was built by Newcomen, a Dartmouth blacksmith. This, in its turn, was developed further by James Watt in the 1760s, and the double-impulse engine was the result. With the addition of James Pickard's crank and connecting rods, the reciprocating motion became a rotary one. A French nobleman had been the first to test a paddle-steamer—this vessel plied the Saône, but any further developments in that country were halted by the outbreak of the French Revolution in 1789. At the same period, John Fitch, in America, was running a steamboat on the Delaware by engines assisted by oars. William Symington, in conjunction with Patrick Miller, built successful paddle-steamers for the Clyde, but the first well-known steam-propelled craft in this country was the *Charlotte Dundas*, constructed for Lord Dundas by Symington in the early years of the century.

Robert Fulton, whose ideas and production of submarines had been rejected by both the French and the British, built the first steam-propelled and armoured warship, having previously built successful paddle-steamers. She was double-hulled, had a single paddle, and was driven by 120 h.p. Armed with thirty 32-pounders protected by nearly five feet of wood, she also carried guns firing 100-lb. projectiles below the waterline. Originally named the *Demologos*, it was intended that she should take part in the War of 1812, but she was never tested in action. Renamed *Fulton*, she was destroyed in an explosion in the Navy Yard at Brooklyn in 1829.

The *Savannah* had been the first ship to cross the Atlantic—in 1818—with the aid of steam power. Four years later, the Admiralty's first steam vessel was built. She was the paddle-wheel tug, *Comet*. During the First Burmese War, brought about by that country's encroachments in British India, HMS *Diana* was the first steam-propelled vessel to take part in an action, capturing thirty of the enemy's warships, long, low vessels reminiscent of galleys. The date was 1824.

Weaponry, too, was undergoing a change, with resulting doubts as to the future of the old 'wooden walls'. Deschiens, a Frenchman, was probably the first to use explosive shells in sea warfare. This was in 1690, but it was not until nearly a century later that Lieutenant Henry Shrapnel of the Royal Artillery demonstrated his version of the weapon at Gibraltar. Basically, it was a canister filled with bullets and a charge, which, when exploding in mid-air, scattered the shot over a large area. The following year, 1788, the first naval victory was won by the use of shellfire. Sir Samuel Bentham, an English constructor in Russian service, fitted out a flotilla of gunboats with these

The Comet
J. Bourne

Inspired by the successful crossing of the Atlantic by the SS *Savannah*, primarily a sailing ship but powered by a steam engine driving a pair of external paddle-wheels, the Admiralty built its first steam vessel four years later, in 1822. This was the paddle-wheel tug, *Comet*, shown above.

devices on a non-recoil principle. The Russians destroyed a Turkish fleet vastly superior in numbers at the mouth of the river Liman where it runs into the Sea of Azov. The British, alarmed by the risk of accidental explosion, always a fear in the wooden ships of the line, did not adopt the shell for some time, but it is believed possible that the blowing up of the French *L'Orient* at the Nile was occasioned by fire igniting shells brought up on deck. The shell required a higher elevation than the cannonball to achieve the same range but, because the centre of the projectile was not always hollowed out uniformly, it was apt to spin or roll in the air. This led to the rifling of guns and the improved efficiency of that armament.

Another weapon which seized the imagination was the rocket. The Chinese had known of the properties of gunpowder for centuries, but Sir William Congreve was the first to harness them in the service of Great Britain. Sir Sidney Smith was an exponent of this unorthodox mode of warfare but, when he joined Collingwood in the Mediterranean, he was given to understand that the Commander-in-Chief did not approve of its use.

> ... I endeavoured to impress on him the inefficacy of that mode of war which is carried on by explosion vessels and sky rockets. I know of no instance of a favourable result from them. They serve merely to exasperate, to harass our own

people, and, by reducing the companies of the ships, to render them unfit for real service when it is wanted.

The first warship adapted for use of rockets was HMS *Erebus*; this was in 1812, and she took part in that war, firing at land targets but, thereafter, the weapon fell into oblivion. Its notorious inaccuracy was its downfall, coupled with its limited range of about 1,500 yards, although it had played a part in numerous actions, including that of 1807 against Denmark. A Frenchman, Henri Joseph Paixhans, advocated the next step in naval gunnery, modifying the thirty-six pounder to fire explosive shells. The British and Americans eventually followed suit.

Propulsion by means of a screw was the next great invention. Both Francis Pettit Smith and John Ericsson, a Swede, took out patents for propelling steam-driven vessels by this method. Although Ericsson had towed members of the Admiralty down the Thames in a screw vessel as a demonstration of its efficacy, he was advised that his invention was impracticable. The United States Consul at Liverpool, along with a naval officer of that country, was watching, however, and they persuaded Ericsson that his livelihood could be found in America. His most famous invention, the *Monitor*, a turret ship, was to become involved in the well-known duel with the screw ship *Merrimack* during the American Civil War.

In spite of the Admiralty's reservations (in 1828 'Their Lordships felt it their bounden duty to discourage to the best of their ability the employment of steam vessels, as they consider the introduction of steam is calculated to strike a fatal blow at the naval supremacy of the Empire.' All that had been requested was that a steamer should be used to carry mail between Malta and Corfu), they had had to keep up with the times or lose their mastery of the seas.

Lord Exmouth (Edward
Pellew) was despatched to
punish the Dey of Algiers for
his atrocities against
Christians, and was joined by
a Dutch fleet under van
Cappellen. After a furious
cannonade which left Algiers
ablaze, the Dey submitted,
handing over 1,200 Christian
slaves. To commemorate the
event, Exmouth was
presented with a massive gold
table ornament depicting the
scene.

II

In spite of the technological advances, Lord Exmouth—formerly Sir Edward Pellew, a dashing sailor—was given a conventional fleet when he was ordered to Algiers to take punitive measures against the ruler of that state for his depredations on British shipping and personnel. News of the expedition had reached the Dey, and 40,000 troops and janissaries had been called in to defend the place. Exmouth's fleet was becalmed so, taking advantage of the weather, he dispatched a boat to the Dey, its occupants making demands on behalf of the Prince Regent—owing to the illness of his father, George III, the future George IV was exercising power—giving the Dey three hours to reply. No satisfactory answer being received, fire commenced at 2.45, not finally ceasing until 11.35 that night. The combined fleet—for a Dutch squadron under the command of van Cappellan was also involved—destroyed the port and the ships of the corsairs. The Dey released something like 3,000 Christian prisoners. Although the severity of the bombardment had served its immediate purpose, it failed to stamp out piracy, and it was not until the 1830s that France conquered Algeria.

III

The Balkan theatre of war—the 'Eastern Question' beloved of historians—was again giving difficulties to statesmen. The Greeks wished to throw off the yoke of Turkish suzerainty, and finally revolted in the Morea. Turkish reprisals were swift, and soon Greece was ablaze. Greece, as the seat of the classics, was held in great reverence by many British philhellines, and their bias towards that country was further inflamed by

*Table-Centrepiece
Commemorating Algiers 1816*

Presented to Admiral Lord
Exmouth by his captains, this
massive table centrepiece
commemorating the bom-
bardment of Algiers is two
feet three inches square at its
base, three feet high, and
made of solid gold. The base
carries the Exmouth arms on
each side, supported by shells
and leaf-work. At all angles of
the base are figures a foot
high of British seamen, two
freeing slaves from fetters,
two fighting Turks. A square
rises from the base; on one
side is an inscription; opposite, a list of the British
ships. The third side shows
the attack and the fourth the
retirement of the triumphant
fleet. On the platform of this
square stands a round tower
surmounted by a smaller one.
Crowning all is a lighthouse
bearing the arms of Algiers
and a battery at each corner.
The whole cost 1,400 guineas.

169

Hood's Ships at Toulon 1793
Thomas Luny

In August 1793 the French Royalists surrendered the town of Toulon to the British commander, Vice-Admiral Lord Hood. Unfortunately, not enough account had been taken of the French Jacobins, both inside and outside the town, and Toulon had to be evacuated, along with 15,000 of the Royalist population, fearful of their fate should the Jacobins retake the place. Many French ships had to be left intact in the harbour, although Suffren's late flagship, *Héros*, was burnt.

the death of Byron at Missolonghi in 1824. The Greeks appealed to Canning, the Foreign Secretary, for help: he found himself in a rather delicate position for, should the Turks be overthrown, Russia might well attain her ambition, a foothold in the Mediterranean. It was decided to persuade the Russians to join in an enterprise against the common enemy. Accordingly, by the Treaty of London of July 1827, Britain, France and Russia demanded that the Egyptians, allies of the Turks, withdraw and the Turks themselves agree to an armistice. Both refused, and on 8 September Turkish and Egyptian reinforcements arrived at Navarino. The British fleet in the Mediterranean was commanded by Admiral Sir Edward Codrington. A veteran of many years' service, he had been a lieutenant in the *Queen Charlotte*, Howe's flagship, at the Glorious First of June, and had commanded the *Orion* at Trafalgar. He was now flying his flag in the *Asia*, an 84-gun ship of the line, in which his son was serving as a midshipman. With the arrival of the Russian and French fleets, under Count Heiden and de Rigny respectively, the Allied force was brought up to ten ships of the line, ten frigates and six smaller craft. Codrington, as the most senior officer, took overall command. It was the first time since Solebay, a century and a half before, that British and French were to fight on the same side. Their purpose was to enforce a blockade against Turkish forces in the Morea, ensuring that no men or *matériel* reached them, while allowing reinforcements for the Greek forces through. When, not unnaturally, the commander of the Turco-Egyptian forces, Ibrahim Pasha, protested that the Greeks were being allowed to

prosecute hostilities while he was not, the answer was that Greece had accepted mediation, while the Turks had not. A truce, however, was arranged so that Ibrahim could again apply to the Sultan as to his intentions. In the meantime, however, reports were received by the Allies that the enemy were laying waste the Peloponnese, and the *Dartmouth* was dispatched to Ibrahim with a letter requiring that these activities cease forthwith. Ibrahim never received this letter, being himself *en route* to the Peloponnese to take command there. The allied admirals therefore decided that the way to stop these depredations was to stand into the Bay of Navarino and, by a show of force, bring Ibrahim to a sense of his obligations.

Just about 2 p.m. on 20 October 1827, Codrington led the combined fleet into Navarino Bay. The only sign of activity was a boat sent from the flagship of Moharrem Bey, the Egyptian brother-in-law of Ibrahim, requesting Codrington to desist from entering the anchorage. This was refused, Codrington saying that he had come to give orders, not to receive them. The Turco-Egyptian fleet was deployed in a great horseshoe, the sixty-five or so vessels covered by shore batteries. Codrington sailed straight towards the centre of the formation, anchoring at 2.10 p.m.

By no means had all the large ships taken their positions when action was precipitated by a foolish act on the part of the Turks. *Dartmouth*, seeing a Turkish crew apparently about to set their ship alight, sent a boat to ask them either to desist or remove the vessel from the vicinity. The boat was fired on, the *Dartmouth* provided

HMS Diana *in the First Burmese War 1824*
J. Moore

HMS *Diana* was the first steam-driven ship to be involved in action—during the First Burmese War which was occasioned by the depredations of the Burmese on British India. The *Diana* was a paddle-steamer, the first ever seen in India, and was bought by the Navy at the instigation of the novelist, Frederick Marryat, who had been a naval man before he turned to writing.

'Poor Billy'—Caricature of 1828

The third son of George III and his Queen, William Henry was early destined for the Navy. His first taste of action was during Howe's relief of Gibraltar, and he was the only Prince of the Blood to visit New York while it was still in British hands. Although he took after his brothers in amatory pursuits, he was equally happy at sea, and was appointed captain of the *Pegasus* in 1786, when he once more made the acquaintance of Nelson in the West Indies. Although he was a strict disciplinarian, he was prone to absent himself from the calls of duty on whims of his own, which accounted for his promotion by list rather than on merit. For years he agitated for a seagoing or an administrative appointment, but nothing was forthcoming except for the ceremonial rank of Admiral of the Fleet. Succeeding to the throne in 1830, he reigned for seven years before the start of the Victorian age.

172

Sir Edward Codrington
Sir Thomas Lawrence

Serving under Howe and Nelson, Codrington received his early training in the best of schools and ended by commanding in the last battle wholly under sail—Navarino, in 1827—a battle which should never have been fought, but, on the Turks firing first, they and the Egyptian fleets were annihilated by the British, French and Russian forces. Codrington was recalled, but commanded the Channel Squadron in 1831 and thereafter was in charge at Plymouth. He died in 1851.

covering fire, and almost immediately action became general. There were no tactics employed in this battle: it was purely and simply a slogging match between individual ships, and no lessons could be drawn from it. The Turkish fleet was almost annihilated, and its loss in killed and wounded was almost three times that of the Allies.

An extraordinary feature of the battle was that none of the five participants was officially at war. Both the French and Russian governments rejoiced at the news of the victory, but Codrington, who had won the fight at a politically inexpedient time, was later recalled. Meeting a bucolic acquaintance in London not long afterwards, he was asked if he had had any good shooting lately. The Admiral's reply was 'Why, yes, I *have* had some rather remarkable shooting,' and passed on his way. He died in 1851, having been allowed to resume his naval career, being promoted Admiral of the Red in 1837 and, after a long struggle, gaining 'pecuniary recompense' for those engaged at Navarino.

Navarino was important for two reasons. First of all, it laid the basis for Greek independence; a monarchy was established in 1832, when the Bavarian Prince Otto ascended the throne. Secondly, Navarino, fought in the same seas as Actium and Lepanto, was the end of an epoch, for it was the last naval battle wholly under sail. Be that as it may, the wind-assisted method of propulsion was a long time in disappearing, and shared in many actions with steam and screw.

Change for change's sake is never popular, and the Admiralty was no exception to this maxim. Reluctance to discard the means by which her Navy had become supreme lay at the bottom of their arguments against steam. Also, early engines were often unreliable and, not unnaturally, the Admiralty wished to be sure what they were about before committing the Navy to this new medium. It was not, therefore, until 1843 that the *Rattler*, a sloop, was fitted with the first screw in a British naval vessel. It was at this time that the argument over the respective merits of paddle-wheel and screw was at its height. Which was better? The Admiralty decided to settle the matter once and for all, and accordingly arranged a contest between the *Rattler* and the *Alecto*, a paddle-wheel sloop of the same size. First, they raced against each other, and the *Rattler* won handsomely. The decisive trial, however, was one in which the *Rattler*, engaging in a tug-of-war with *Alecto*, towed her rival stern first at $2\frac{1}{2}$ knots. The contest was over. Screw had won an impressive victory over paddle. An additional attraction of the screw was that it left room on the main deck for guns and masts whereas the paddle had taken up valuable space, and was also vulnerable to gunfire. However conclusive the *Rattler* trial and others of the same nature proved to be, it was a long time before steam was considered other than an auxiliary to sail.

Naval gunnery, improved by new techniques, increased its range and efficiency. The great guns were cast in the foundry of Sir William Armstrong at Elswick on the Tyne, and the new shell-firing cannon sounded the death-knell of the old wooden walls.

The Crimean War was the final fling of the sailing ship in battle. The use of steam had obviated the need to wait for wind and tide to get into position against an enemy; the means of propulsion was well protected; and the greater range of naval gunnery, as well as increased accuracy, had all combined to change the facet of war at sea. The battle bringing these facts home to the controlling authorities was that off Sinope between the Russians and the Turks at the end of 1853. Dispute over the custodianship of the Holy Places in Jerusalem—under Ottoman rule—caused the rift between the two countries, Russia, as always, being keen to use any opportunity to secure entry into the Mediterranean. The Turkish fleet, under the command of Hussein Pasha, lay in the harbour of Sinope and, after an engagement of about six hours, it was almost totally destroyed by a Russian squadron using shell as their most effective weapon.

Tardy the Admiralty may have been at first in establishing a Navy driven by steam, but in the *Illustrated London News* of 28 January 1854, it was stated that:

> The progress of our Royal steam navy is wonderful: England possesses more marine steam power in her Royal Navy than all steam fleets of the world could furnish. A few years since we only possessed some 14,000 h.p.; but on 1 January the British navy included no less than 202 steam vessels of all classes; whilst nominal steam power of machinery in those ships represented more than that of 55,300 horses, with a reserve of 2800 h.p. available for other Royal ships.

Plate 1

Fitting out.—

"He hails in life's advancing day"
"Amusive hopes & prospects gay"
"Nor in the wide horizon round"
"Can e'er one little speck be found"
    "to cloud the scene" *anon*

'Fitting Out'

This cartoon, published in 1835, shows the contents of the seaman's chest of a midshipman of those times. While his womenfolk are in a state of collapse, the future Nelson is totally and happily unaware of what awaits him in his new life, though some of the bottles and boxes give clues.

Alarmed by Russian expansion in the Black Sea, Britain and France, both with their own interests to protect, joined forces and sent a fleet to the area. The Baltic Fleet, as the British component was known, had not one ship solely dependent on sail, twelve of them being screws and available as either steamers or sailers or a combination of the two. A correspondent writing for the *Illustrated London News* at the end of March 1854 described what happened when the *Neptune* joined the accumulation of ships waiting to proceed under the command of Sir Charles Napier.

Shortly after 8 o'clock, the *Neptune* of the 120 guns, one of the finest models of naval architecture in the world, which for more than twenty years had been in harbour, was towed out to Spithead by a small steamer. It was a strange sight to see that majestic hull . . . taken as a helpless prisoner by a petty steam tug, which could have been stowed away without inconvenience in any part on the deck of the noble vessel . . . Here was one of the finest line of battleships in the world lying sluggishly at the mercy of the reluctant breeze, when lo! a little black magician appears; and taking the huge leviathan by the fin, coolly places her in the proper

order of departure. It is quite clear that sailing line-of-battleships will soon be matters of history in this country.

The anonymous writer was quite right, and the success of the French before the Kinburn Forts in October 1855 hastened the demise of the sailing ship. The French Emperor, Napoleon III, had learned the lessons of Sinope and the failure to bombard Sevastopol into submission from the sea, as the ships could not get within range owing to the dangers of Russian shellfire. He had had constructed three floating batteries for service in the Baltic, the *Dévastation*, *Tonnante* and *Lave*. They successfully destroyed Russian outworks while sheltering behind their $4\frac{1}{2}$-inch iron protection and suffered only two mortalities with less than two dozen wounded. The first ironclads in action had proved their worth and settled the fate of the sailing ship.

IV

The end of the age of fighting sail coincided with the beginning of an age of startling progress. The reluctance of the Board of Admiralty to adopt new measures was soon overtaken by events, and they found themselves propelled into a new era where iron took the place of wood and steam that of wind, although it was as late as 1871 that the first British battleship, HMS *Dévastation*, was launched without sails. Less than a century after Trafalgar, a battle fought in the heyday of sail, the first British submarine was in commission.

A sailing ship was a thing of beauty—not unequalled in their own way by her sisters today—and many stirring episodes took place during her era, but the world was changing fast, and soon there was no room for her particular qualities in an increasingly technological age. It is pleasant to reflect, however, that she has survived in various forms, and that more and more young people are benefiting from sea training under sail.

A SHORT BIBLIOGRAPHY

Anderson, R. C. *Naval Wars in the Baltic* 1522–1850

Apps, Michael. *The Four Ark Royals*. William Kimber, 1976

Corbett, Julian. *Drake and the Tudor Navy* (2 vols). Longmans, 1912

Dugan, James. *The Great Mutiny*. Deutsch, 1966

Garrett, Richard. *The British Sailor*. Wayland, 1974

Hattersley, Roy. *Nelson*. Weidenfeld & Nicolson, 1974

Howarth, David. *Sovereign of the Seas: The Story of British Sea Power*. Collins, 1974

Howarth, David. *Trafalgar: The Nelson Touch*. Collins, 1969

Jenkins, E. H. *A History of the French Navy*. Macdonald & Jane's, 1973

Lewis, Michael. *A History of the British Navy* 1793–1815. Allen & Unwin, 1959

Lewis, Michael. *The Navy of Britain*. Allen & Unwin, 1948

Lewis, Michael. *A Social History of the Navy* 1793–1815. Allen & Unwin, 1960

Lewis, Michael. *The Navy in Transition* 1814–1864. Hodder & Stoughton, 1965

Lloyd, C. C. *St Vincent and Camperdown*. Batsford, 1963

Lloyd, C. C. *The British Seaman*. Collins, 1968

Mackesy, Piers. *The War in the Mediterranean* 1803–10. Longmans, 1957

Mahan, Alfred. *The Influence of Sea Power Upon History*. Sampson Low, 1890

Mahan, Alfred. *Major Operations of Navies in the War of American Independence*. Sampson Low, 1913

Marcus, G. *Hearts of Oak*

Mattingly, Garrett. *The Defeat of the Spanish Armada*. Cape, 1959

Naval Chronicle, The, 1799–1819. 40 vols.

Ollard, Richard. *Pepys*. Hodder & Stoughton, 1974

Oman, Carola. *Nelson*. Hodder & Stoughton, 1947

Owen, J. H. *War at Sea Under Queen Anne*. 1938

Pope, Dudley. The Great Gamble: Nelson at Copenhagen. Weidenfeld & Nicolson, 1972

Richmond, H. W. *The Navy in India* 1763–1783. 1931

Ryan, A. N. *Saumarez Papers: Selection from the Baltic Conference* 1808–12. Navy Records, 1968

Sanderson, Michael. *Sea Battles: A Reference Guide*. David & Charles, 1973

Spinney, David. *Rodney*. Allen & Unwin, 1969

Terraine, John. *Trafalgar*. Sidgwick & Jackson, 1976

Warner, Oliver. *Trafalgar*. Batsford, 1959

Warner, Oliver. *The Glorious First of June*. Batsford, 1961

Warner, Oliver. *The Life and Letters of Vice-Admiral Lord Collingwood*. OUP, 1968

Warner, Oliver. *With Wolfe to Quebec*. Collins, 1972

Warner, Oliver. *Nelson*. Weidenfeld & Nicolson, 1975

Warner, Oliver. *The British Navy: A Concise History*. Thames & Hudson, 1975

Warner, Oliver. *Great Naval Actions*. David & Charles, 1976

Warner, Oliver. *Command at Sea*. Cassell, 1976

ILLUSTRATION ACKNOWLEDGEMENTS

The illustrations in this book are the copyright property of the persons and institutions as listed. The publishers wish to express their appreciation of permission to reproduce these illustrations granted by the various owners, trustees, directors or other governing bodies.

INDEX

English ship
13th C.

Hansa Cog (Nef)
14th C.

Caravel ~ early 15th C.

Carrack
15th C.

Galleass ~ 16th C.

Sovereign of the Seas
1637

Later renamed Royal Sovereign

0   100   200   300 feet